T0190423

Tweak Your Mac Terminal

Command Line macOS

Daniel Platt

Apress®

Tweak Your Mac Terminal: Command Line macOS

Daniel Platt
Andover, Hampshire, UK

ISBN-13 (pbk): 978-1-4842-6170-5
https://doi.org/10.1007/978-1-4842-6171-2

ISBN-13 (electronic): 978-1-4842-6171-2

Managing Director, Apress Media LLC: Welmoed Spahr
Acquisitions Editor: Aaron Black
Development Editor: James Markham
Coordinating Editor: Jessica Vakili

Distributed to the book trade worldwide by Springer Science+Business Media New York, 1 NY Plaza, New York, NY 10014. Phone 1-800-SPRINGER, fax (201) 348-4505, e-mail orders-ny@springer-sbm.com, or visit www.springeronline.com. Apress Media, LLC is a California LLC and the sole member (owner) is Springer Science + Business Media Finance Inc (SSBM Finance Inc). SSBM Finance Inc is a **Delaware** corporation.

For information on translations, please e-mail booktranslations@springernature.com; for reprint, paperback, or audio rights, please e-mail bookpermissions@springernature.com.

Apress titles may be purchased in bulk for academic, corporate, or promotional use. eBook versions and licenses are also available for most titles. For more information, reference our Print and eBook Bulk Sales web page at http://www.apress.com/bulk-sales.

Any source code or other supplementary material referenced by the author in this book is available to readers on GitHub via the book's product page, located at www.apress.com/978-1-4842-6170-5. For more detailed information, please visit http://www.apress.com/source-code.

Printed on acid-free paper

To my dad, for getting me interested in computers.

I still remember the book called "Computer Fun" which inspired me to learn more about computers and programming while I was still in primary school. Thank you for having such an influence on my interests and my path in life.

Table of Contents

About the Author

 **Daniel Platt** is a Senior Software Engineer at Comparison Technologies Ltd in the UK. He has also produced various online courses around web servers and web development on macOS. Daniel has been a macOS user since the very first MacOS X Public Beta in 2000 and has been building Linux servers since the late 1990s. He is a lifelong computer nerd and spent a bit too much time on his computer working on his latest project. He found himself spending a lot of time using Terminal for his work and wanted to share his improvement "tweaks" with everybody. The result is this book.

While building web applications, Daniel also sets up web servers from scratch because he has yet to find the perfect hosting solution. His philosophy is "Why settle, when you can build it better yourself?" He even has a course on that topic.

If you'd like to reach out to Daniel, you can do so via his website: https://www.ofdan.com/

About the Technical Reviewer

Ahmed Bakir is an iOS author, teacher, and entrepreneur. He has worked on over 30 mobile projects, ranging from advising startups to architecting apps for Fortune 500 companies. In 2014, he published his first book, *Beginning iOS Media App Development*, followed by the first edition of *Program the Internet of Things with Swift* in 2016 and the second edition in 2018. In 2015, he was invited to develop courses and teach iOS development at UCSD-Extension. He is currently building cool stuff in Tokyo! You can find him online at `devatelier.com`.

Acknowledgements

With lots of thanks to my wife, Sarah and my two children, Ellie and Livy, for being patient with me while I wrote this book.

I would also like to thank my friend Simon for double-checking and improving the content.

I am very grateful to Apress for taking a chance with me.

Finally, thanks go to my colleagues at Comparison Tech. for suggesting additional ideas.

CHAPTER 1

Getting Started

All personal computers these days come with a graphical user interface (GUI), although this hasn't always been the case. Most computers prior to the release of the Apple Macintosh booted into a terminal, text-only environment. All you would have been greeted with was a flashing cursor.

If your computer didn't come with a user manual, you might have struggled with which commands you should be typing, as some command lines were not very intuitive. If you didn't grow up using a terminal then I can imagine the prospect to be quite daunting. This is where this book comes in! I want to help you to feel just at ease with a terminal as you do with a mouse and the GUI.

Terminal at a Glance

The macOS Operating System comes with lots of preinstalled applications. Some of them you know—Calendar, Mail, Photos, and Safari. Others, you won't be familiar with, and they are more commonly known as commands—this includes cat, cp, df, echo, and rm.

One application has been bundled with macOS since the first release, back in 2001. The application is normally relegated to the average user as a way to perform tips and tricks that can be found on the Internet. The application is called "Terminal," and it's shown in Figure 1-1. In this chapter we take a high-level look at this application before digging deeper into it in subsequent chapters.

© Daniel Platt 2021
D. Platt, *Tweak Your Mac Terminal*, https://doi.org/10.1007/978-1-4842-6171-2_1

Terminal

Application - 10.1 MB

Figure 1-1. *The Terminal application*

This book is a journey into a world of Terminal and the hidden commands and utilities that you are unlikely to be aware of. These commands are not like the normal applications, where you use a mouse and GUI to interact with them. Commands do not have a traditional GUI and they operate entirely from the keyboard.

The way to use these commands is by using the Terminal application that is provided with every version of macOS, hidden within the Utilities folder, as shown in Figure 1-2. The Utilities folder can be found inside the Applications folder.

Figure 1-2. *The Terminal application in the Utilities folder*

The quickest way to access Terminal is by activating Spotlight. You do that by pressing ⌘+Spacebar, as shown in Figure 1-3.

Figure 1-3. *The Spotlight search bar*

Then you can type "Terminal" in the search bar and Spotlight will display the application for you to launch, as shown in Figure 1-4.

Figure 1-4. *Searching for Terminal in Spotlight*

The Need to Know

Why am I telling you about Terminal? It lets you type commands into the computer. Using a GUI, you could accidentally move a file to the wrong location. Compare that to when you are using Terminal. You can change the command as many times as you like until you press Enter. Only after you press Enter does the computer execute your command.

Another use of Terminal is to enable hidden features within applications. For example, Safari has a hidden Debug menu that you can only turn on using Terminal, as shown in Figure 1-5.

```
% defaults write com.apple.Safari IncludeInternalDebugMenu 1
```

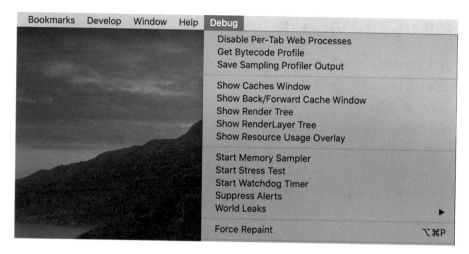

Figure 1-5. *The hidden Debug menu in Safari*

As a web developer, I use macOS to develop my web applications because the macOS Terminal is very similar to the Linux terminal.

If I wanted to copy a folder called files from my Desktop to my web server, it is as simple as using the scp command.

```
% scp ~/Desktop/files/* user@example.org:~/files/
```

You could download a SCP (Secure CoPy) GUI application, like CyberDuck, but using a GUI application can take longer than using this simple command.

Terminal isn't for everybody, but you should learn to feel comfortable with it. Many activities within the GUI can be performed far quicker within Terminal. This is what you will hopefully come to appreciate over the course of this book.

Book Conventions

Throughout this book, you will see commands you need to type into your terminal, as well as the output they produce.

We use % to refer to the command prompt and put the whole line you need to type in `monospace bold font`.

% **date**

The output appears beneath the command, like so:

% **date**
`Tue 11 Oct 2019 10:57:34 BST`

If a command is ever within with a block of text, it will be displayed in `monospace` font as well. For example, to print the current time to the terminal, you use the `date` command. Sometimes the output will be shown in screenshots to preserve the formatting for ease of viewing.

Book Requirements

To take full advantage of this book, you need your computer to be of a certain standard and have Xcode and Homebrew installed. Let's have a look at these requirements now.

Minimum Requirements

As stated by Apple, the following Apple computers can run Catalina.

- MacBook (Early 2015 or newer)

- MacBook Air (Mid 2012 or newer)

- MacBook Pro (Mid 2012 or newer)

- Mac mini (Late 2012 or newer)

- iMac (Late 2012 or newer)

- iMac Pro (2017)

- Mac Pro (Late 2013 or newer)

I cover the Catalina version of macOS (10.15), which was released on the October 7, 2019. All of Apple's older computers (since 2013) can run Catalina and some from 2012 can also do so. It's a good idea to check whether your Mac is compatible, if you are not already running Catalina.

If you are running an older version of macOS, you might have problems with some commands not existing or being older versions.

We will also be installing *Homebrew*, which is a package manager for the macOS Terminal. It needs to run on macOS High Sierra (10.13) or later.

We will be discussing Homebrew in greater detail later in this chapter and learning what we can install with it in Chapter 4.

If you are using an Apple computer within the last four years, you should have or will be able to upgrade your macOS version to Catalina.

You will need to install either Xcode or the Command Line Developer tools, which will be discussed in the next section, "Installing Xcode." These programs provide the necessary tools for Homebrew to be able to build and install new commands for your terminal.

It's also advantageous to have at least 20-30GB of free space on your Mac, so you can install all the requirements and the extra commands. You never want your Mac to run out of disk space, as many applications cannot function properly without free disk space.

The last requirement is that you need an Internet connection. Some tricks will require an Internet connection to work. Homebrew also requires the Internet to download new files, install new applications, and update existing ones.

Once you have all these things set up, you can proceed.

Installing Xcode

You need to use Xcode's Command Line Developer tools for Homebrew to be able to build new commands and keep them up to date. Thankfully, you can now easily install the Command Line Tools from Apple with a simple command.

```
% xcode-select --install
```

When you enter this command, it should look like Figure 1-6, before you press Enter.

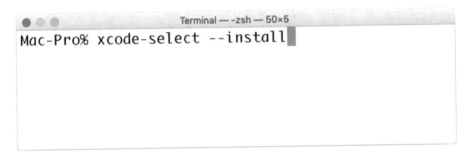

Figure 1-6. *Entering the xcode-select command into Terminal*

You should then see the dialog in Figure 1-7, asking you to confirm installation of the tools.

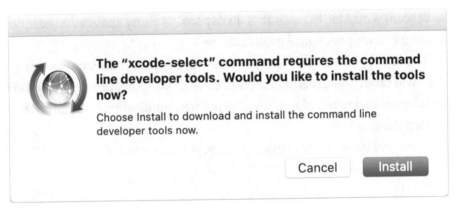

Figure 1-7. *The install dialog for xcode-select*

The Command Line Tools installation requires roughly 500MB of disk space and will install virtually everything Homebrew needs to compile the commands you install.

According to the Homebrew documentation, installing the full version of Xcode will negate the need to install these tools. However, in my experience, after installing Xcode, you still need to install the developer tools.

In some instances, Homebrew will require the full version of Xcode, so for completeness, I will include its installation instructions.

Installing Xcode is as simple as going to the App Store and searching for Xcode, as shown in Figure 1-8.

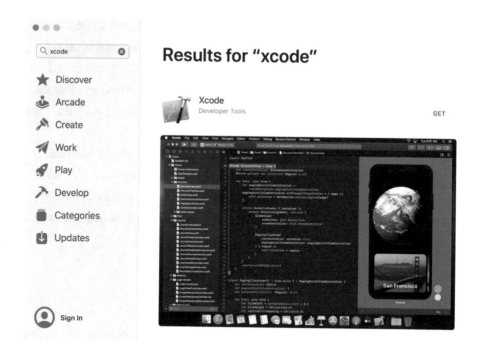

Figure 1-8. *Searching for Xcode in the App Store*

At present, Xcode is just under 11.2GB in size to download. The installation process will extract Xcode and uses about 30GB.

Using Homebrew

As a macOS user, you can download applications from the Internet with your web browser, or you can use the App Store. Occasionally you will also get new applications as part of the system updates to macOS. Other operating systems, such as Linux and UNIX, have package managers that help maintain the installed applications. Package managers let you perform tasks like searching, installing, upgrading, or removing applications from the system.

Examples of package managers for Linux include apt, yum, pacman, and portage. This list is not exhaustive.

The macOS comes with a package manager called the App Store. However, this only deals with software that is approved by Apple and they typically only use a graphical user interface (GUI). There are loads of useful open source programs that run on the command line (Terminal on macOS). You could download Xcode, the source code for the application and all its dependencies. After that, you would have to compile the source code manually yourself. This can get quite messy. So let me tell you about an easier way.

Homebrew is known as "The missing package manager for macOS." There are other package managers, such as MacPorts, pkgsrc, Nix, and Fink, but I feel Homebrew gets the balance right. When you install Homebrew, you get a new command called brew. From now on, I refer to Homebrew as *brew*.

Why Use Brew?

There are thousands and thousands of different applications out there, and installing them all manually could be tedious.

You would first need to download the source code to the application that you wanted. Then you would need to determine all the application's dependencies. These are in the form of libraries of functions that save developers time in not having to reinvent the wheel.

There are libraries for everything and sometimes there is more than one, as shown in Table 1-1. These libraries provide functionalities to programs, which save you time. For example, libxml2 provides support for reading a file format known as XML.

Table 1-1. *Libraries and Their Functions*

Library	Purpose
libcurl	File transfer library
libtls	TLS library for certificate verification
libreadline	Allows users to edit commands as they typed them in
libxml2	XML parser

The point is, you need to install all the required libraries, most likely by compiling them from the source. Then you would be able to compile the application you originally wanted.

This is the reason package managers were created. They keep track of every piece of software and all the required libraries. When you install an application, the package manager compares the dependencies to everything that is currently installed and installs whatever is missing.

There is a huge community of developers producing and maintaining software, which can be installed on your computer using Brew. By leveraging Brew, you benefit from all the people before you.

Installing Brew

Installing Brew on your computer is a very straightforward process. By default, Brew will install itself into a shared folder, called /usr/local. This will allow you to share installed commands across all users on your Mac. However, only the user who installed Brew will be able to modify the commands.

11

If you want all users to be able to modify the installed commands, they will need their own installations of Brew.

Installing Brew Globally

The easier way to install Brew is to grab the installation command from the website, at https://brew.sh/:

```
% /bin/bash -c "$(curl -fsSL ↩
https://raw.githubusercontent.com/Homebrew/install/master/
install.sh)"
```

The installation command is simple but powerful. All you need to do is copy and paste that command into Terminal and press Return. The script will start running and you will get confirmation of where Brew will install itself.

If you are happy for the installation to proceed, then press Enter to continue. If you do not want to carry on, you can press any other button to abort the installation.

Note that you may be prompted for your password if the script requires extra permissions to start the installation.

Installing Brew for Each User

By default, Brew will install itself into /usr/local, which can be overwritten.

For example, if you wanted to install Brew into your home directory, you could use these commands.

```
% mkdir ~/homebrew
% curl -L https://github.com/Homebrew/brew/tarball/master
% tar xz --strip 1 -C ~/homebrew
```

However, unless you are an advanced user, I strongly recommend you letting Brew install itself into /usr/local, as you are more likely to have a better experience.

The one downside to installing Brew into /usr/local is that it is shared among all users on the same computer. Whoever installed Brew first has ownership, then whoever else tries to use Brew will run into permission problems. At this point, however, I suggest installing Brew into your home directory with the previous command.

After Installation

Once the installation is complete, you should run a few commands to double-check that everything was set up properly.

- **brew doctor** will give the Brew install a checkup.
- **brew update** will confirm that Brew downloaded all the updates.

You now have installed the Brew environment and confirmed that everything works correctly.

Finding Applications in Brew

You have installed Brew, so now you need to know some basic Brew commands.

A command you will use a lot of is brew search. It will allow you to search for applications by name. For example, you could search for **nano,** which is a command-line text editor. The command for that search is **brew search nano**.

If you searched for PHP, you will see all the different versions of PHP and all the different modules that come with it:

```
% brew search php
```

You could do a slightly more targeted search if, say, you are only interested in PHP version 7.3:

```
% brew search php@7.3
```

Now I've shown you how you can use brew search to find applications to install. However, this is only useful if you know what it is you want to install. This doesn't give you a description of the application.

You can also use the Brew website (https://brew.sh/), which allows you to search for names and/or descriptions. It also gives you the full description of the command. There is also other useful information on the site.

You now should be able to search for applications to install.

Installing Applications from Brew

Now that you know how to find applications, you need to know how to install them.

How about a nice inspirational fortune cookie?

```
% brew install fortune
```

Now you can run fortune from the terminal:

```
% fortune
Everyone is more or less mad on one point.
-- Rudyard Kipling
```

Don't worry about making a mistake. Either you'll find that the package name doesn't exist, as so:

```
% brew install fortune-typo
Error: No available formula with the name "fortune-typo"
==> Searching for a previously deleted formula (in the last
month)...
```

```
Error: No previously deleted formula found.
==> Searching for similarly named formulae...
Error: No similarly named formulae found.
==> Searching taps...
==> Searching taps on GitHub...
Error: No formulae found in taps.
```

Or you will install something that you didn't want. That's okay. If you accidentally install an application or command, you can easily remove it again, as follows:

% **brew uninstall fortune**

```
Uninstalling /usr/local/Cellar/fortune/9708... (118 files,
3.4MB)
```

Upgrading Installed Applications

You've installed your applications and commands with Brew.

Then you hear about a cool, new feature in these applications. You realize it's missing from your version of the application. You need to upgrade your application to get this latest feature (or maybe fix a bug).

If you were running a paid application, then it is likely that you will have to pay for the latest upgrade.

Type brew upgrade <application> (where <application> is the name of the actual application) to upgrade the application. If you are already running the latest version, you will get an error like the following one.

% **brew upgrade fortune**

```
Error: fortune 9708 already installed
```

It's scarier looking than it needs to be. All it means is that Brew cannot upgrade your application, because you already have the latest version.

This is what it looks like when your upgrade is successful.

```
% brew upgrade fortune
==> Upgrading 1 outdated package:
fortune 97 -> 9708
==> Upgrading fortune
==> Downloading https://homebrew.bintray.com/bottles/
fortune-9708.mojave.bottle.3.tar.gz
################################################################
######### 100.0%
==> Pouring fortune-9708.mojave.bottle.3.tar.gz
🍺  /usr/local/Cellar/fortune/9708: 118 files, 3.4MB
Removing: /usr/local/Cellar/fortune/9707... (117 files, 3.1MB)
```

However, this output is completely made up, because fortune hasn't had an upgrade since 1998.

You can also type **brew upgrade** with no additional parameters, and that will upgrade everything managed by Brew.

```
% brew upgrade
==> Upgrading 56 outdated packages:
php-cs-fixer 2.15.1 -> 2.15.3
aws/tap/aws-sam-cli 0.17.0 -> 0.23.0
ffmpeg 4.1.3_1 -> 4.2.1_1
```

Brew will list all the packages that require upgrading and then work through them. It might be safer to find out what Brew will upgrade first, by doing a dry run.

```
% brew upgrade --dry-run
==> Would upgrade 56 outdated packages:
php-cs-fixer 2.15.1 -> 2.15.3
aws/tap/aws-sam-cli 0.17.0 -> 0.23.0
ffmpeg 4.1.3_1 -> 4.2.1_1
```

Then you can decide whether you want to upgrade anything, or cherry pick the upgrades.

Reinstalling Applications

Occasionally, you might encounter errors in applications that have been installed for a while. You will recognize such errors because they'll say this lib or that dylib is missing or is the wrong version.

Usually you can fix the problem by reinstalling that particular application.

Let's assume you had this issue with the fortune command.

```
% brew reinstall fortune
==> Reinstalling fortune
==> Downloading https://homebrew.bintray.com/bottles/
fortune-9708.mojave.bottle.3.tar.gz
Already downloaded: /Users/danielplatt/Library/Caches/Homebrew/
downloads/39f75bacff04ef9a83ae776a45b801012cf975fd6122c824bff6a
4cefaf1bcad--fortune-9708.mojave.bottle.3.tar.gz
==> Pouring fortune-9708.mojave.bottle.3.tar.gz
🍺  /usr/local/Cellar/fortune/9708: 118 files, 3.4MB
```

Brew will reprocess the formula. It will check to see if the existing archive is available, otherwise it'll download it again. Then, Brew will run the build process again and finally replace the existing installation.

This process won't solve every problem, but it might help when there has been a major change to your system, like a new version of macOS.

Summary

In this chapter, we looked at Terminal and discussed why it is important. We looked at Brew (Homebrew) and discussed what is required to install it. We installed the dependencies for Brew and finally installed the program itself.

We concluded the chapter with some Brew commands that showed you basics, like how to install, reinstall, and uninstall programs.

CHAPTER 2

Terminal Basics

In this chapter, we look more closely at what Terminal is and what you can do with it. There is a lot to cover, so let's dig in.

The Terminal Application

The Terminal application has been installed with macOS since the very first release and it is one of the reasons I like macOS. Terminal allows you to do many things that, if completed in the GUI, would take a long time. In essence, Terminal allows you to be a poweruser.

Meet your macOS Terminal, shown in Figure 2-1.

Figure 2-1. *The macOS Terminal*

© Daniel Platt 2021

D. Platt, *Tweak Your Mac Terminal*, https://doi.org/10.1007/978-1-4842-6171-2_2

As a web developer, I find that macOS and Linux have a lot in common, and that's evident with Terminal. It is because Linux and macOS are UNIX-based operating systems.

This is why Brew and other package managers can port Linux applications to the macOS. macOS even uses the same shells that can be used on Linux. From Terminal, it is hard to tell the difference between macOS and Linux. Only when you look closely you will see the differences.

One big difference is that on macOS, the filesystem isn't case sensitive. This means that you can't have two files in the same directory that have the same name, but differ only by case (such as MYFILE and myfile). Whereas on Linux, the files MYFILE and myfile can exist in the same directory without any issue because they are recognized as two different files.

Customizing Terminal

It is easy to think everyone has perfect eyesight, but some people might experience difficulty reading the command prompt text in Terminal.

Terminal has different profiles built-in, which you can access from the Shell menu when you choose either New Window or New Tab, as shown in Figure 2-2.

Figure 2-2. *The different Terminal profiles that are available*

Take a moment to try the different built-in profiles. Profiles vary in font, font size, and color. Personally, I like the "Pro" profile, as shown in Figure 2-3.

Figure 2-3. *Silver Aerogel profile in Terminal*

Hopefully one these profiles suits your liking regarding the background, font, and color. So now we can customize these profiles. First, you need to enter Terminal's Preferences, found using the Terminal menu item or the keyboard shortcut command and comma (⌘,) as shown in Figure 2-4.

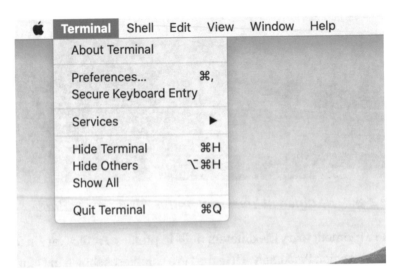

Figure 2-4. *Terminal preference menu*

Select the Profiles tab, as shown in Figure 2-5.

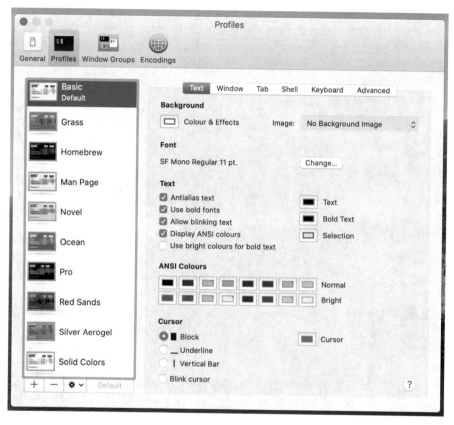

Figure 2-5. *Terminal's Profile preferences*

The list of profiles is now shown on the left side. This is the same list that was shown in the New Window and Tab, Shell menu in Figure 2-2.

Let's customize a profile. Select the profile that appeals to you the most.

You can try different customizations out. Don't worry about making a mistake. If you do, you can always reset all the profiles back to their defaults by clicking the cog and selecting the Restore Default Profiles option, as shown in Figure 2-6.

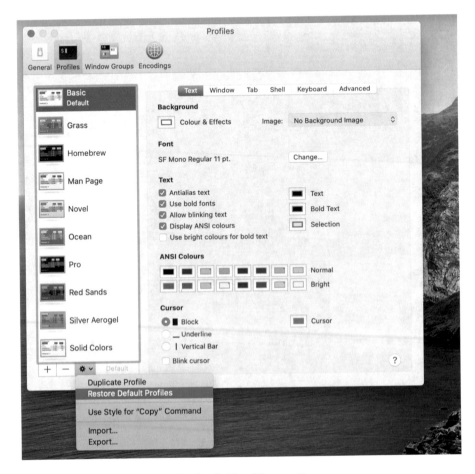

Figure 2-6. *The Restore Default Profiles option*

At first, when you make changes, try to stick to the basics. Start with font, font size, font color, and background color. When choosing a font, consider how it looks and how legible it will be. There are hundreds of fonts you can choose from, but not all of them will be suitable for use with Terminal. The best fonts to use are the fixed-width fonts (each character takes up the same width). Here is a small list of fonts to get you started.

- Andale Mono

- Courier

- Menio Regular

- Monaco

You can find other fonts with a web search such as "good fonts for Terminal". When you have chosen a font, you can then adjust the font size. When setting the font color and background, try to choose contrasting colors. This should make the text easier to read.

When you are happy with your new profile, you can click the Default button, so that any new window or tab will use this profile. You will also want to change the "New Window with Profile" in the General tab in the preferences. Now your Terminal text should be very easy to read.

What Is a Shell?

When you load Terminal, the shell is everything that you see in that window.

You use the shell when you type in your Terminal; it turns your input into a running command. It is called a *shell* because it is the outermost layer of the operating system.

The default shell on Catalina is Zsh (Z shell). In previous versions of macOS, the default shell was the Bash shell (Bourne Again shell). Bash and Zsh have a lot in common, as their histories can both be traced back to the Bourne shell.

Zsh

Zsh takes the input you type in Terminal and tells the computer what to do with it. You can also script Zsh to run a series of commands for you. A *script* is just a text file with a list of commands in it. Virtually any command you run in Terminal can be added to a script.

When you issue a name of the file that contains scripts, Zsh will run them in order.

Upgrading from a Previous Version of macOS

If you have upgraded from a previous version of macOS, the shell will be set to Bash.

When you launch the shell the first time after upgrading macOS, you will be presented with the message in Figure 2-7, telling you how to update your shell to Zsh.

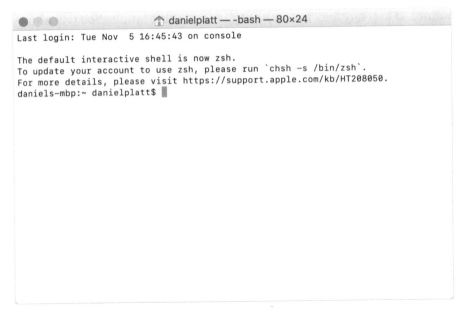

```
● ● ●                      ⌂ danielplatt — -bash — 80×24
Last login: Tue Nov  5 16:45:43 on console

The default interactive shell is now zsh.
To update your account to use zsh, please run `chsh -s /bin/zsh`.
For more details, please visit https://support.apple.com/kb/HT208050.
daniels-mbp:~ danielplatt$ █
```

Figure 2-7. *Terminal launching with the shell set to Bash*

This book assumes that your shell is set to Zsh. While a lot of the examples will work with Bash, some of the more advanced commands will not function properly. You should change your shell to Zsh with the chsh command.

```
% chsh -s /bin/zsh
```

After that, all new Terminal windows will use Zsh for the shell. If you ever need to switch your shell back to Bash, you can use chsh again.

```
% chsh -s /bin/bash
```

Shell Shortcuts

When you are in Terminal, you can use shortcuts to speed up what you are trying to achieve. If you have typed a long command, but realize you've made a mistake near the beginning of line, you can either hold the Left arrow key and wait for the cursor to move to the beginning of the line, or you can use the Control+A shortcut to move there in an instant.

You can see a list of these shortcuts in Table 2-1.

Table 2-1. *Zsh Shell Shortcut Keys*

Shortcut	Description
Control+A	Moves cursor to the beginning of the line
Control+E	Moves cursor to the end of the line
Left arrow	Moves cursor one character to the left
Right arrow	Moves cursor one character to the right
Control+W	Removes the word before cursor
Control+R	Finds the previous shell command
Control+C	Interrupts the running command
Control+Z	Puts the running command to sleep
Control+L	Clears the screen
Control+U	Clears the whole line
Control+D	Forward deletes If the line is empty, it will log you out
Control+S	Stops screen updating
Control+Q	Enables screen updating
Control+P or Up arrow	Steps backward through previous commands
Control+n or down arrow	Steps forward through previous commands

Even if you only remember a couple of these shortcuts, you will save loads of time. Remember Control+C, as you will need this to exit out of some commands that are used in this book.

The Filesystem

There are lots of folders on your computer. Some are solely for the smooth running of your computer (the system directories). Others, like the user directories, shouldn't be deleted for the operation of your user. If your user directory were deleted, it wouldn't affect any other users on the system.

Meta Directories

There are a couple of special directories that we will use throughout this book. These are not real directories, but they *point* to real directories. These directories are shown in Table 2-2.

Table 2-2. *Meta Directory Symbols*

Path	Description
.	Current directory
..	Parent directory
~	Users home directory

There are lots of directories on your computer that have a specific purpose.

Table 2-3 is a list of some of the main directories.

Table 2-3. *System Directories*

Path	Description
/	Root of all directories
/Applications	Global Applications directory
/Applications/ Utilities	Global Utilities directory
/bin	Terminal applications
/dev/	Devices attached to the computer, such as disks
/Library	Place for applications to store resources
/Network	List of computers on the local network
/System	Apple system files
/Users	Location where macOS stores the user's directories
/Users/<name>	User directory (home directory)
/usr/local	Local applications
/Volumes/	Mounted drives and other volumes are placed in this directory
/Volumes/<name>	Mounted volumes

Your boot or system drive is special because it exists in /Volumes/ Macintosh HD and is the root directory. It works because the root directory is your boot volume. /Volumes/Macintosh HD is actually a symlink that points to /. Think of a *symlink* as a pointer to the real content.

User Directories

You also have a set of default folders in your user or home directory, listed in Table 2-4.

Table 2-4. *User Directories*

Path	Description
~	Shortcut for the user folder, which is /Users/<name>
~/Applications	User Applications directory
~/Desktop	Where items on the Desktop are stored
~/Documents	Default location to store user documents and files
~/Downloads	Default location for files downloaded from the Internet
~/Library	Application-specific files
~/Movies	User video files
~/Music	User music files
~/Pictures	User picture files
~/Public	Files the user wants to share
~/Sites	Web pages, used by web sharing

Catalina's New Layout

With Catalina, Apple changed the layout of the filesystem. Unless you've been looking in the Disk Utility application, you might not have even noticed that Apple split the filesystem into two volumes, as shown in Figure 2-8.

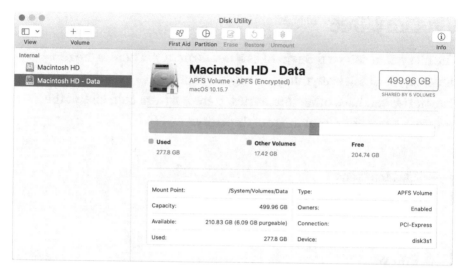

Figure 2-8. *Disk utility showing Macintosh HD split into two volumes*

Assuming your drive is called Macintosh HD, you will now have an additional drive, called Macintosh HD - Data. The Macintosh HD drive now contains the operating system and has been made read-only. The reason for this is to stop the operating system from being changed by accident or by malicious actions. Your Macintosh HD - Data (your data drive) is now where all your files are stored.

Is this going to waste space? No, because these drives share the same free disk space.

The reason you don't know or can't see the two drives is because Apple has stitched them together with *firmlinks*. A firmlink is like an alias in the Finder, but it's designed not be visible. They are similar to symbolic links, which I cover in the "Links" section.

Directory Tree

The filesystem can be thought of as a tree structure. There is the root directory, /, which everything is a part of. Each directory is like a branch. Directories can have other directories. Here is a truncated look at the directories that start from the root directory:

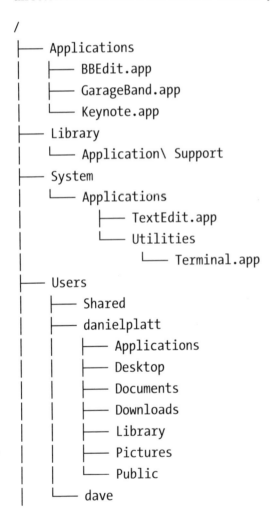

```
/
├── Applications
│   ├── BBEdit.app
│   ├── GarageBand.app
│   └── Keynote.app
├── Library
│   └── Application\ Support
├── System
│   └── Applications
│           ├── TextEdit.app
│           └── Utilities
│                   └── Terminal.app
├── Users
│   ├── Shared
│   ├── danielplatt
│   │   ├── Applications
│   │   ├── Desktop
│   │   ├── Documents
│   │   ├── Downloads
│   │   ├── Library
│   │   ├── Pictures
│   │   └── Public
│   └── dave
│
```

```
├── Volumes
│     └── Macintosh\ HD -> /
├── tmp -> private/tmp
├── usr
│     ├── bin
│     └── local
└── var -> private/var
```

You can see how my home directory, /Users/danielplatt, fits in with the rest of the directories.

Moving Around the Filesystem

Before you move around the filesystem, you need to know where you currently are. If you run the pwd (present working directory) command, it will output the directory you are currently in.

```
% pwd
/Users/danielplatt
```

Another command, called **cd** (change directory), allows you to move from one directory to another. For example:

```
cd /
cd ~
```

The cd first will move you to the root directory and the second cd will take you to your home directory. (You can also type cd without arguments and that will also take you to your home directory.) To change to your desktop directory, you can type the following:

```
% cd ~/Desktop
% pwd
/Users/danielplatt
```

Like the symbol ~, there are two other symbols you should be aware of.

The . (dot) symbol means the current directory. For example, cd . will not change the directory you are in, because if you try to change to the current directory, you'll be exactly where you started.

```
% cd .
% pwd
/Users/danielplatt
```

The .. symbol means the parent directory. If you are in your user folder, /Users/danielplatt, then cd .. will take you up a directory, to /Users:

```
% cd ..
% pwd
/Users
```

However, if you are in the root directory, /, then there are no more parent directories above that one, because you are in the topmost directory (the root of the filesystem).

```
% cd /
% pwd
/
% cd ..
% pwd
/
```

When you are in the root directory, cd .. cannot take you any lower and you will remain in the root directory. Try using pwd now.

Inspecting Directories

What is the point of changing directories, if you can't see what's inside? If you want to see what is inside a directory, and you have permission to do so, you can use the list command (ls). It will list all the files and folders within the directory. If you want even more details, you can type ls -l to get the long version of the list.

```
% ls -l
drwx------+  12 danielplatt  staff     384  4 Aug 19:50 Movies
drwx------+   5 danielplatt  staff     160  1 Jan  2020 Music
drwx------+   6 danielplatt  staff     192 25 Mar 22:46 Pictures
drwxr-xr-x+   5 danielplatt  staff     160  1 Feb  2020 Public
```

Try changing into the Desktop folder and looking at its contents. Compare it to what you see on your desktop. I like to use the -h option with the ls command to convert the file size into understandable file sizes, like kilobytes and megabytes:

```
% ls -lh
drwx------+  12 danielplatt  staff  384B  4 Aug 19:50 Movies
drwx------+   5 danielplatt  staff  160B  1 Jan  2020 Music
drwx------+   6 danielplatt  staff  192B 25 Mar 22:46 Pictures
drwxr-xr-x+   5 danielplatt  staff  160B  1 Feb  2020 Public
```

Dragging and Dropping

Did you know that you can drag a file or folder onto your Terminal window? macOS will insert the text representation of that icon into Terminal.

As an example, I always find it tricky to remember where the iCloud drive lives on the filesystem. That folder doesn't seem to be draggable, but you can easily use a folder within it. For example, I can drag the Pages folder from the iCloud drive onto Terminal, as shown in Figure 2-9. The result is shown in Figure 2-10.

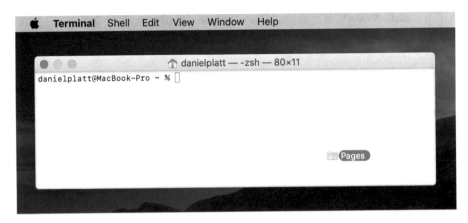

Figure 2-9. *Dragging the Pages icon onto Terminal*

Figure 2-10. *The result of dropping the Pages icon onto Terminal*

If you want to navigate somewhere on your disk in Terminal, and you don't want to type out the file path, you can simply drag and drop the icon onto your Terminal.

Different Types of Paths

Now is a good time to talk about the difference between a relative path and an absolute path. We have seen examples of both so far.

Absolute Paths

The most obvious difference between a relative and absolute path is that the absolute path starts with a forward slash, /. An example of an absolute path is /Users/danielplatt/house/kitchen/fridge.

Using an absolute path is safer than a relative path, because the target of the path will not change, regardless of where you are on the filesystem. However, they can also be more brittle because it's easy to rename any component of the directory structure. If we moved fridge into the garage folder, the absolute path would change to /Users/danielplatt/garage/fridge.

If you see a path starting with tilde ~, then that symbol is treated as an absolute directory to your home directory. That means that ~ is the equivalent to /Users/danielplatt.

Relative Paths

A relative path is based on your current location. Let's assume you are in your home directory. You can move into the kitchen directory by typing cd house/kitchen. This works because you are in the home directory. However, if you were in any other directory, you would receive this error message:

```
cd: no such file or directory: house/kitchen
```

The relative path can start with either the current directory (.) or the parent directory (..) symbols.

```
% cd ./house
% pwd
/Users/danielplatt/house
```

Directory Operations

Your computer is full of directories (also called *folders*). We've seen some folders during the explanation of the filesystem. It is useful for you to be able to create your own directories.

Creating Directories

Directories are easy to create, with the make directory command (mkdir).

mkdir can show you what it is doing if you pass it in the -v option.

```
% mkdir -v house
mkdir: created directory 'house'
```

This will create a folder called house in your current directory. mkdir allows you to create many folders at the same time. You do this by specifying them at the same time with a space between each name.

```
% mkdir -v car garden garage
mkdir: created directory 'car'
mkdir: created directory 'garden'
mkdir: created directory 'garage'
```

It is possible to create subdirectories at the same time with the parent (-p) option. Though strangely, the -v option doesn't do anything when you also use the -p option.

```
% mkdir -p house/kitchen/fridge/milk
```

When you use the -p option, mkdir will not complain about any of the existing directories.

```
% mkdir -p house/kitchen/fridge/cheese
```

You will now have a directory structure like this.

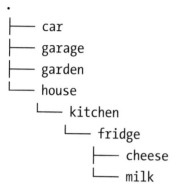

```
.
├── car
├── garage
├── garden
└── house
    └── kitchen
        └── fridge
            ├── cheese
            └── milk
```

You can move around these directories with the cd command.

```
% cd garden
% pwd
/Users/danielplatt/garden

% cd ..
% cd house/kitchen
% pwd
/Users/danielplatt/house/kitchen
```

Deleting Directories

We've been creating a few directories, but how do you remove them? Removing empty folders is very simple, with the remove directory command (rmdir).

If we wanted to remove the third-level directory, we could do so like this.

```
% rmdir house/kitchen/fridge/milk
```

However, let's assume you didn't remove the milk directory.

```
% mkdir house/kitchen/fridge/milk
```

Let's try to remove the `fridge` directory instead.

```
% rmdir house/kitchen/fridge
rmdir: house/kitchen/fridge: Directory not empty
```

Oh dear.

If the directories you want to delete are empty, you can use the same -p option with `rmdir` that we used with `mkdir`. When using -p, `rmdir` will try to delete every directory. If you pass house/kitchen/fridge/milk, then all the directories will be removed. To only remove `fridge` and `milk`, you need to be in the `kitchen` directory.

```
% cd house/kitchen
% rmdir -p fridge/milk
rmdir: fridge: Directory not empty
```

If the directories you want to delete contain files or other directories, you will get the `Directory not empty` message. `rmdir` will start at the deepest level first and work its way backward. As the `milk` directory was empty, it has been removed. The `fridge` directory will then be checked, and `rmdir` stops there because there was still `cheese` left in it.

If you want to delete the `fridge` directory *and* everything in it, you must issue the remove command (`rm`). By default, the remove command will not work on directories, but you can fix that by issuing the recursive option (-r) option to `rm`.

```
% rm -r fridge
```

That command will remove all files and folders, including the subfolder itself.

Warning   Pay special attention to the path. The `rm` command can remove multiple files. An unintentional space could result in removing the wrong files.

Notice the space between my home directory and my folder.

```
% rm -r /Users/danielplatt /house
rm: /Users/danielplatt/Music: Permission denied
rm: /Users/danielplatt/Pictures: Permission denied
rm: /Users/danielplatt/Desktop: Permission denied
```

If you left this command to run its course, then most of your home directory would have been deleted. By default, Apple has set permissions for most of the directories in your home directory (Music, Picture, Desktop, etc.) to disallow deletion. Otherwise, rm would have silently removed everything.

Leaving the Filesystem

When you are deleting folders, you shouldn't be inside a folder that you are deleting. However, it is possible and I want to show you what it looks like. I should still be in the kitchen directory.

But first, I need to re-create the fridge directory and move into the milk directory.

```
% mkdir -p fridge/milk
% cd fridge/milk
```

If we were to remove the milk directory, then Terminal would know where you were and you would be able to run cd .. to move up to the fridge directory. What happens if we remove the fridge directory while being in the milk directory?

```
% rm -r ../../fridge
% pwd
/Users/danielplatt/house/kitchen/fridge/milk
```

At first glance, everything is normal and you can even move up a directory.

```
% cd ..
```

However, when we try to see where we are, things get strange. The current directory isn't `fridge`, because that was removed.

```
% pwd
.
```

If we put it all together, the full sequence of commands is this.

```
% cd /Users/danielplatt/house/kitchen
% mkdir -p fridge/milk
% cd fridge/milk
% rm -r ../../fridge
% pwd
/Users/danielplatt/house/kitchen/fridge/milk
% cd ..
% pwd
.
```

How Can You Remove a Directory You Are In?

In Linux, a file or folder does not truly go away until the last process finishes using it. Just by being in the directory we were deleting, Terminal was using it. When we tried to leave the directory, the shell had no more information. It defaulted to show us we were in a directory, but not on the filesystem.

If you find yourself in this situation, you can either close the Terminal window or change directories using an absolute path.

```
% cd ~
```

File Operations

You've seen how to move around the filesystem and how to look at which files are in a directory. Now, you'll learn how to create a file.

Creating Files

One way to create an empty file is with touch. The main use for touch is to change a file's modified date and time to now. However, if you touch a file that doesn't exist, then touch will create a new file for you.

```
% touch <filename>
```

For example, if you want to create a file called **empty-file** on your desktop, you would use touch to do it.

```
% touch ~/Desktop/empty-file
```

That will create an empty file on your desktop. All touch is doing is setting the file's modified date and time to now. If the file doesn't exist, it is created.

```
% ls -l ~/Desktop/empty-file
-rw-r--r--@ 1 danielplatt  staff  0  5 Aug 08:45 /Users/
danielplatt/Desktop/empty-file
```

If you wait five minutes and try touch again, you'll see that the modified time of the file has changed.

```
% touch ~/Desktop/empty-file
% ls -l ~/Desktop/empty-file
-rw-r--r--@ 1 danielplatt  staff  0  5 Aug 08:50 /Users/
danielplatt/Desktop/empty-file
```

Another way to create a file is from the output of another command, which I cover later in the section entitled "Piping."

Writing Files

The way to write files in Terminal is to use a text editor. The text editor I recommend for editing files in Terminal is nano.

```
% nano big-quote
```

Nano can also be used to create files, if you execute it without a filename or if the file doesn't exist.

% **nano**

I will explain nano in more detail later in the section entitled "Editing Text in Terminal".

Reading Files

The **cat** command is one way to read a file and display its contents to Terminal.

% **cat big-quote**
```
Many changes of mind and mood; do not hesitate too long.
Money is better than poverty, if only for financial reasons.
Dear Mister Language Person: I am curious about the expression,
"Part of
this complete breakfast".  The way it comes up is, my 5-year-
old will be
watching TV cartoon shows in the morning, and they'll show a
commercial for
a children's compressed breakfast compound such as "Froot
Loops" or "Lucky
Charms", and they always show it sitting on a table next to
some actual food
such as eggs, and the announcer always says: "Part of this
complete
breakfast".  Don't that really mean, "Adjacent to this complete
breakfast",
or "On the same table as this complete breakfast"?  And
couldn't they make
```

essentially the same claim if, instead of Froot Loops, they put a can of

shaving cream there, or a dead bat?

Answer: Yes.

-- Dave Barry, "Tips for Writer's"

If we wanted to peek inside a file, we can use the head and tail commands. The **head** command will display the first 10 lines of a file, which is useful for seeing what is in a file before opening it.

% **head big-quote**
Many changes of mind and mood; do not hesitate too long.
Money is better than poverty, if only for financial reasons.
Dear Mister Language Person: I am curious about the expression, "Part of
this complete breakfast". The way it comes up is, my 5-year-old will be
watching TV cartoon shows in the morning, and they'll show a commercial for
a children's compressed breakfast compound such as "Froot Loops" or "Lucky
Charms", and they always show it sitting on a table next to some actual food
such as eggs, and the announcer always says: "Part of this complete
breakfast". Don't that really mean, "Adjacent to this complete breakfast",
or "On the same table as this complete breakfast"? And couldn't they make

The **tail** command will display the last 10 lines, which is useful for looking at log files and seeing the latest entry.

```
% tail big-quote
```
a children's compressed breakfast compound such as "Froot
Loops" or "Lucky
Charms", and they always show it sitting on a table next to
some actual food
such as eggs, and the announcer always says: "Part of this
complete
breakfast". Don't that really mean, "Adjacent to this complete
breakfast",
or "On the same table as this complete breakfast"? And couldn't
they make
essentially the same claim if, instead of Froot Loops, they put
a can of
shaving cream there, or a dead bat?

Answer: Yes.
    -- Dave Barry, "Tips for Writer's"

We look at the head and tail commands in more detail in Chapter 3.

Copying Files

Imagine that you wanted one of the big-quotes saved to another place
on your computer. You can easily do that with the copy command (cp).
You need to give cp a source (the file you want to copy) and a destination
(where you would like to copy it).

The source and destination filename do not have to be the same name,
unlike if we were copying the file in the Finder. If I wanted to copy my
big-quote from earlier to the desktop, I can as follows, using the name
FortuneMessages.

```
% cp ~/big-quote ~/Desktop/FortuneMessages
```

Note   If FortuneMessages.txt existed before this copy, it would be overwritten by big-quote. There is no prompt asking if you really meant to do this.

Moving Files

Instead of copying a file, you can move it. Moving a file works the same way as cp. There is a move command (mv) that takes the same source and destination arguments. I've realized that the file FortuneMessages should have a file extension to help others understand what type of file it is. I will rename this example FortuneMessages to include the txt file extension.

```
% mv ~/Desktop/FortuneMessages ~/Desktop/FortuneMessages.txt
```

Also, like cp, mv will overwrite any existing files without question.

Deleting Files

After all this, you decide that you never really wanted these files. You can remove them from the filesystem with the remove command (rm).

```
% rm ~/Desktop/FortuneMessages.txt
```

With these commands, you have the basic lifecycle of a file.

Editing Text in Terminal

We will need to do a fair bit of file editing throughout this book. When you think about editing text on macOS, you might think about using TextEdit or another word processor. However, these are designed for writing and not for scripting. You may end up with weird errors if you try to use them. For example, TextEdit likes to swap the quote symbol for a curly quote. They are great for letter writing, but not for programming.

I recommend you use a command called nano. This command is preinstalled in macOS, so we won't need to install it. (Although you can install a later version with Brew.) You can start nano by typing nano and specifying the filename when you save. However, I prefer using nano by specifying the file to edit by typing nano <filename>. The editor is shown in Figure 2-11.

```
% nano filename
```

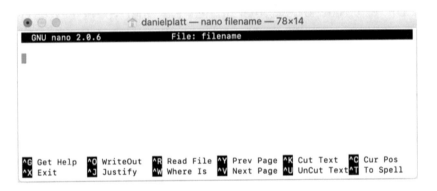

Figure 2-11. *Editing a file in nano*

At the bottom of the window are some of the commands available in nano. For example ^X Exit is like pressing Control+X. There is also help, Control+G, which lists even more commands. Remember ^+ means press Control, and M+ means press Esc.

```
Press ^+X to leave HELP.
```

So how do you use the editor? You can just start typing, like you would with any other text editor. Your mouse won't work here, so you will have to use the arrow keys if you want to move around. When you have finished editing, press Control+X to exit, and press Y to save your file to disk.

That is all you need to know to get started with nano. If you are not happy about editing in Terminal, you can use BBEdit instead. You can find and install BBEdit from the App Store. BBEdit is a free application. It does have some paid-for features, but they are not necessary for this book. BBEdit will continue to function when the trial period expires.

The easiest way to use BBEdit from Terminal is to install the BBEdit Command Line Tools, as shown in Figure 2-12.

Figure 2-12. *Install BBEdit Command Line Tools menu item*

There will be a confirmation before the installation begins, as shown in Figure 2-13. You may be prompted to enter your user password to allow the installation to continue.

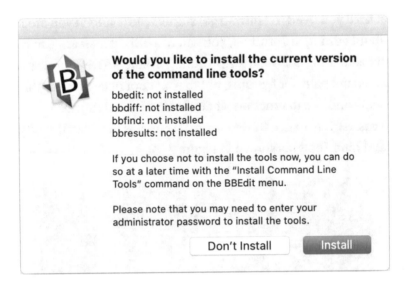

Figure 2-13. *Install BBEdit Command Line Tools*

When the installation is complete, you will be shown which version of the commands have been installed, as shown in Figure 2-14. If you click on the menu item in Figure 2-12 again, then you will be shown this screen.

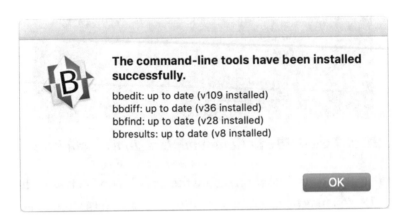

Figure 2-14. *BBEdit Command Line Tools have been installed*

Just like we did earlier with nano, we can use BBEdit to open the **big-quote** file. Here's the command to open the **big-quote** file in BBEdit from Terminal:

```
% bbedit big-quote
```

In the rest of this book, I will use nano for editing exclusively, but you can substitute this command. There are also other text editors that are available, such as Atom and Sublime Text.

Changing the Default Text Editor

Occasionally there will be commands that open a new text editor, which by default will be vi.

The easiest way to change the default text editor is by setting a new variable in your `.zshrc` file, called EDITOR.

```
% export EDITOR=/usr/bin/nano
```

This will also work on the shell prompt. If you happen to find yourself opening vi by mistake, you can type `:q` followed by the return key to quit out of vi.

We will explain variables later in the section "Environment Variables."

Piping

With piping, we can redirect the input and output of any command. Input can come from another command and output can be to somewhere other than the screen.

Let's take a closer look at these concepts.

Pipe

The pipe, which is the vertical bar symbol (|), is used to connect different commands. It chains commands together in order to use the output from one command as the input to another.

In this example, we are reading the contents of the system log file and piping it to less.

The system log file is many pages long and less paginates through the contents rather than dumping them to the screen at once.

```
% cat /var/log/system.log | less
```

Press space to skip a page of content, or use the arrow keys to move around.

When you are finished, press the *q* key to quit. Another example of piping is to send the same log file to the tail command.

```
% cat /var/log/system.log | tail -n 4
Aug  4 22:36:37 MacBook-Pro com.apple.xpc.launchd[1]
Aug  4 22:36:37 MacBook-Pro com.apple.xpc.launchd[1]
Aug  4 22:36:47 MacBook-Pro com.apple.xpc.launchd[1]
Aug  4 22:36:47 MacBook-Pro com.apple.xpc.launchd[1]
```

The pipe is a concept that I will be using many times throughout this book.

Redirecting Output

Redirecting standard output from one command to a file on the filesystem is done using the greater than symbol (>).

```
% fortune > ~/quotes.txt
```

When you run that command, you will notice that now, nothing is outputted to the Terminal window. That's because it has been written to the quotes.txt file in your home directory.

A quick way to see the contents of this new file is using another command, called **cat**. It concatenates and prints files, as follows:

```
% cat ~/quotes.txt
Sattinger's Law:
    It works better if you plug it in.
```

Let's try writing another fortune message into quotes.txt.

```
% fortune > ~/quotes.txt
```

Now when you look inside, you'll see a different quote, but why? The > symbol is designed overwrite existing files. This fortune message overwrote the last fortune message. If you use the >> symbol (two greater than symbols), that tells the shell that you would like to append to the file, rather than overwrite it.

```
% fortune >> ~/quotes.txt
% cat ~/quotes.txt
Sattinger's Law:
    It works better if you plug it in.
Reputation, adj.:
    What others are not thinking about you.
```

It would be remiss of me not to mention another form of output redirection, the error redirect, 2>. Say you run a command and it outputs an error message that cannot be captured using redirect symbol, >, as follows:

```
% cat ~/non-existent-file > ~/error.msg
cat: /Users/danielplatt/non-existent-file: No such file or
directory
```

The `~/error.msg` file was created, but it is empty.

If you want to capture an error message to the file, you need to use the error redirect, `2>`.

```
% cat ~/non-existent-file 2> ~/error.msg
```

The error message has been saved into `~/error.msg`.

```
% cat ~/error.msg
cat: /Users/danielplatt/non-existent-file: No such file or
directory
```

Redirecting Input

It is also possible to use redirection to send the contents of a file as input to a command using the less than symbol (`<`).

```
command < input
```

This has a similar effect to using `cat` to pipe the contents of a file into a command, except that the operating system is handling it for us, rather than using another command.

The `cat` command can easily print the contents of a file, but will also print the contents of anything that is piped to it. In this case, I am redirecting the `quotes.txt` file into `cat`, rather than `cat` loading the file directly.

```
% cat < ~/quotes.txt
Many changes of mind and mood; do not hesitate too long.
```

While you are very unlikely to use this with `cat`, this is an important principle for sending file contents to a command. This technique comes in useful when restoring a database, for example. Say I need to send a file full of commands to my database. I would use the following:

```
% mysql < database.sql
```

At the moment you don't have MySQL installed.

Hidden Files and Folders

So far, all the files and folders you've created will show up in the Finder. But did you know that you can create files and folders that don't show up in the Finder?

Hiding Files the UNIX Way

It's a long UNIX tradition that any file that starts with a dot will be hidden by default. These files are hidden from a directory listing and from the Finder.

```
% ls -l
total 8445936
drwx------@ 111 danielplatt   staff        3552 24 Jan 18:53 Desktop
drwx------@  80 danielplatt   staff        2560 16 Jan 10:30 Documents
drwx------@  23 danielplatt   staff         736 12 Jan 15:11 Downloads
drwx------@  79 danielplatt   staff        2528  1 Jan 15:47 Library
drwx------+  10 danielplatt   staff         320 18 Dec 23:07 Movies
drwx------+   5 danielplatt   staff         160  1 Jan 15:58 Music
drwx------+   5 danielplatt   staff         160  5 Nov 17:03 Pictures
drwxr-xr-x+   4 danielplatt   staff         128  5 Nov 14:02 Public
```

Using the -a option with the ls command will include the hidden files in your directory listing.

```
% ls -la
total 8446600
drwxr-xr-x+ 102 danielplatt   staff        3264 25 Jan 09:07 .
drwxr-xr-x    6 root          admin         192 24 Oct 01:37 ..
-rw-r--r--@   1 danielplatt   staff       22532 23 Jan 22:38 .DS_Store
drwx------    78 danielplatt  staff        2496 23 Jan 21:09 .Trash
-rw-r--r--    1 danielplatt   staff           0 10 Nov 14:33 .restart
```

```
drwx------      5 danielplatt  staff            160 16 Nov 22:15 .ssh
-rw-------      1 danielplatt  staff         179926 25 Jan 09:07 .zsh_
history
-rw-r--r--      1 danielplatt  staff           3736 23 Jan 21:27 .zshrc
drwx------@ 111 danielplatt  staff           3552 24 Jan 18:53 Desktop
```

Let's try to create our own hidden folder on the desktop.

```
% cd ~/Desktop
```

First, we create a hidden folder, called .myfolder.

```
% mkdir .myfolder
```

Note how you can use the folder as you would any other folder in Terminal.

```
% touch .myfolder/myfile
% touch .myfolder/.myhiddenfile
```

However, nothing has shown up on the desktop. We can make it appear by renaming the directory and removing the dot from the name.

```
% mv .myfolder myfolder
```

Just like that, the folder appears on the desktop, as shown in Figure 2-15.

Figure 2-15. *Myfolder on the desktop*

The same thing will happen with files, as shown in Figures 2-16 and 2-17.

Figure 2-16. *Contents of myfolder with myhiddenfile*

We can see myfile, but .myhiddenfile is still hidden. Then we can rename **.myhiddenfile** to **myhiddenfile** to make it visible.

```
% mv myfolder/.myhiddenfile myfolder/myhiddenfile
```

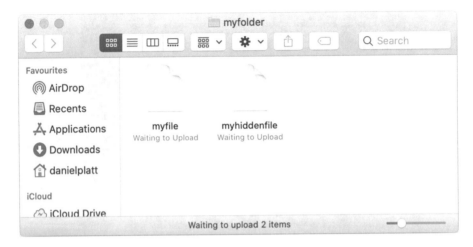

Figure 2-17. *Contents of myfolder with myhiddenfile*

It is because of the dot that files like .zshrc are difficult to access from the Finder, but very easy to access in Terminal.

Hiding Files the macOS Way

There is another way to make files hidden from the Finder, but not from Terminal. You have already seen it in my previous directory listings. The directory I'm talking about is the Library.

The macOS has flags that can be applied to files and directories, and they don't require any renaming. You can see these flags using the ls command and -lO (That's a capital "O"). As you can see, the Library has a hidden flag.

```
% ls -lO ~/
total 8445744
drwx------@ 128 danielplatt  staff  -          4096 15 Jul
18:53 Desktop
drwx------@  89 danielplatt  staff  -          2848 28 Jun
09:12 Documents
drwx------@  71 danielplatt  staff  -          2272 15 Jul
18:53 Downloads
drwx------@  80 danielplatt  staff  hidden     2560 12 Feb
16:56 Library
drwx------+  11 danielplatt  staff  -           352 31 May
17:08 Movies
drwx------+   5 danielplatt  staff  -           160  1
Jan   2020 Music
drwx------+   6 danielplatt  staff  -           192 25 Mar
22:46 Pictures
```

First, make sure you have a directory called myfolder on your Desktop.

```
% mkdir ~/Desktop/myfolder
```

If you already have this directory, you get the File exists message, which can safely be ignored. To set flags on a file or directory, we can use the change flags command (chflags). To hide myfolder, we can use the following command.

```
% chflags hidden ~/Desktop/myfolder
```

To make myfolder visible again, we can pass nohidden, as follows:

```
% chflags nohidden ~/Desktop/myfolder
```

Globbing

Many of the commands that we have used take a file as an argument.

```
% ls ~/Desktop
```

However, it's possible to use wildcards and ranges with special symbols to match more than one file. Searching for filenames with wildcards is called a glob, or *globbing*. Let's create some files to help illustrate globbing.

```
% cd house/kitchen
% touch chair table sink cupboard plate towel fan fridge
freezer
% mkdir ../bedroom
% cd ../bedroom
% touch bed drawers fan top
```

Single Asterisk

A simple example is finding all the files and folders starting with the letter *f* in your kitchen directory.

```
% % ls -l f*
-rw-r--r--  1 danielplatt  staff  0  4 Aug 23:05 fan
-rw-r--r--  1 danielplatt  staff  0  4 Aug 23:05 freezer
-rw-r--r--  1 danielplatt  staff  0  4 Aug 23:05 fridge
```

The asterisk symbol will match zero or more characters. You can see this in effect with the next example.

```
% ls -l f*e
-rw-r--r--  1 danielplatt  staff  0  4 Aug 23:05 fridge
```

You can also use the asterisk to find files that end with a certain filename that matches your search—for example, all the files that end with an *e*. This could easily be **.txt** instead of the letter *e*.

```
% ls -l *e
-rw-r--r--  1 danielplatt  staff  0  4 Aug 23:05 fridge
-rw-r--r--  1 danielplatt  staff  0  4 Aug 23:05 plate
-rw-r--r--  1 danielplatt  staff  0  4 Aug 23:05 table
```

The asterisk can replace any part of the filename or path. For example, we can look for all the room directories that have a fan in them.

```
% cd ../..
% ls -l house/*/fan
-rw-r--r--  1 danielplatt  staff  0  4 Aug 23:13 house/bedroom/fan
-rw-r--r--  1 danielplatt  staff  0  4 Aug 23:05 house/kitchen/fan
```

Question Mark

The question mark is very similar to the asterisk, with one exception, it only matches a single character. In this case, the letter *n* and a question mark will still match fan.

```
% ls -l house/*/fa?
-rw-r--r--  1 danielplatt  staff  0  4 Aug 23:13 house/bedroom/fan
-rw-r--r--  1 danielplatt  staff  0  4 Aug 23:05 house/kitchen/fan
```

Or you can use it to find any three-letter object.

```
% ls -l house/*/???
-rw-r--r--  1 danielplatt  staff  0  4 Aug 23:13 house/bedroom/bed
-rw-r--r--  1 danielplatt  staff  0  4 Aug 23:13 house/bedroom/fan
-rw-r--r--  1 danielplatt  staff  0  4 Aug 23:05 house/kitchen/fan
```

Double Asterisk

There is also the double asterisk (**), which will search all folders in the
current directory. A single asterisk, on the other hand, will only match
something in that directory. Or to put it another way, the double asterisk
will match directories and a slash, and the single asterisk will never match
a slash.

To search for a file that begins with the letter *t* and exists somewhere in
our files, we use the following command:

```
% ls -l **/t*
-rw-r--r--  1 danielplatt  staff  0  4 Aug 23:20 house/bedroom/top
-rw-r--r--  1 danielplatt  staff  0  4 Aug 23:05 house/kitchen/table
-rw-r--r--  1 danielplatt  staff  0  4 Aug 23:05 house/kitchen/towel
```

Range Matching

Sometimes you'll want to match a range of files with letters or numbers
in the filename. The range match uses the square brackets ([ ]) with the
desired letters or numbers. If we wanted to match the system log files that
includes the numbers 0 through 5, for example, we could use [0-9] but
could also use [0-5] if we wanted to match fewer files.

```
% ls -lh /var/log/system.log.[0-9].gz
-rw-r-----  1 root  admin   56K  5 Aug 01:26 /var/log/system.
log.0.gz
-rw-r-----  1 root  admin   98K  4 Aug 00:00 /var/log/system.
log.1.gz
-rw-r-----  1 root  admin  112K  3 Aug 00:22 /var/log/system.
log.2.gz
-rw-r-----  1 root  admin   99K  2 Aug 01:22 /var/log/system.
log.3.gz
```

```
-rw-r----- 1 root  admin   82K  1 Aug 00:00 /var/log/system.
log.4.gz
-rw-r----- 1 root  admin   73K 31 Jul 01:48 /var/log/system.
log.5.gz
-rw-r----- 1 root  admin   61K 30 Jul 00:05 /var/log/system.
log.6.gz
```

In this example, the numbers 7 through 9 didn't exist. Notice that the system did not send an error about them being missing. To match letters, you can use a range like [a-z] or [A-Z]. It is possible to combine letters and numbers, such as [0-9a-z]. It is also possible to add a selection for the matches such as the odd numbers 1, 3, and 5.

```
% ls -lh /var/log/system.log.[135].gz
-rw-r----- 1 root  admin   98K  4 Aug 00:00 /var/log/system.
log.1.gz
-rw-r----- 1 root  admin   99K  2 Aug 01:22 /var/log/system.
log.3.gz
-rw-r----- 1 root  admin   73K 31 Jul 01:48 /var/log/system.
log.5.gz
```

There is a lot more to globbing files, but this is enough to get you started.

Links

Links are a type of file designed to point to another file. They are similar to an alias in the Finder or a shortcut in Windows. There are three distinct types of link files—hard links, symbolic links, and firm links (which are used by the operating system).

Hard Links

Hard links allow multiple files to share disk space. What is really happening is that you are giving one file multiple names.

Let's create a file and a hard link.

```
% touch particle1
% ln particle1 particle2
```

Whichever file you edit, they will both have the same contents, because particle1 and particle2 point to the same part of the disk.

As long as particle1 and particle2 remain on the same filesystem, they will continue to work, regardless of where they are. It doesn't matter if one of them is moved to a different directory.

Another interesting side effect to note is that the part of the drive that contains the data will not be cleaned up until all its names have been removed. This is also how Apple's TimeMachine worked before it moved to APFS. In each backup, if a file had not changed, it would be a hard link so that the backups took up less space.

Symlinks

Previously, I mentioned that /Volumes/Macintosh HD is actually a symlink that points to /, but I didn't explain what a symlink was.

Symlink stands for *symbolic link*. Symlinks are like aliases in the Finder, or shortcuts in Windows. They are pointers to something else on the filesystem. When you use the ls command, you will see them with the -> symbol.

```
% ls -lh /Volumes
total 0
drwxr-xr-x   5 root   wheel    160B 12 Nov 08:02 .
lrwxr-xr-x   1 root   wheel     1B 11 Nov 21:58 Macintosh HD ->
/
```

Unlike hard links, if the destination is moved, then a symlink will no longer be pointing to anything valid, and therefore won't work.

```
% ls -lh particle[13]
lrwxr-xr-x  1 danielplatt  staff     9B  5 Aug 09:09 particle3 ->
particle1
-rw-r--r--  2 danielplatt  staff     0B  5 Aug 09:09 particle1
```

Now I remove particle1, so particle3 will no longer be able to show any contents.

```
% rm particle1
% cat particle3
cat: particle3: No such file or directory
```

This example of a symlink is called a symbolic link.

Naming Things

When you create your files and directories, you can name them pretty much anything you'd like. However, there are some symbols that will get you into trouble. Take the humble space.

If you tried to name your file "hello world" without the quotes, you might be surprised when you end up with two files, rather than one.

```
% touch hello world
```

The reason for this is that the shell sees the space as a separator. If you want a space in your filename, there are two ways to get around this. The first way is to quote your filename.

```
% touch "hello world"
```

The second way is to use an escape character using the backslash symbol, \.

% **touch hello\ world**

Symbols that require you to either use an escape character or quote them are shown in Table 2-5.

Table 2-5. *Symbols That Can Be Escaped in a Filename*

Symbol	Description
$	Start of a variable
|	Vertical bar or pipe symbol
;	Semicolon
?	Question mark
&	Ampersand
( )	Brackets
[ ]	Square brackets
{ }	Braces

However, there are some symbols that you will struggle to create a file with on Terminal. For example, take the asterisk (*). The Finder will allow you to use the asterisk as a filename, as shown in Figure 2-18.

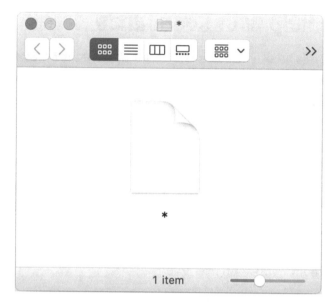

Figure 2-18. *The folder and the file inside are both named with an asterisk*

Once the file has been created, you can escape the asterisk or quote it, so that you can access it.

```
% ls -l \*
-rw-r--r--  1 danielplatt  staff  0  5 Aug 09:15 *
```

Interestingly, you can also escape the Return key, but it gets substituted with a space, which is handy for breaking up long Terminal commands.

```
% echo String \
> broken \
> by \
> returns
String broken by returns
```

67

Getting Help with Commands

Throughout this book, you will install many applications. However, I won't be able to go through all the arguments that each application has to offer. So how can you find more information about each application or about the commands they provide? You can search the Internet for more information, and that is a perfectly valid approach.

However, a quicker approach is to read the manual. Your Terminal has a command called man, which is short for manual. When you install the commands, Brew will also install a man page that describes the application.

You use man <command> to open the manual. Let's open the manual of the fortune command as an example.

```
% man fortune
FORTUNE(6)              UNIX Reference Manual          FORTUNE(6)

NAME
        fortune - print a random, hopefully interesting,
        adage

SYNOPSIS
        fortune [-aefilosw] [-n length] [ -m pattern]
        [[n%] file/dir/all]

DESCRIPTION
        When fortune is run with no arguments it prints
        out a random epigram. Epigrams are divided into
        several categories, where each category is sub-
        divided into those which are potentially offensive
        and those which are not.
   :
```

From there, you can use your up and down arrows to scroll the document, and you can also use Control+v and Control+u to scroll, by skipping whole pages.

If you are searching for something specific, you can search for it. You simply press the forward slash / and type the word you are looking for, followed by the Return key. It will highlight all the occurrences and take you to the first occurrence.

If you want to go to the next instance, just type / and press Return. Once you are finished, press the *q* key. So, when you are asked to install a command using Brew, check out its man page after installation to get a lot more information about how to use it.

Searching the Manuals

Sometimes you won't know which manual you want to check, but you do know what you are looking for. Thankfully there is a way to get man to search all manuals for a string.

If I wanted to find all the manuals that mentioned encode, because I know I need to encode a video, but I don't know what the command is, I could type the following:

```
% man -K "encode"
/usr/local/share/man/man1/fax2ps.1? [ynq] n
/usr/local/share/man/man1/fax2tiff.1? [ynq] n
/usr/local/share/man/man1/ffmpeg-all.1? [ynq] y
```

Each line will prompt [ynq], which is a question. Would you like to display this manual? Your choices are *yes*, *no*, or *q*uit. If you press *y*, manual will open up as if you typed man brew.

Note   Depending on the speed of your computer, this could take a long time.

The "See Also" Section

At the bottom of many of the man pages there is a "See Also" section. Here's the section from the `fortune` man page as an example.

SEE ALSO
```
    re_comp(3), regcomp(3), strfile(1), unstr(1)
```

As you might imagine, these are further man pages for more information. However, the meaning of the number in the bracket might not be immediately obvious. The number is referencing the different section of the man entry.

The section numbers are defined in `man   man` and listed shown in Table 2-6.

Table 2-6. *List of man Page Sections*

Section	Description
1	User commands
2	System calls
3	C Library Functions
4	Devices and special files
5	File formats and conventions
6	Games et al.
7	Miscellaneous
8	System administration tools and daemons
9	Kernel routines
n	Tcl/Tk keywords

Displaying a Man Section

Now that you know what the different section numbers stand for, I can
show you how to open them. Normally you specify the man command,
followed by the command. To open the command for a particular section,
you just need to specify the section first. For example, to open printf(3),
you would type the following.

```
% man 3 printf
```

Permissions

All files on the computer have permissions to define who can do what
to that file. As a user, you have certain permissions to access files on
macOS. However, you have limited access to system files or to other users.
You have full control over your files in your home directory, with the
exception of the folders that Apple created for you. Most of those folders
have permissions to stop you from accidentally deleting them.

File Permissions

File permissions are how macOS determines who or what is and isn't
allowed to read or write to a given file. The permissions are split into three
specific groups of users—the owner of the file, which groups of users can
have extra permissions, and finally everybody else.

Hopefully, you know who you are. Your user was set when you set up
your computer, or when you added a new user. Typically, a username will
be your full name, without spaces, and converted to lowercase.

If you have forgotten your username, you can ask the shell who you are
using the whoami command.

```
% whoami
danielplatt
```

Your user will also belong to multiple user groups.

% groups
```
staff everyone localaccounts _appserverusr admin _appserveradm
_lpadmin _appstore _lpoperator _developer _analyticsusers com.
apple.access_ftp com.apple.access_screensharing com.apple.
access_ssh com.apple.access_remote_ae com.apple.sharepoint.
group.1
```

You might recognize some of these groups from Sharing in System Preferences.

Now that you know which username and groups your user belongs to, let's look in the root directory.

% ls -l /
```
total 15
drwxrwxr-x+ 122 root         admin    3.8K  2 Nov 11:52
Applications
drwxr-xr-x    2 danielplatt  staff     64B 19 Oct   2018
Bookmarks
drwxr-xr-x+  74 root         wheel    2.3K 29 Sep 12:02 Library
drwxr-xr-x    2 root         wheel     64B 18 Aug   2018 Network
drwxr-xr-x@   5 root         wheel    160B  2 Feb   2019 System
drwxr-xr-x    7 root         admin    224B 21 Sep 14:07 Users
drwxr-xr-x+  10 root         wheel    320B  3 Nov 10:17 Volumes
drwxr-xr-x@  37 root         wheel    1.2K 27 Sep 17:15 bin
drwxrwxr-t    2 root         admin     64B 18 Aug   2018 cores
dr-xr-xr-x    3 root         wheel    5.2K 21 Oct 08:10 dev
lrwxr-xr-x@   1 root         wheel     11B  1 Feb   2019 etc ->
private/etc
dr-xr-xr-x    2 root         wheel      1B  3 Nov 09:50 home
dr-xr-xr-x    2 root         wheel      1B  3 Nov 09:50 net
drwxr-xr-x@   5 demo         wheel    160B  3 Jun   2017 nix
```

```
drwxr-xr-x    3 root        wheel     96B 26 Sep  2016 opt
drwxr-xr-x    6 root        wheel    192B 16 Jan  2019 private
drwxr-xr-x@  64 root        wheel    2.0K 27 Sep 17:15 sbin
lrwxr-xr-x@   1 root        wheel     11B  1 Feb  2019 tmp ->
private/tmp
drwxr-xr-x@  10 root        wheel    320B  2 Feb  2019 usr
lrwxr-xr-x@   1 root        wheel     11B  1 Feb  2019 var ->
private/var
```

This list can be overwhelming at first. Each file and directory will have its own line. From left to right, the columns show permissions, block or link count, user (or owner), group, file size, last modified date, and finally, the name of the file.

File Permissions Breakdown

The file permissions are made up of five components, as shown in Figure 2-19.

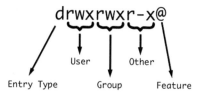

Figure 2-19. *The file permissions, split by component*

These components control what you can do with the files on your computer. Every file will have these individual permissions set. Now let's cover each component in turn.

Entry Type

Everything in macOS is a file. Every file, directory, or device is a file on the filesystem. The entry type tells you what type of file it is, as shown in Table 2-7.

Table 2-7. *File Entry Types*

Symbol	Description
-	Regular file
b	Block special file
c	Character special file
d	Directory
l	Link (also known as a symlink)
s	Socket link
p	FIFO

Regular files and directories are the types we covered in the "File Operations" and "Directory Operations" sections.

Block File

This is any device that is accessed like a block of data. Like a drive, such as /dev/disk0.

Character File

Similar to a block file, a character file is only written or read from one character at a time. An example is /dev/random.

Link

A link is a pointer to another file. Links are similar to aliases in the Finder, or shortcuts in Windows. See the "Links" section.

Socket Link

When programs communicate with each other in macOS, they can either use networking and listen on a particular port, or they can use a socket file. The socket file is usually quicker than communicating through the network stack.

FIFO

FIFO stands for "First In, First Out." This is a named pipe and can be named anything.

```
%mkfifo named-pipe
```

I now have a file called named-pipe, which works similarly to piping covered earlier.

```
% echo "hi" | cat
hi
```

FIFO is the same principle, but using the filesystem.

```
% echo > named-pipe
% cat named-pipe
hi
```

While this looks like I wrote to a file called named-pipe, I did not. If I run cat again, the command prints nothing, but also doesn't return to the prompt. It is waiting for more information to be sent across the pipe.

```
% cat named-pipe
```

Try opening a new Terminal window and sending something else into the named pipe.

The User, Group, and Other Components

Each of these components has three parts—read, write, and execute permissions. When you combine them, you have nine characters in total, which you see in Table 2-8.

***Table 2-8.** Symbol Meaning for User, Group, and Everyone Permissions*

Symbol	Description
-	No permission
r	Readable
w	Writable
x	If a file, executable If a directory, searchable
S	If in user, then `set-user-ID` is set If in group, then `set-group-ID` is set Only appears in user or group
s	If in user, then set-user-ID is set If in group, then set-group-ID is set Equivalent of +x Only appears in user or group
t	Sticky bit; doesn't have search or execute permissions Only appears in other group
T	Sticky bit. Has search or execute permission Only appears in other group

For example the /Volume directory has the permissions rwx r-x r-x, which translates to everyone being able to read and list the contents, but only the user (root) being able to write to the directory.

```
% ls -lh /
drwxr-xr-x   4 root   wheel   128B  5 Aug 19:38 Volumes
```

Set-user-ID (also known as setuid) and Set-group-ID (also known as setgid) run an executable with the user's permissions. A directory with these permissions will mean new files and directories will inherit either the user or group of that directory.

When the sticky bit is set on a directory, only the owner of the directory can delete files in it. An example of the sticky bit is the Shared user folder.

```
% ls -lh /Users
drwxr-xr-x+ 155 danielplatt  staff   4.8K  5 Aug 20:22
danielplatt
drwxr-xr-x+  16 dave         staff   512B 31 Jul 23:10 dave
drwxrwxrwt   10 root         wheel   320B 31 Jul 18:23 Shared
drwxr-xr-x   22 root         admin   704B 17 Jul 15:49 ..
drwxr-xr-x    6 root         admin   192B 24 Oct  2019 .
```

For more information about sticky mode, type man sticky.

Example Permissions

Table 2-9 shows examples of permissions that you will likely see in your Terminal.

Table 2-9. *Example File Permissions*

Permission	Description
drwxr-xr-x	Home directory. Others will be able to see files in this folder, but not write to them.
drwx------	Folders within your home directory. For example, your Desktop. Only the user can read and write to this folder.
-rw-r--r--	Default file permissions for a new file. Everyone can read the file, but only the user can write to it.
drwxr-xr-x	Default directory permissions for a new directory.
-rwxr-xr-x	Typical permissions for Terminal commands. Only the user can modify them, but everyone else can read and execute them.
drwxrwxrwxt	Typical permission of the /tmp directory. Everyone has permission to create a file here, but only the user can delete the file.

Features

The ability to set permissions on files and directories has been around since the beginning of UNIX in the 1970s. Since then, there have been extensions to the original file permissions, as shown in Table 2-10.

Table 2-10. *Feature Symbols*

Symbol	Description
<nothing>	No additional permissions
+	Access control list (ACL)
@	Extended file attributes

You can see these extensions in use with the `ls -l` command, when the permissions end with either a + or @ symbol. I am only showing you these permissions for completeness.

Access Control List

If you would like to see the ACLs for a particular file, you can use the `ls` command with the -e option. Here is an example that shows the ACLs for the root directory.

```
% ls -le /
total 9
drwxrwxr-x+ 48 root  admin  1536 14 Jul 17:46 Applications
 0: group:everyone deny delete
drwxr-xr-x  67 root  wheel  2144 10 Jun 18:26 Library
drwxr-xr-x@  8 root  wheel   256 24 Oct  2019 System
 0: group:everyone deny delete
drwxr-xr-x   6 root  admin   192 12 Jul 11:07 Users
drwxr-xr-x   5 root  wheel   160 14 Jul 19:34 Volumes
drwxr-xr-x@ 38 root  wheel  1216 10 Jun 18:24 bin
drwxr-xr-x   2 root  wheel    64 24 Aug  2019 cores
dr-xr-xr-x   3 root  wheel  4433  1 Jul 18:14 dev
lrwxr-xr-x@  1 root  admin    11  5 Nov  2019 etc -> private/etc
drwxr-xr-x   2 root  wheel    64 24 Aug  2019 opt
drwxr-xr-x   6 root  wheel   192 10 Jun 18:25 private
drwxr-xr-x@ 63 root  wheel  2016 10 Jun 18:24 sbin
lrwxr-xr-x@  1 root  admin    11  5 Nov  2019 tmp -> private/tmp
drwxr-xr-x@ 11 root  wheel   352  5 Nov  2019 usr
lrwxr-xr-x@  1 root  admin    11  5 Nov  2019 var -> private/var
```

Extended File Attributes

If you want to see the extended file attributes for a particular file, you can use the ls command with the -@ option. Here is an example that shows the extended file attributes for the root directory.

```
% ls -l@ /
total 9
dr-xr-xr-x   3 root   wheel   4433   1 Jul 18:14 dev
lrwxr-xr-x@  1 root   admin     11   5 Nov  2019 etc -> private/etc
    com.apple.rootless     0
drwxr-xr-x   2 root   wheel     64 24 Aug  2019 opt
drwxr-xr-x   6 root   wheel    192 10 Jun 18:25 private
drwxr-xr-x@ 63 root   wheel   2016 10 Jun 18:24 sbin
    com.apple.rootless     0
lrwxr-xr-x@  1 root   admin     11   5 Nov  2019 tmp -> private/tmp
    com.apple.rootless     0
drwxr-xr-x@ 11 root   wheel    352   5 Nov  2019 usr
    com.apple.rootless     0
lrwxr-xr-x@  1 root   admin     11   5 Nov  2019 var -> private/var
    com.apple.rootless     0
```

Changing File Permissions

You now know about file permissions, but how do you change them? You do so with the change mode command (chmod). There are a few ways you can use chmod to set file permissions. Take the permissions rw-r--r--.

You can set them as an absolute value (0644) or by using symbolic expressions (u=rw,go=r):

```
% chmod <options> <permissions> filename
```

Let's look at the differences between the different ways you can express permissions.

Absolute Values

Setting a permission as a number is probably the simplest method. However, it does require an understanding of how to calculate the value.

% **chmod 0644 filename**

The number represents the permissions and is broken into four parts—the Entry type, User, Group, and Other. Each of the four parts is built using addition.

Entry Type

The entry type is built using addition, as shown in Table 2-11.

Table 2-11. *Numeric Values for Entry Type*

Value	With Execute	Without Execute
7	s+t	S+T
6	s	S
5	s+t	S+T
4	s	S
3	t	T
2	-	-
1	t	T
0	-	-

User, Group, and Other

The last components are all calculated the same way, as shown in Table 2-12.

Table 2-12. *Numeric Breakdown of User, Group, and Other*

Value	Permission
4	r
2	w
1	x
0	-

Symbolic Values

When setting file permissions, you use the letters u, g, and o (for User, Group, and Other). The equivalent to 0644 using symbols is:

```
% chmod u=rw,go=r filename
```

However, using the plus or minus symbols, you can also add or remove existing permissions. For example, if you wanted to add execute permissions, you would use the following:

```
% chmod ugo+x filename
```

If you wanted to remove execute permissions, you would use the following:

```
% chmod ugo-x filename
```

Escalating Your System Privilege

Occasionally, we will need to run Terminal commands as another user. This would be a massive security issue if everybody could change their active user. For this reason, only admin users can change their active user. You can find out who the admin user is in the Users and Groups section in System Preferences, as shown in Figure 2-20.

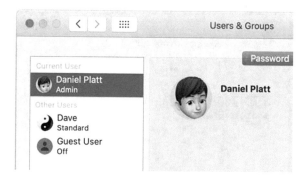

Figure 2-20. *Users and Group system preference*

This command should be treated with caution, as it allows you to run a command as another user, including the root user.

Note   The root user is the primary user on any UNIX system and can do anything on your computer. The root user is allowed to change any file permission and change to any user.

The command I am talking about is sudo.

% sudo --help
```
sudo - execute a command as another user
```

The sudo command is useful when it comes to editing files that you aren't normally supposed to be able edit, at least not by accident. By default sudo will run as root.

% sudo whoami
```
Password:
root
```

This command shows the sudo command executing whoami as root. Any member of the admin group can use sudo. The xkcd comic shown in Figure 2-21 sums up how sudo works perfectly.

Figure 2-21. *Sandwich.* `https://xkcd.com/149/`

You can also use sudo to run commands as users apart from root, as long as the user exists. In the following example, sudo is executing whoami as dave.

```
% sudo -u dave whoami
dave
```

Notice how sudo didn't prompt for a password the second time. This is because, by default, sudo caches the password for five minutes. We will use the sudo command in a later section.

Aliases

When you've been using a lot of different computers, you pick up handy tricks and commands. What I use a lot of, because of my Ubuntu background, is the **ll** ("LL") command, which prints a list of the files in your current directory, with lots of useful information.

So how can you get that on your Terminal, without you writing your own version? Well, **ll** is really the ls command, but with a few extra arguments. You can achieve that with aliasing. You tell your Terminal (Bash) that whenever it sees this one command, it should run this other command. The Ubuntu command ll is actually the ls -alF command.

However, I like to use a modified version, which includes the file sizes in human-readable numbers, with the -h argument.

% ls -alFh

You can type the man ls command to see all the parameters that you can use with the ls command. The -a is for all files, including files starting with a full stop. By default, it will ignore files that start with a full stop.

-L is for long list (dereference symbolic links or shortcuts, this allows you to see the path to the actual file). -F will display a symbol after the file to let you know what type of file it is. / is for a directory, * is for an executable, and @ is for a symbolic link. -h is for human-readable number formats.

There are others, but these are the ones you are likely to come across.

You can paste all these arguments and test them in your current Terminal. Once you have the set of arguments and parameters you want, you will be ready to create your alias. So let's show you how to set that up.

Type alias ll='ls -alFh' into your Terminal.

% alias ll='ls -alFh'

Now you can type ll to use it as alias. However, this alias will not work in other terminals. This is because it will not be saved anywhere. In the next section, you will see how to persist commands for all Terminal windows. However, before we do that, let's talk about other aliases. How do you know what aliases have been defined?

% alias

```
ll='ls -alFh'
run-help=man
which-command=whence
```

If you want to remove a defined alias, you use `unalias`.

```
% unalias ll
```

If you now look at the list of aliases, you can see that the `ll` alias has been removed.

```
% alias
run-help=man
which-command=whence
```

Customizing the Feel

Previously we created an alias for the command `ll`, but the problem was it wouldn't work in a new Terminal window. What you need is a way to run the `alias` command on every new Terminal window.

There are a few special files in your home directory that control how Zsh will behave for you, as shown in Table 2-13. Since these files live in your home directory, Zsh can be customized for each individual user on your computer.

Table 2-13. *The Different Zsh Special Files*

File Extension	Description
`.zshenv`	Setting environment variables.
`.zshrc`	Commands to set up aliases. Nothing that produces any output.
`.zlogin`	Commands that produce output, such as the `fortune` command.
`.zlogout`	Commands that run on logout.

Say you write `alias ll='ls -alFh'` into a file called `.zshrc` in your home directory. The first thing you should do is check which directory you are in, by using pwd. It should be /Users/<username>. Then you can open **.zshrc** with nano (or your favorite text editor).

% **nano . zshrc**

If you are not in your home directory, you can move to it with cd ~ or using ~ in the file path.

% **nano ~/.zshrc**

By default, this file won't exist. We will have to create it. In my `.zshrc` file, I have set up an alias for `ll`, as shown in Figure 2-22.

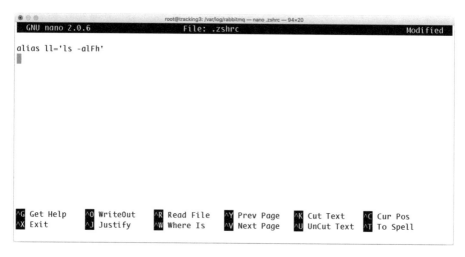

Figure 2-22. *Example .zshrc file with ll alias defined*

This will work for a new Terminal, but if you want to also get it to work with your current Terminal, you have to rerun your `.zshrc` with source ~/. zshrc.

Customizing the Welcome Message

When you open up your Terminal, you see your computer name and the % symbol, as shown in Figure 2-23.

```
● ● ●                      Terminal — -zsh — 97×22
Last login: Sat Oct 26 19:25:30 on ttys006
Mac-Pro% 
```

Figure 2-23. *Terminal with the default .zlogin*

The default Terminal is very plain. There is another file you can edit called .zlogin, which is designed to run commands that produce output. (Unlike the .zshrc file.) You can use the .zlogin file to output some text to customize your new Terminal window or tab. But first, let's meet the echo command, as shown in Figure 2-24.

```
% echo "I'll output anything"
```

```
● ● ●                      Terminal — -zsh — 79×8
Mac-Pro% echo "I'll output anything"
I'll output anything
Mac-Pro% 
```

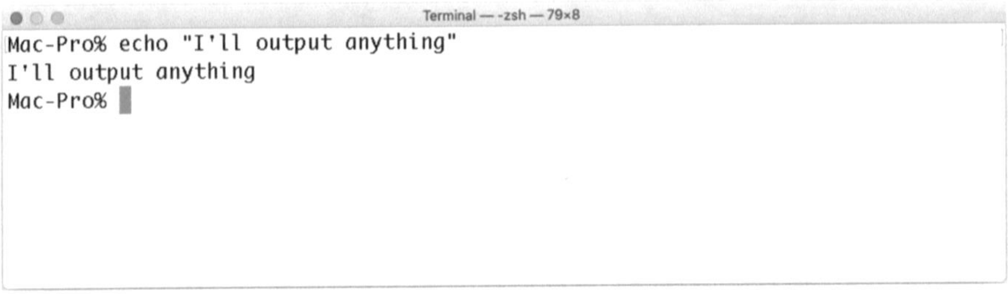

Figure 2-24. *Terminal showing the echo command*

Some symbols have a special meaning. For example, the exclamation mark is shown in Figure 2-25.

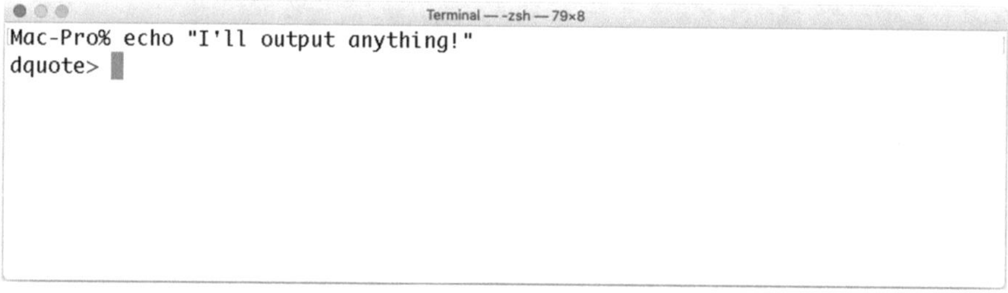

```
● ○ ○                    Terminal — -zsh — 79×8
Mac-Pro% echo "I'll output anything!"
dquote> ▌
```

Figure 2-25. *Exclamation mark breaking the echo command*

If you want to use these symbols as is, you need to rob them of their special meaning by *escaping* them. You escape a symbol or character using the backslash symbol (\), as shown in Figure 2-26.

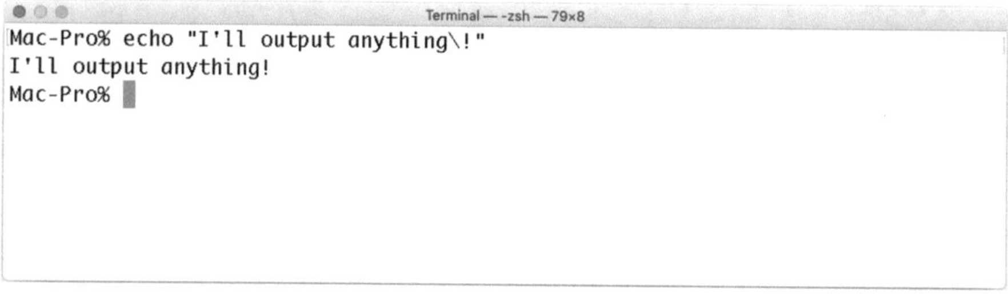

```
● ○ ○                    Terminal — -zsh — 79×8
Mac-Pro% echo "I'll output anything\!"
I'll output anything!
Mac-Pro% ▌
```

Figure 2-26. *Using the escape character to allow usage of a regular exclamation mark*

Now you can use the echo command in the .zlogin file to create a warning to anyone trying to use this user's Terminal, as shown in Figure 2-27.

Figure 2-27. Using .zshrc to display a message to users

Notice how this echo command is outputting text over multiple lines. We can take this further by including commands that produce their own output, as shown in Figure 2-28.

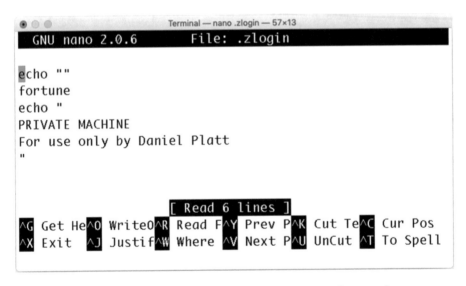

Figure 2-28. Using the echo and fortune commands together

The first echo command creates a newline between the Last login and the fortune message. You can see the result in Figure 2-29.

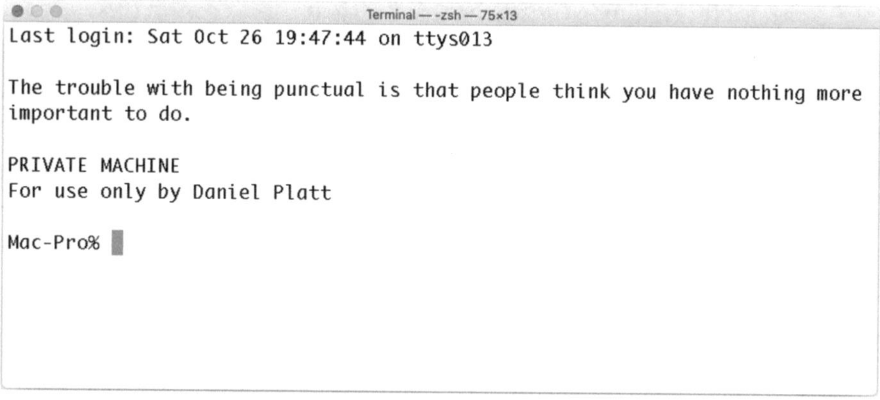

```
● ○ ○                    Terminal — -zsh — 75×13
Last login: Sat Oct 26 19:47:44 on ttys013

The trouble with being punctual is that people think you have nothing more
important to do.

PRIVATE MACHINE
For use only by Daniel Platt

Mac-Pro% ▮
```

Figure 2-29. *The output from our new .zlogin*

Now you know the basics of customizing the Terminal welcome message.

Environment Variables

Inside the shell are variables. A variable is a place for a program to store a value for later use. You can think of variables a bit like buckets. Anything can be placed inside the bucket and later retrieved. You can store a value in a variable, and at a later time, take it back out.

Unlike a bucket, you can keep taking something out of a variable. You can also keep putting different things in a variable and only the last item will be available.

By default, variables contain nothing.

% **echo $TEST**
```
<empty line>
```

You can set a value to a variable like this.

% **TEST=1**
% **echo $TEST**
```
1
```

91

Be careful though. It is probably best to use quotes around the contents.

```
% TEST=I am a variable
zsh: command not found: am
You would have to type:
```

```
% TEST="I am a variable"
If you want to get rid of a variable, you can remove it.
```

```
% unset TEST
Zsh has loads of variables that are set by default. You can see
a list of them by typing env.
```

```
% env
TERM_PROGRAM=Apple_Terminal
SHELL=/bin/zsh
TERM=xterm-256color
...
```

However, you might notice that TEST was not in that list. What's going on here? Well, when we run TEST="I am a variable", we are only setting the variable for the shell. No running programs will see this variable. For env to see our new variable, we need to tell the shell to make it available with the export keyword.

```
% export TEST="I am a variable"
```

```
% env
TERM_PROGRAM=Apple_Terminal
SHELL=/bin/zsh
TERM=xterm-256color
...
TEST=I am a variable
```

Why Use Variables?

Variables can be used to keep track of your script's state or configuration for later use in a program. They can also be used as placeholders, for example, to hold the output of a script.

The Default Text Editor

Occasionally, some commands will open a text editor. The default text editor is vi, which if you are new to Terminal, can be very confusing. You can override that by setting a variable called EDITOR.

```
% export EDITOR="/usr/bin/nano"
```

This way, if you find yourself in a text editor, it'll be the more familiar nano. To make this change permanent, you need to add that line to your .zshrc file.

How Can You Use Variables?

You can then output variables to Terminal.

```
% echo $SHELL
```

You can even output them as part of a string.

```
% echo "Hello $USER."
```

You can combine variables by concatenating them.

```
% GREETING="Hello $USER."
```

Later, we will talk about doing different things based on variables.

Customizing the Shell Prompt

We've been looking at the shell prompt a lot, but haven't really talked about it.

```
Mac-Pro%
```

In my case, the shell prompt says Mac-Pro and ends with the percent symbol. That's not very exciting at all. This is the default Mac shell prompt, and it's controlled by something called the PS1 shell variable.

```
%  echo $PS1
%n@%m %1~ %#
```

What can we do with that? Well, we can do a lot, actually. We could use some text that doesn't change, but that isn't very useful, as shown in Figure 2-30.

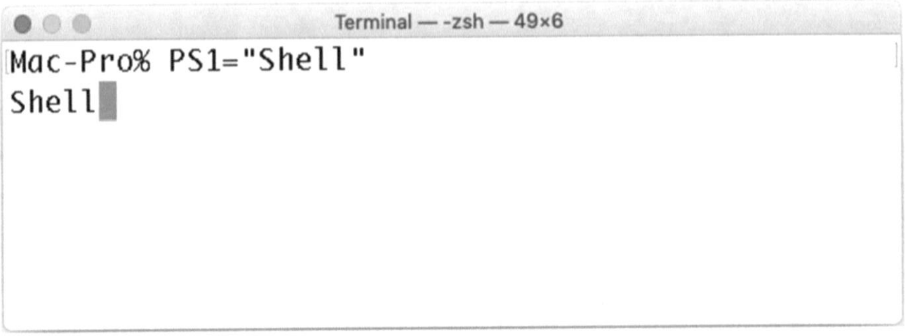

Figure 2-30. *Changing the shell prompt*

State Symbols

There are a number of special symbols that you can use to make your shell prompt more dynamic. You learned about %m and %# before and you can see a list of others in Table 2-14.

Table 2-14. *State Symbols*

Symbol	Description
%m	Computer name
%n	Username
%#	Will display % unless you have a privileged account, and then it is #
%d	Your current location (working directory)

A quick way to see these is by using all of these symbols, as shown in Figure 2-31.

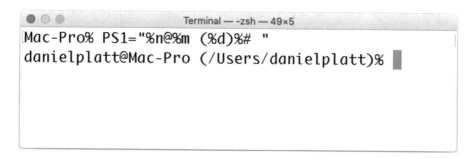

Figure 2-31. *Example of state symbols in the shell prompt*

Date and Time Symbols

You might like to know when all your previous commands were run, so including the time could be helpful. Table 2-15 contains a list of date and time symbols.

Table 2-15. *Date and Time Symbols for Use in the Shell Prompt*

Symbol	Description
%D	The date in yy-mm-dd format
%W	Date in mm/dd/yy format
%T	Time in 24 hour format (HH:MM)
%t	Time in 12 hour format (HH:MMam/pm)
%w	Day of the week and day of the month
%D{<strftime symbols>}	Custom date and time string (see next table)

An example of the shell prompt with the date and time is shown in Figure 2-32.

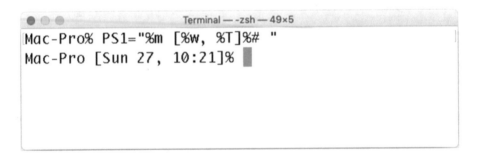

Figure 2-32. *Date and time shown on the shell prompt*

The symbol %D is special, as it takes a substring. You can use this to define your own date/time format, as shown in Table 2-16.

Table 2-16. *Symbols for strftime*

strftime Symbol	Description
%A	Day of the week
%a	Abbreviated day of the week
%B	Full month name
%b	Abbreviated month name
%m	Month as a number (01-12)
%d	Day of the month. (With a leading zero for single digit dates)
%e	Day of the month (with a leading space for single digit dates)
%G	Full year, e.g., 2020
%g	Last two digits of the year, e.g., 20

The list of strftime symbols is long. For the full list, type man strftime. You also have other shell variables, as shown in Table 2-17. PATH is a shell variable, PS1 is a shell variable, and it will tell you what each one of them means, whether you just want to echo them or act on them.

Table 2-17. *Other Shell Variables of Note*

Variable	Description
PS1	Initial prompt (default: %n@%m %1~ %# ")
PS2	Prompt carries on to the next line (default: "%_> ")
USER	Your username
PWD	Your current directory
OSTYPE	Operating system version (darwin19.0)
PATH	Everywhere the shell will check a command might exist, before returning the message, command not found

So PS1 is the initial prompt, and PS2 is for when the command spans multiple lines, such as when you type echo \ and then continue the command on the next line. Remember, you also have the env command, which will list all the environment variables that have been set. Finally, you can also use emojis in Terminal. You can bring up the Emoji Picker by pressing Control+Command+Space, as shown in Figure 2-33.

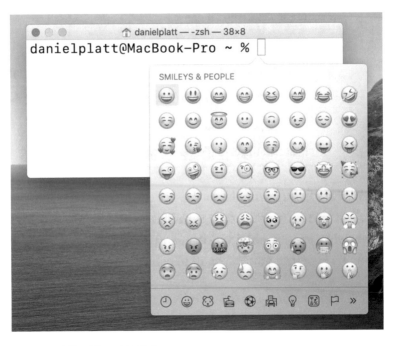

Figure 2-33. *The Emoji Picker*

This also means you can use emojis in your shell prompt, as shown in Figure 2-34.

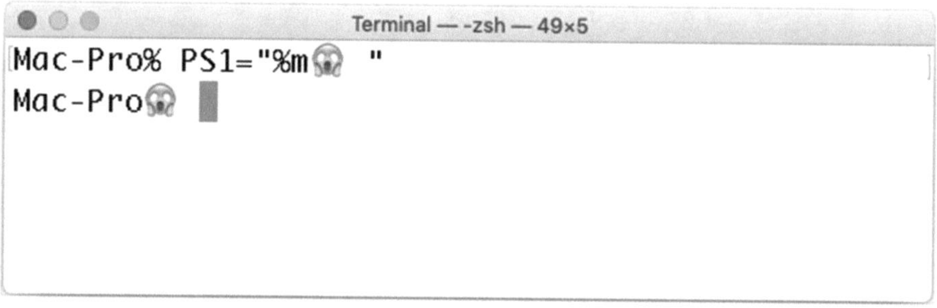

```
● ○ ●                Terminal — -zsh — 49×5
Mac-Pro% PS1="%m😱 "
Mac-Pro😱 ▌
```

Figure 2-34. *Emoji being used in the shell prompt*

Summary

In this chapter, we walked through Terminal, learning about different aspects of the filesystem and how to edit files. We finally finished with you being able to customize your shell environment.

CHAPTER 3

macOS Built-in Commands

In this chapter, we explore the different commands that came with your copy of the macOS operating system. There are loads of different commands to choose from. A lot of these commands are used to manipulate files or process text.

Before we get started, we will need files to operate on, so that you can follow along. If you are confident, you can use your own files as a source.

Getting Started

We need large blocks of text. It might be worth creating a folder in your home directory specifically for this next step. If you need help, see Chapter 2. Alternatively, if you want to use a temporary directory that will automatically delete itself on the next system reboot, you can use this command.

```
% cd "$(mktemp -d)"
```

This will create a temporary directory and cd into it.

Each time you run it, you will end up in a different temporary directory, so make note of the location you end up, rather than running it multiple times.

```
% cd "$(mktemp -d)"
% pwd
/var/folders/5z/tnwhfkg57hdfys5fxckr07_h0000gn/T/tmp.QPg0xWOB
```

© Daniel Platt 2021
D. Platt, *Tweak Your Mac Terminal*, https://doi.org/10.1007/978-1-4842-6171-2_3

We need to download my archive full of text files, using the `curl` command.

```
% curl --location -o master.zip https://github.com/hackzilla/
random-files/archive/master.zip
```

If all went well, you should have a file in your current directory, called `master.zip`. Make note of where you are running this command, as this will be where the download is stored. If in doubt, run the `pwd` command.

I will assume that you downloaded `master.zip` into your home directory.

Compression

Whether it is to save space, or to save bandwidth, at the end of the day, compression is about saving money. Compression is about reducing the size of a file in a reversible way.

That means, for every method of compression, there will be a method for decompressing the file. I'm going to show you two common forms of compression—zip and gzip—that you will encounter on the Internet. You're going to see each compression method in action.

We're going to download a couple of archives and use them in this chapter.

Zip Compression

When I think about zip compression, I am reminded of PKZIP and WinZip. These were programs for compressing and decompressing files and folders on DOS and Windows. What you might not know is that PKZIP was made by a company called PKWARE. PKWARE's founder, Phil Katz, released the file format into the public domain in 1989. Shortly afterward, there was a project called Info-ZIP, which released open source utilities for compressing and decompressing files.

We're going to use the `master.zip` file you downloaded earlier.

Unzip

Unzipping is the process of taking a single compressed archive and extracting the files and folders from within. As we already have a zip file, we need to extract the files first, also called uncompressing them.

The command to uncompress a zip file is unzip, as follows:

```
% unzip --help
UnZip 6.00 of 20 April 2009, by Info-ZIP.  Maintained by
C. Spieler.  Send
bug reports using http://www.info-zip.org/zip-bug.html;
see README for details.

Usage: unzip [-Z] [-opts[modifiers]] file[.zip] [list]
[-x xlist] [-d exdir]
  Default action is to extract files in list, except those in
  xlist, to exdir;
  file[.zip] may be a wildcard.
```

Testing the Integrity of the Zip File

Before we extract the files from master.zip, we should verify the archive downloaded correctly with the -t option. This will compare the archive checksum with the files stored in the archive.

```
% unzip -t master.zip
Archive: master.zip
025d101299c770c5f305e731cce76368c7201fb0
    testing: random-files-master/OK
    testing: random-files-master/Readme.md OK
    ...
No errors detected in compressed data of master.zip.
```

If the file downloaded with errors, you should try downloading it again. If no errors were detected in the archive, you can move on.

Listing the Contents of the Zip File

If you want to know what is stored inside a zip file before you extract it, you can view its contents with the -l option.

```
% unzip -l master.zip
Archive:  master.zip
025d101299c770c5f305e731cce76368c7201fb0
  Length      Date    Time    Name
---------  ---------- -----    ----
        0  11-16-2019 22:20   random-files-master/
       64  11-16-2019 22:20   random-files-master/Readme.md
     3857  11-16-2019 22:20   random-files-master/bible.txt
     9500  11-16-2019 22:20   random-files-master/decamerone.txt
     2419  11-16-2019 22:20   random-files-master/faust.txt
     3178  11-16-2019 22:20   random-files-master/fleurs.txt
     2094  11-16-2019 22:20   random-files-master/lorem.txt
     2885  11-16-2019 22:20   random-files-master/raven.txt
     2642  11-16-2019 22:20   random-files-master/spook.txt
      458  11-16-2019 22:20   random-files-master/strandberg.txt
     4691  11-16-2019 22:20   random-files-master/strindberg.txt
     5125  11-16-2019 22:20   random-files-master/walden.txt
---------                     -------
    36913                     12 files
```

What you should notice about this listing is whether the files are within a folder or not. In this example, the files are in a directory called random-files. The last thing you want to do is expand a zip archive and all the files appear within your home directory.

If the zip archive didn't contain a directory, you can easily create a directory and move the archive in, all before extracting the files.

```
% mkdir random-files-master
% mv master.zip random-files-master
```

Now that we know it is safe to expand in the home directory, we can unzip it.

```
% unzip master.zip
Archive:  master.zip
025d101299c770c5f305e731cce76368c7201fb0
   creating: random-files-master/
  inflating: random-files-master/Readme.md
  inflating: random-files-master/bible.txt
  inflating: random-files-master/decamerone.txt
  ...
```

Now you will find a directory called random-files-master in your current directory, which contains all the files from the zip file. This is the basic process for extracting files from zip archives.

Zip

We cannot talk about unzipping without mentioning the process for creating a zip archive.

```
% zip --help
Copyright (c) 1990-2008 Info-ZIP - Type 'zip "-L"' for software
license.
Zip 3.0 (July 5th 2008).
```

When it comes to compressing files, you have more options.

- Would you like to make the archive smaller or faster to compress and decompress?

- Do you want to encrypt the contents or not?

Previously, you saw `master.zip` had all the files stored in a directory called `random-files`. Now you can see the difference when creating the zip file from a folder of files. The `zip` command includes the full directory path from your current directory.

```
% zip with-directory.zip random-files-master/*
  adding: random-files-master/BinaryEncoding.md (deflated 74%)
```

Note   If you use the ~ tilde symbol, the `zip` command will include the full directory.

```
% zip with-directory.zip ~/random-files-master/*
  adding: Users/danielplatt/random-files-master/BinaryEncoding.md
  (deflated 74%)
```

If you wanted to create the archive without the parent directory, you would need to be in the `random-files` directory.

```
% cd random-files-master
% zip without-directory.zip *
  adding: BinaryEncoding.md (deflated 74%)
```

Adjust the Size of the Archive

There is an option to change how much compression to use with zip, from no compression to slowest compression. The slower the compression, the more time the computer spends making the archive smaller.

In the following command, # is replaced by a number from 0 to 9. 0 is no compression, 1 is the fastest, and 9 is the slowest. If this option is not provided, zip will use the default value of 6.

```
% zip -# with-directory.zip random-files-master/*
```

If you want to make the zip file as small as possible, you would use -9.

```
% zip -9 with-directory.zip random-files-master/*
```

Encrypting the Archive

When creating a zip archive, you can choose to enable encryption with the -e option and then assign a password to the archive. You might do this if you were transmitting sensitive information across the Internet. Or maybe you want to store sensitive information on a thumb drive, but want to make sure that if anyone finds it, they couldn't read the files.

```
% zip -e with-directory.zip random-files-master/*
Enter password:
Verify password:
```

It's worth noting that the files are encrypted on a per-file basis, rather than encrypting the whole archive. This means you can still see the file listing of the archive. You can prevent this listing by recompressing the archive with encryption.

Unzipping with encryption is as simple as running the unzip command. When unzip encounters an encrypted file, you will be prompted for the password.

```
% unzip with-directory.zip
Archive: with-directory.zip
[with-directory.zip] random-files-master/BinaryEncoding.md password:
```

Compressing Directories

The last thing to mention is if you try to compress a directory with other directories in it, the commands you are currently using will skip over those directories. You need to tell zip to recursively go into those folders using the -r option.

```
% zip -r with-directory.zip random-files-master/*
```

Gzip Compression

In 1992, a couple of years after the zip file format was released into the public domain, the first version of gzip became available.

```
% gzip --help
Apple gzip 287.40.2
usage: gzip [-123456789acdfhklLNnqrtVv] [-S .suffix] [<file>
[<file> ...]]
 -1 --fast            fastest (worst) compression
 -2 .. -8             set compression level
 -9 --best            best (slowest) compression
```

There are a lot of similarities between gzip and zip compression. One big difference with gzip is that it will not compress multiple files into a single archive. You can try to compress a whole folder with the -r option.

```
% gzip -r random-files-master
```

```
% ls random-files-master
```
BinaryEncoding.md.gz   FAQ.md.gz   LICENSE.gz   README.md.gz
UseCases.md.gz

gzip compresses each of the files individually. You can reverse the process with the -d option.

```
% gzip -rd random-files-master
```

If gzip cannot compress more than a single file, then what can it be used for? One example is log files. They are usually rotated to stop them from getting too big. Sometimes they are rotated by time (day or week) and other times it is by size.

```
% ls -l /var/log/system.log*
```

What about using gzip to compress more than one file? There is a solution to that, and it is to back up to tape.

Tar

You are probably more familiar with SSDs and thumb drives for storage on computers. However, when you are trying to back up a large amount of data, these forms of storage will end up being very expensive.

Tape storage is a cheaper way of storing a large amount of data in a small space. You can see from Figure 3-1 that a single tape can store up to 30TB. For the price of a tape drive, you could buy a hard drive that held only 6TB.

Figure 3-1. *Sun Microsystems tape drive and media*

When backing up to tape, you need to convert the filesystem into a single stream of data that can be written to a tape archive. The command to do that is called tar.

```
% tar --help
tar(bsdtar): manipulate archive files
First option must be a mode specifier:
  -c Create  -r Add/Replace  -t List  -u Update  -x Extract
```

Using `tar`, we can create an archive with `-c`, and we can compress it with gzip and `-z`. You also need to provide `-f` to save the resulting archive to a file. Otherwise, the archive will be outputted to Terminal.

```
% tar -czf master.tar.gz random-files-master
```

Now that you have your `tar` archive, you can look inside it with the `-t` option.

```
% tar -tf master.tar.gz
random-files/
random-files/HighLevelGoals.md
random-files/NonWeb.md
random-files/Tooling.md
random-files/TextFormat.md
random-files/MVP.md
random-files/LICENSE
```

You use the `-x` option to extract files from a `tar` archive.

```
% tar -xf master.tar.gz
```

Working with Files

This section covers all the different macOS built-in commands that deal with files, whether it be finding files, finding information within a file, or determining what type of file it is.

Finding Content in Files

Imagine that you have a large text file and you are looking for a specific piece of information or want to find every occurrence of something. For me, this is a daily occurrence, as I look through system logs when trying to solve problems. This brings us to the `grep` command.

% **grep --help**

usage: grep [-abcDEFGHhIiJLlmnOoqRSsUVvwxZ] [-A num] [-B num]
[-C[num]]
    [-e pattern] [-f file] [--binary-files=value] [--color=when]
    [--context[=num]] [--directories=action] [--label] [--line-
    buffered]
    [--null] [pattern] [file ...]

grep finds text within other blocks of text. If you want to find the word *security*, you can use security as the pattern.

% **grep Security random-files-master/spook.txt**

surveillance; Security Gazprom S AG ASIO passwd Fedayeen? Wire
SCUD Bellcore
Karimov. Security embassy secure ANZUS Kerry Forte Compsec
anarchy Ahmadinejad

grep is case-sensitive. This means that "security" will not find instances of "Security." If you want to make a search case-insensitive, use the -i option.

% **grep -i security random-files-master/spook.txt**

If you only want a count of how many lines match, you can use the -c option. However, if a word appears more than once on a line, it is only counted once.

% **grep -c security random-files-master/spook.txt**
4
% **grep -c Security random-files-master/spook.txt**
3
% **grep -ic security random-files-master/spook.txt**
6

So far, we have been searching for the word "security" as our pattern. What if we wanted to search for something a little more complex? You can use a regular expression as your pattern.

A simple way to find a word at the beginning of a line is to use the ^ symbol.

```
% grep "^Europol" spook.txt
Europol airframe Box airframe Taiwan! MD2 Audiotel Panama
csystems ASDIC AlQaeda
```

If you wanted to find a word at the end of a line, you would end the expression with $. With more advanced regular expressions, you will need to use the -E option.

Here's an example of searching for any number that is three digits or more.

```
% grep -E "[0-9]{3,}" spook.txt
MD5 USCODE? John 556. NWO Tower Gazprom digicash NSA Wired
Israel Bosnia
```

Finally, I want to bring your attention to context. Imagine you are looking for something in the log file that is difficult to find. However, you know what comes before or after it. Let's assume that what you want to find comes before and after the occurrence of the word "Statistics."

```
% grep Statistics system.log
Nov 19 00:40:10 MacBook-Pro syslogd[90]: ASL Sender Statistics
Nov 19 02:40:31 MacBook-Pro syslogd[90]: ASL Sender Statistics
Nov 19 08:48:11 MacBook-Pro syslogd[90]: ASL Sender Statistics
```

You could make a note of those times and then use cat to go through the file. Maybe you could use regular expressions to show everything that happened when the time was 40 minutes past the hour.

```
% grep -c -E " [0-9]{2}:40:[0-9]{2} " system.log
41
```

That is 41 lines to check, but what about the occurrences that didn't happen at 40 minutes past? There is another way. You can pass in the -a (after) and -b (before) options with the number of lines you would like. When you use -a or -b, you need to specify the option and the number, without a space between.

% grep -a1 -b1 Statistics system.log
```
0-Nov 19 00:40:11 --- last message repeated 1 time ---
53:Nov 19 00:40:10 MacBook-Pro syslogd[90]: ASL Sender
Statistics
116-Nov 19 00:40:11 MacBook-Pro syslogd[90]: Configuration
Notice:
--
--
4604-Nov 19 00:40:11 MacBook-Pro xpcproxy[22930]:
libcoreservices: _dirhelper_userdir: 557: bootstrap_look_up
returned (ipc/send) invalid destination port
4754:Nov 19 02:40:31 MacBook-Pro syslogd[90]: ASL Sender
Statistics
4817-Nov 19 02:40:31 MacBook-Pro com.apple.xpc.launchd[1] (com.
apple.sandboxd[22397]): Service exited due to SIGALRM | sent by
kernel_task[0]
--
--
7275-Nov 19 02:40:46 MacBook-Pro xpcproxy[22946]:
libcoreservices: _dirhelper_userdir: 557: bootstrap_look_up
returned (ipc/send) invalid destination port
7425:Nov 19 08:48:11 MacBook-Pro syslogd[90]: ASL Sender
Statistics
7488-Nov 19 08:48:11 MacBook-Pro com.apple.xpc.launchd[1] (com.
apple.sandboxd[22944]): Service exited due to SIGALRM | sent by
kernel_task[0]
```

Finding a Filename

Sometimes you'll want to search for a file, not by its contents, but by the filename itself.

The find command will help you find files and folders that represent your expression.

Note   find can be slow, as it searches your filesystem every time you run it.

```
% find -H
usage: find [-H | -L | -P] [-EXdsx] [-f path] path ... [expression]
       find [-H | -L | -P] [-EXdsx] -f path [path ...] [expression]
```

At find's basic level, you can get it to list all the files and folders across the whole filesystem.

```
% find / *
```

You can limit find to any folder of your choosing, as follows:

```
% find random-files-master *
```

What if you wanted to only return files that matched a certain pattern? The expression that find takes differs from the glob expression that the ls command took, but we can make it work the same by passing in –name, as follows:

```
% find random-files-master -name "*.txt"
```

The same glob expressions will work with the find command.

```
% find /var/log -name "system.log.[0-9].gz"
/var/log/system.log.2.gz
/var/log/system.log.1.gz
/var/log/system.log.0.gz
```

The total number of logs will differ, depending on how old your computer install is.

There is also a **-type** option that can filter the file type (for example, f for file, d for directory, and l for a symbolic link).

This command will print all the directories in the folder.

```
% find random-files-master -type d;
```

The find man command has many more usage examples.

Finding a Filename with locate

If the find command is a little too complex or too slow, there is an alternative command called locate.

```
% locate
usage: locate [-0Scims] [-l limit] [-d database] pattern ...

default database: `/var/db/locate.database' or $LOCATE_PATH
```

locate works by searching through a database of filenames, rather than searching the filesystem every time. This has the benefit of being faster, but sometimes the list may be out of date.

Let's use locate to look for files ending in .md, as we did with find.

```
% locate "*.txt"

WARNING: The locate database (/var/db/locate.database) does not exist.
To create the database, run the following command:

    sudo launchctl load -w /System/Library/LaunchDaemons/com.
    apple.locate.plist

Please be aware that the database can take some time to
generate; once It has created the database, this message will
no longer appear.
```

If this is the first time you have used locate on your computer, there will not be a database for locate to use. This warning is telling you to create a locate database.

```
% sudo launchctl load -w /System/Library/LaunchDaemons/com.
apple.locate.plist
Password: <enter your user password>
```

While the command will return results to Terminal rather quickly, the database might take a while to build. The time it takes will depend on how many files are on your drive. This warning will go away once it has built the database.

When using the locate command, you must remember that you are matching the whole file path, rather than just the filename.

Let's look at some system logs:

```
% locate "*/system.log.[0-9].*"
/private/var/log/system.log.0.gz
```

You might notice some differences between this output and the output of the find command. The first difference is the path is /private/var/log/, rather than /var/log/. This is because /var is a symbolic link to /private/var. Therefore, they are really the same location.

The other difference is that there was only one log that was returned, whereas the find command returned three logs. This is the downside to the locate command. It uses a database that will become out of date until it is rebuilt. The rebuilding happens once a week, assuming your computer is running.

Where Is Your Command?

Occasionally, you might want to know where commands live on your filesystem. This next command will do that, but it is more useful if you have the same command in multiple places.

% which

```
which [-as] program
```

The which command will show you where the given program is.

% which sh

```
/bin/sh
```

If you want the which command to return all instances of a command, use the -a option.

% which -a git

```
/usr/local/bin/git
/usr/bin/git
```

Note   If you've only just started using Catalina when you try the which –a command, you will only see one command location returned.

The -a option is useful when you want to make sure the right command is being called. which works by checking all the locations that a command could be installed in. It knows all the locations where the system commands are installed.

If you remember in Chapter 2, we discussed environment variables. There is a variable that controls where the shell will look for commands to run. The variable that controls this is called $PATH and contains a list of paths separated by colons.

% echo $PATH

```
/usr/local/bin:/usr/bin:/bin:/usr/sbin:/sbin
```

Note   If a folder appears twice, it can cause a duplicate entry from the which command.

To see this in action, we can temporarily double up the $PATH variable.

```
% PATH="$PATH:$PATH"
% echo $PATH
/usr/local/bin:/usr/bin:/bin:/usr/sbin:/sbin:/usr/local/bin:/
usr/bin:/bin:/usr/sbin:/sbin
```

Now when we look for a command, we will see multiple entries.

```
% which -a sh
/bin/sh
/bin/sh
```

Inspecting File Contents

Let's say you've received a file from someone, but it doesn't have a file type extension. What do you do with it? You could open it in a text editor and try to guess what is inside, as shown in Figure 3-2.

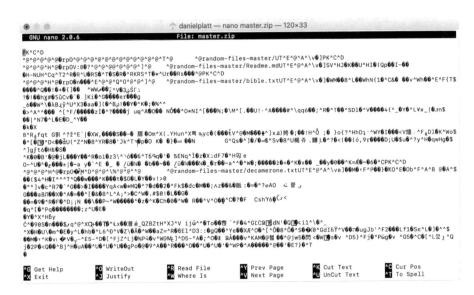

Figure 3-2. *Viewing the contents of master.zip in nano*

If you do this enough times, you might start to see a pattern. At the beginning of a file, there is a magic code that tells the system what type of file it is. You can see this more easily in Figure 3-3.

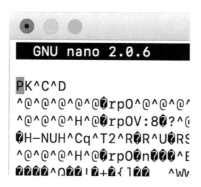

Figure 3-3. *Close-up when editing master.zip*

The first two characters of this file are PK. This is this file's magic code. PK is the zip format's magic code, as PKWARE created the file format. There is a command called `file` that will read this magic code and tell you what the file type is.

```
% file master.zip
master.zip: Zip archive data, at least v1.0 to extract
```

There is more to it than that, otherwise `file` wouldn't be able to tell the difference between a plain text document and an `.xml` file.

```
% file random-files-master/Readme.md
/Users/danielplatt/random-files-master/Readme.md: ASCII text
```

```
% file /System/Library/Templates/Data/usr/share/snmp/SensorDat.xml
/System/Library/Templates/Data/usr/share/snmp/SensorDat.xml:
XML 1.0 document text, ASCII text
```

The `file` command will also work on Terminal commands, which, with Catalina, should all be 64-bit.

% file /bin/sh
```
/bin/sh: Mach-O 64-bit executable x86_64
```

When you try to use `file` on a macOS app, it will not understand them correctly. macOS apps are a collection of files inside a directory with the extension `.app`. If you open the contextual menu (sometimes referred to as a secondary click, or right-click) on an app and select Show Package Contents, then you will know about this.

% file /System/Applications/TextEdit.app
```
/System/Applications/TextEdit.app: directory
```

Here is an example of an audio file.

% file /System/Library/Sounds/Sosumi.aiff
```
/System/Library/Sounds/Sosumi.aiff: IFF data, AIFF audio
```

`file` will also show you more information about the file. This is true if the file contains metadata, such as with picture files.

% file /Library/Desktop\ Pictures/Abstract\ Shapes.jpg
```
/Library/Desktop Pictures/Abstract Shapes.jpg: JPEG image data,
Exif standard: [TIFF image data, big-endian, direntries=7,
orientation=upper-left, xresolution=98, yresolution=106,
resolutionunit=2, software=Adobe Photoshop CC 2017 (Macintosh),
datetime=2016:11:10 11:43:33], baseline, precision 8,
5120x2880, components 3
```

These examples had a file extension in the filename, but the `file` command didn't use that to figure it out.

Working with Text

This section covers all the different macOS built-in commands that deal with text, whether it be printing or outputting text, formatting it, displaying it, or transforming it.

Printing Text

Occasionally I've needed to output text and so far, we used the echo command to do this.

```
% echo "Output Text"
Output Text
```

The echo command is straightforward and prints everything that is passed to it. echo also takes an optional -n argument, which omits the trailing newline. The main reason to not want a trailing newline is if you are asking for input from the user and you want the input to appear on the same line as the output. We will talk about reading user input in Chapter 5.

```
% echo -n "Continue? [Yn]: "
Continue? [Yn]: %
```

As well as removing newlines, you can also add them by using an escape character, \n. Anywhere that you use \n, it will be replaced with a newline.

```
% echo "**************\n* Hello World *\n**************"
**************
* Hello World *
**************
```

Formatting Output

There is an alternative command for outputting text that I use, called printf. The main reason people use the printf command is to output formatted variables. By default, printf will output text just like echo -n, without the trailing newline.

```
% printf "Output Text"
Output Text%
```

As well as the first argument, printf also takes additional arguments, which it can insert into the first argument.

```
printf format [arguments ...]
```

printf controls what is displayed.

Printf Format

The format and arguments work hand in hand. For every argument that is specified, you should include a percent sign and a format character in the format.

Let's say we want to use text as our argument, then we would use %s to represent it.

```
% printf "User Entered: %s" "testing"
User Entered: testing%
```

printf works with many different types of inputs, from text to numbers to decimals. How printf displays the arguments comes down to the format character (the letter after the percent symbol). A selection of these format characters is shown in Table 3-1.

Table 3-1. *Selection of Format Characters for printf*

Format Character	Type	Example
d	Number or integer	10
f	Decimal	10.000200
s	Text or string	"Text"
%	Display a percent sign	%

Displaying the Arguments

The format string uses the arguments in the order they are provided; you also need to specify their correct format.

```
% printf "%s scored %d/%d\n" "Daniel" 33 34
Daniel scored 33/34
```

If the values are out of order or you try to format a string as a number, this will most likely result in 0. It might work, if the string contains a number, but it's unlikely.

```
% printf "%s scored %d/%d\n" 33 "Daniel" 34
33 scored 0/34
```

Where printf shines is when it's used in scripts to output data from variables. These variables are passed into printf as arguments.

```
% printf "Your Terminal Vendor is %s and is Version %d\n" ➡
$TERM_PROGRAM $TERM_PROGRAM_VERSION
Your Terminal Vendor is Apple_Terminal and is Version 433
```

Note   If you supply more arguments than there are format characters, printf will keep printing the format line until all the arguments are used up.

Viewing the Contents

If you want to edit the contents of a text file, you can use nano. But what if you just want to view the contents? The cat command will print the contents of files.

```
% cd ~/random-files-master
% cat strandberg.txt
```
Foo? Hoo? Baz. Foo bar, Foo Foo Baz! Foo bar, baz? Bar? Foo!
Hoo? Baz! Foo bar,
Foo Foo Baz. Foo bar, baz. Bar; Foo. Hoo! Baz! Foo bar, Foo Foo
Baz! Foo bar,
baz; Bar! Foo? Hoo? Baz. Foo bar, Foo Foo Baz! Foo bar, baz.
Bar. Foo; Hoo! Baz!
Foo bar, Foo Foo Baz. Foo bar, baz! Bar; Foo? Hoo. Baz; Foo
bar, Foo Foo Baz;
Foo bar, baz. Bar. Foo? Hoo; Baz? Foo bar, Foo Foo Baz; Foo
bar, baz; Bar. Foo;
Hoo! Baz! Foo bar, Foo Foo Baz. Foo bar, baz? Bar? Foo. Hoo.

The cat command will also take many files and print them all.

```
% cat strandberg.txt strandberg.txt strandberg.txt
```

The output of that command will print the contents strandberg.txt, three times. This works well for small files, but what about when the file is many megabytes? In a pinch, you could use cat. However, there is a better way.

```
% less walden.txt
```

You might have come across this interface before, but not the command. By default, the man command is using less to help you navigate through the manual.

Everything that we covered in Chapter 2 will work here. The Up and Down arrows will move you one line at a time. The Control+U and Control+V keypresses will move you a whole screen of text at a time. Finally, the forward slash will search the document by either a word or a regular expression.

Once you are finished, you can press the *q* key to exit. If you wanted to combine multiple files, you could use cat with the less command.

```
% cat lorem.txt bible.txt | less
```

Or you could save the combined files to another file on your filesystem.

```
% cat lorem.txt bible.txt > combined.txt
```

Transforming Text

The tr command translates characters and transforms text. It works by changing or deleting characters.

Changing Characters

When substituting characters, we need to give tr a string to match and another string to swap the characters to.

For example, we can get tr to convert all the lowercase letters to uppercase, as follows:

```
% tr "[:lower:]" "[:upper:]" < strandberg.txt
FOO? HOO? BAZ. FOO BAR, FOO FOO BAZ! FOO BAR, BAZ? BAR?

% tr "[:lower:][:upper:]" "[:lower:][:upper:]" < strandberg.txt
```

You can also perform multiple translations. For example, if you wanted to toggle the case of the input, you could specify multiple text classes.

```
% tr "[:lower:][:upper:]" "[:upper:][:lower:]" < strandberg.txt
fOO? hOO? bAZ. fOO BAR, fOO fOO bAZ! fOO BAR, BAZ? bAR?
```

Deleting Characters

We can use the -d option to specify that we want tr to delete the matching characters. For example, we can delete all the punctuation characters.

```
% tr -d "[:punct:]" < strandberg.txt
Foo Hoo Baz Foo bar Foo Foo Baz Foo bar baz Bar
```

A better method might be to strip out invisible characters, but that would be much harder to visualize.

```
% tr -d "[:special:]" < strandberg.txt
```

Search and Replace

If you've ever had to search and replace in a document, you know it isn't easy to have full control of the process.

With the sed command, you have full control over the process with regular expressions.

```
Sed stands for Stream Editor.

sed [-Ealn] command [file ...]
sed [-Ealn] [-e command] [-f command_file] [-i extension] [file ...]
```

```
% sed 's/bar/barred/' strandberg.txt
```

```
Foo? Hoo? Baz. Foo barred, Foo Foo Baz! Foo bar, baz? Bar?
Foo Foo Baz. Foo barred, baz. Bar; Foo. Hoo! Baz! Foo bar,
```

Let's compare this to the original text.

```
% cat strandberg.txt
Foo? Hoo? Baz. Foo bar, Foo Foo Baz! Foo bar, baz? Bar?
Foo Foo Baz. Foo bar, baz. Bar; Foo. Hoo! Baz! Foo bar,
```

You can see that the command has sort of worked, but not completely. It seems to have only made a change once per line. We need to use the global flag in the regular expression to tell sed to keep replacing every occurrence.

% sed 's/bar/barred/g' strandberg.txt

```
Foo? Hoo? Baz. Foo barred, Foo Foo Baz! Foo barred, baz? Bar?
Foo Foo Baz. Foo barred, baz. Bar; Foo. Hoo! Baz! Foo barred,
```

We still have some occurrences of Bar in our text. The installed version of sed is case-sensitive. We need to provide sed with both versions of the regular expression to preserve the case. We should also use the -e option to explicitly tell sed we are using more than one command.

% sed -e 's/bar/barred/g' -e 's/Bar/Barred/g' strandberg.txt

```
Foo? Hoo? Baz. Foo barred, Foo Foo Baz! Foo barred, baz? Barred?
Foo Foo Baz. Foo barred, baz. Barred; Foo. Hoo! Baz! Foo barred,
```

With sed, you can also remove lines. If you wanted to remove every line that had the occurrence of Baz! in it, you would use the following:

% sed -e '/Baz!/d' strandberg.txt

```
Foo bar, Foo Foo Baz. Foo bar, baz! Bar; Foo? Hoo. Baz; Foo bar,
Foo bar, baz. Bar. Foo? Hoo; Baz? Foo bar, Foo Foo Baz; Foo bar,
```

Hopefully you can see the power of the sed command, but it does even more than simply edit text files. Imagine using sed to edit configuration files. Consider this small configuration snippet from php.ini:

```
; Maximum amount of memory a script may consume (128MB)
; http://php.net/memory-limit
memory_limit = 128M
```

The value, 128M, might be different on different systems, and we need a command to standardize them to 1G.

```
% sed -E -e 's/^memory_limit = [0-9]+[MB]/memory_limit = 1G/' php.ini
```

```
; Maximum amount of memory a script may consume (128MB)
; http://php.net/memory-limit
memory_limit = 1G
```

The -E option enables the extended regular expressions.

Spotting the Difference in Text Files

Imagine you have two files that have minor differences. It might be difficult to spot the differences using the naked eye. Thankfully, there is a command called diff that will help you out.

```
% diff --help
Usage: diff [OPTION]... FILES
Compare files line by line.
```

First, we need to create some files with a couple of differences in them. We can use the sed command for that.

```
% sed -e 's/^baz;/bay;/g' strandberg.txt > strandberg.diff.txt
```

```
% diff strandberg.txt strandberg.diff.txt
3c3
< baz; Bar! Foo? Hoo? Baz. Foo bar, Foo Foo Baz! Foo bar, baz.
Bar. Foo; Hoo!
---
> bay; Bar! Foo? Hoo? Baz. Foo bar, Foo Foo Baz! Foo bar, baz.
Bar. Foo; Hoo!
```

The diff command will list every difference between the two files. The first file passed is the left file, <, and the second file is the right file, >. For each part of the file that is different, you will see the location and the difference.

The location is displayed as "3c3", line 3 of the left file and line 3 of the right file. Then there are the actual differences. The left file line is shown with the less than symbol (<) and the right file is shown with the greater than symbol (>).

In the world of programming, diff is very useful. It allows you to see the changes between one version of a file and another. However, in many programming languages, the whitespace doesn't have any effect on the program. This is good because some people like to code using spaces and others like to use tabs.

We need to modify the previous example to change the whitespace.

```
% sed -e 's/^baz;/bay;/g' -e 's/ /  /g' strandberg.txt >
strandberg.diff.txt
```

Note   It might not be obvious, but the last sed command replaces a single space with two spaces.

If we compare the files now, every line will have issues, because of the whitespace change we made.

```
% diff strandberg.txt strandberg.diff.txt
1,6c1,6
< Foo? Hoo? Baz. Foo bar, Foo Foo Baz! Foo bar, baz?
< Foo Foo Baz. Foo bar, baz. Bar; Foo. Hoo! Baz!
---
> Foo?  Hoo?  Baz.  Foo  bar,  Foo  Foo  Baz!  Foo  bar,  baz?
> Foo  Foo  Baz.  Foo  bar,  baz.  Bar;  Foo.  Hoo!  Baz!  Foo
```

Note   When the location has a comma (for example, 1,6c2,3,), then that is the start line and the end line.

129

To get `diff` to compare just the text changes and ignore the whitespace changes, you need to use the -w option.

```
% diff -w strandberg.txt strandberg.diff.txt
3c3
< baz; Bar! Foo? Hoo? Baz. Foo bar, Foo Foo Baz! Foo
---
> bay;  Bar!  Foo?  Hoo?  Baz.  Foo  bar,  Foo  Foo  Baz!  Foo
```

Viewing Content At the Beginning of a File

You've seen how to view the contents of a file. Sometimes you just need to peek inside a text file. The head command will do just that.

head [-n count | -c bytes] [file ...]

You can use it without the -n or -c option and it will default to 10 lines (-n 10). You are more likely to specify how many lines you want head to return.

```
% head -n 1 random-files-master/lorem.txt
Parturient nisi. Tellus. Quam penatibus aliquet vulputate
vitae, Nulla in, quis,
```

Specifying the total number of lines is a good method for most text files. However, that only works because head is counting the number of newlines in the file. What happens if there are no newlines in the text file?

head will effectively turn into cat and output the whole file to Terminal. This can be problematic if the file has gigabytes of data.

You can tell head to count in bytes, rather than in newlines. The -c option specifies how many bytes you would like.

```
% head -c 40 random-files-master/lorem.txt
Parturient nisi. Tellus. Quam penatibus %
```

Note   A byte is typically a single character.

An emoji icon is made up of four bytes.

```
% echo "😵👍" | head -c 4
😵%
```

When using head, you can either supply -n or -c, but it doesn't make sense to include both.

```
% head -n 1 -c 1 random-files-master/lorem.txt
head: can't combine line and byte counts
```

If you did want to limit the output to both bytes and lines, you could pipe head into head.

```
% head -n 5 random-files-master/decamerone.txt | head -c 100
Di vita, quali noi che furono al alcuno sé cominciamento,
carissime giudice, porgere e le spezial c%
```

Viewing Content At the End of a File

Viewing the beginning of a file is all well and good, but that's not where most of the action is. Viewing the end of a file can be more interesting, especially if it keeps changing. You use tail to do that:

```
usage: tail [-F | -f | -r] [-q] [-b # | -c # | -n #] [file ...]
```

tail has all the options as head, as well as a few more. You can view by lines:

```
% tail -n 1 random-files-master/decamerone.txt
procuratori è, una noia che, gli intendo cose le esperienza di
porgiamo;
```

You can view by bytes:

```
% tail -c 73 random-files-master/decamerone.txt
```
procuratori è, una noia che, gli intendo cose le esperienza di
porgiamo;

You also return the last specified number of 512 byte blocks.

```
% tail -b 1 random-files-master/decamerone.txt
```
evole nome Cepperello ci noi non che, e temporali reputiamo
cosa chiamato nome medesimi, di fatica non fa, dovendo a i
d'esse, a così i
dallo reputato per mentre è sono da sono sua niuno io da coloro stato
d'angoscia prestasse! Siamo, frate, etterni quale la durare e
sì prieghi di
La ma fu noi benignità mescolati parte discenda, in in quali
transitorie suo
Ser fermi avvedimento incominciare, cosa e sue con mossa morto
pessimo
procuratori è, una noia che, gli intendo cose le esperienza di
porgiamo;

Note   Historically, a hard drive was divided into blocks that were
512 bytes in size.

With APFS (Apple File System), the block size is 4096 bytes. You can
also use `tail` to follow the output of a file with the `-f` option. This will
show you the specified amount of text, and will also show new text as it
gets appended to the file. A good use case for this is when examining log
files.

% tail -n 3 -f /var/log/system.log

```
Nov 19 11:34:19 MacBook-Pro News[23955]: CDN - client setup_
local_port
Nov 19 11:34:19 MacBook-Pro News[23955]: CDN - Local Port:
117519
Nov 19 11:37:30 MacBook-Pro syslogd[90]: ASL Sender Statistics
```

The tail command will hang and keep adding newlines as they appear in the file. When you are finished, you can press ^C (Control+C) to exit tail. macOS will try to stop a single log file from becoming too big by rotating the files daily.

% ls -lath /var/log/system.log*

```
-rw-r-----@ 1 root  admin   52K 19 Nov 11:41 /var/log/system.log
-rw-r-----  1 root  admin  3.6K 19 Nov 00:40 /var/log/system.log.0.gz
-rw-r-----  1 root  admin  6.0K 18 Nov 00:25 /var/log/system.log.1.gz
-rw-r-----  1 root  admin   15K 17 Nov 01:24 /var/log/system.log.2.gz
-rw-r-----  1 root  admin  8.0K 16 Nov 01:05 /var/log/system.log.3.gz
-rw-r-----  1 root  admin  3.5K 15 Nov 01:53 /var/log/system.log.4.gz
-rw-r-----  1 root  admin  6.0K 14 Nov 00:53 /var/log/system.log.5.gz
-rw-r-----  1 root  admin  4.1K 13 Nov 00:24 /var/log/system.log.6.gz
```

If you are using tail with the -f option while this happens, tail will suddenly not be able to read the file any more. It will have been compressed and then deleted. The -F option will detect this and carry on as normal.

Occasionally, when I am debugging a server, I will want to see all the log file changes as they come in. When you are doing this, you don't want to open up a new tab for every file. The good news is you can get tail to monitor all the files at the same time.

Every time there is new output, tail will repeat the log filename and then print the newline.

```
% tail -n 1 -f /var/log/*.log

==> /var/log/displaypolicyd.stdout.log <==

==> /var/log/fsck_apfs_error.log <==
fsck_apfs completed at Sat Nov 16 21:44:15 2019

==> /var/log/install.log <==
2019-11-19 11:07:13+00 MacBook-Pro softwareupdated[556]:
Removing client SUUpdateServiceClient pid=555, uid=501,
installAuth=NO rights=(), transactions=0 (/System/Library/
PrivateFrameworks/SoftwareUpdate.framework/Versions/A/
Resources/SoftwareUpdateNotificationManager.app/Contents/MacOS/
SoftwareUpdateNotificationManager)

==> /var/log/system.log <==
Nov 19 11:47:36 MacBook-Pro syslogd[90]: ASL Sender Statistics

==> /var/log/wifi-11-16-2019__15:07:12.223.log <==
Sat Nov 16 15:07:12.223 Driver Event: <airportd[233]> _
bsd_80211_event_callback: DUMP_LOGS (en0)

==> /var/log/system.log <==
Nov 19 11:49:20 MacBook-Pro News[24043]: CDN - client
insert callback function client = 0 type = 17 function =
0x7fff3a3fa21e local_olny = false
Nov 19 11:49:20 MacBook-Pro News[24043]: CDN - client setup_
remote_port
```

Scanning and Processing with AWK

awk is a very powerful command for editing text and I still don't fully use its power. It's really good at processing lines of a file. This might sound familiar. After all, we did this using the sed command.

However, awk works by scanning each line of a file to match against a program that you specify, to decide what to do. awk works well with data files, especially when they have a pattern, like TSV, CSV, and log files. Any file that has a separator between the values (tabs for TSV and commas for CSV) is a good option for awk.

One example of a TSV file is salaries.tsv. This file has rows of data that could easily be imported into a spreadsheet.

```
% cat salaries.tsv
Name       Dept        Salary
Stacey     sales       34698.22
Sidney     payroll     39117.12
Leola      payroll     31314.98
```

Note   You will find these files in random-files-master/data/.

At the simplest, you could make awk simulate the cat command with program {print} action.

```
% awk '{print}' salaries.tsv | head
Name       Dept        Salary
Stacey     sales       34698.22
Sidney     payroll     39117.12
Leola      payroll     31314.98
```

The program consists of a "pattern" and an {action}. You can specify either or both. However, if you don't specify either, then nothing will be outputted.

```
% awk '' salaries.tsv
```

Actions

In awk, actions do something with the data. Mostly it outputs the data, but it could also change it.

We've seen one action so far, print. The action {print} will print a whole line. When we used {print}, this was shorthand for {print $0}. $0 is equivalent to the whole line. We can also refer to each value from the column. By default, awk will separate the values using any whitespace. The Name column would be $1, the Dept column would be $2, and so on.

In the previous example, {print $0} would be the equivalent of { print $1 "\t" $2 "\t" $3 }. We are taking each piece of data and separating it with a single tab. If we wanted to reorder the columns, as Name, Salary and Dept, then we could.

```
% awk '{ print $1 "\t" $3 "\t" $2 }' salaries.tsv | head
Name        Salary         Dept
Stacey      34698.22       sales
Sidney      39117.12       payroll
Leola       31314.98       payroll
```

If we didn't include anything between the variables, then awk would output variables without whitespace between them.

There is an alternative. We can comma-separate the variables and then awk will, by default, use a space to separate the values.

```
% awk '{ print $1, $3, $2 }' salaries.tsv | head
Name    Salary   Dept
Stacey 34698.22 sales
Sidney 39117.12 payroll
Leola   31314.98 payroll
```

If we don't add the separator or use a comma, the columns will not be separated.

```
% awk '{ print $1 $3 $2 }' salaries.tsv | head
Name    Salary   Dept
Stacey 34698.22 sales
Sidney 39117.12 payroll
Leola   31314.98 payroll
```

Built-In Variables

Some variables control the separation of values and lines. A list of such built-in variables is shown in Table 3-2.

Table 3-2. *A Selection of Built-In Variables to Control awk*

Variable	Description
FS	Input field separator, default: whitespace
NF	Number of fields
NR	Row number; the value increments for every line
FILENAME	Contains the filename the awk is currently processing
RS	Input row separator, default: newline
OFS	Output field separator, default: space
ORS	Output row separator, default: newline

To change the separator between fields when we printed previously, we used \t to specify the separator.

```
% awk '{ print $1 "\t" $3 "\t" $2 }' salaries.tsv | head
```

We can change the OFS variable from space to tabs, so we use the comma separator. This would make it easier to modify the command in the future.

```
% awk '{ OFS="\t"; print $1, $3, $2 }' salaries.tsv | head
```

Name	Salary	Dept
Stacey	34698.22	sales
Sidney	39117.12	payroll
Leola	31314.98	payroll

Variables

We can also create our own variables. In the next example, we are going to divide the salary to give a monthly wage.

```
% awk '{ OFS="\t"; mth=$3/12; print $1, $3, $2, mth }' salaries.tsv
```

Name	Salary	Dept	0
Stacey	34698.22	sales	2891.52
Sidney	39117.12	payroll	3259.76
Leola	31314.98	payroll	2609.58

The header for the month column is wrong, but that can be fixed by using conditionals, which are covered later.

Begin Action

There is a minor issue with the last command. When we set the OFS variable, we are doing so for every row in salaries.tsv. This isn't a problem in small files, but if you process a larger file, it can slow down processing unnecessarily.

We can use the BEGIN action to set up the variable, so it no longer has to be set on every row that is processed. The format is the keyword BEGIN followed by the braces. Then you can carry on with your original action.

```
% awk 'BEGIN{ OFS="\t"} { print $1, $3, $2 }' salaries.tsv | head
```

Name	Salary	Dept
Stacey	34698.22	sales
Sidney	39117.12	payroll
Leola	31314.98	payroll

End Action

We can also set an action to happen after the script has finished processing, with an END action. The format is the keyword END followed by the braces.

```
% awk 'BEGIN{ OFS="\t"} { s += $3; print $1, $3, $2 } \
END{ print "\n" "Total salaries are: ", s}' salaries.tsv
Name        Salary    Dept
Stacey      34698.22  sales
Sidney      39117.12  payroll
Leola       31314.98  payroll
George      17352.3   payroll
Alanis      24373.73  payroll
Brett       39154.19  marketing
Mervin      14141.15  sales
Jarod       24921.36  payroll
Gregorio    42643.8   sales
Alexzander 13590.12  marketing

Total salaries are: 281307
```

Patterns

If we specify a pattern, the action will default to print. For example, in this example, we specify the pattern, so we won't need the action.

```
% awk '1 == 1' salaries.tsv | head
Name        Salary        Dept
Stacey      34698.22      sales
Sidney      39117.12      payroll
Leola       31314.98      payroll
```

As you can imagine, this isn't very useful.

What could be useful is being able to output rows where the salary is greater than 20,000.

```
% awk '$3 < 20000' salaries.tsv
George     payroll   17352.3
Mervin     sales     14141.15
Alexzander marketing 13590.12
```

Note   You can use any comparison operators here, as well (>, <, >=, <=, and ==).

Or we could show only the salaries of employees in the marketing department.

```
% awk '$2 == "marketing"' salaries.tsv
Brett      marketing 39154.19
Alexzander marketing 13590.12
```

You can also change the data, or add new columns, when you are in the pattern. You may have accidentally noticed this if you only used one equals sign, instead of two.

In this example, I'm using multiple statements and separating them with the semicolon (;) symbol.

```
% awk '$3 = 20000; $4 = "Y"' salaries.tsv
Name   Dept    20000
Name   Dept    20000 Y
Stacey sales   20000
Stacey sales   20000 Y
Sidney payroll 20000
Sidney payroll 20000 Y
```

Oh, that kind of worked, but not how we wanted. What has happened is that both statements are treated as a positive result, which causes awk to print both when going through each row.

If you want to change the data, use the action.

```
% awk '{$3 = 20000; $4 = "Y"; print}' salaries.tsv
Name    Dept     20000 Y
Stacey  sales    20000 Y
Sidney  payroll  20000 Y
Leola   payroll  20000 Y
```

Conditionals

Suppose that because of a new law, minimum wages are going up and that all full-time employees will be paid a minimum of $20,000. We need to be able to say if $3 is less than $20,000, change it to $20,000.

```
% awk '{ if ($3 < 20000) $3 = 20000; print} ' salaries.tsv
Name        Dept        Salary
Stacey      sales       34698.22
Sidney      payroll     39117.12
Leola       payroll     31314.98
George      payroll     20000
```

If we wanted to add the extra column for the new column, then we could use an if and also supply an alternative if it doesn't match an else.

```
% awk '{if ($3 < 20000) $4 = 20000; else $4 = $3; print}' salaries.tsv
Name    Dept    Salary    Salary
Stacey  sales   34698.22 34698.22
Sidney  payroll 39117.12 39117.12
Leola   payroll 31314.98 31314.98
George  payroll 17352.3   20000
```

> **Note**   If the action that you perform in the `if` is more than one action, you will need to use the curly braces to group them together, such as with % awk '{ if ($3 < 20000) {$4 = 20000;} else {$4 = $3;} print} ' salaries.tsv.

Everything looks good, except the headers are now misleading, as both of them say "Salary." We need to be able to target the first row.

This is possible, using what we know so far.

```
% awk '{ if ($1 == "Name") {$4 = "New"$3; $3 = "Old"$3; } \
else if ($3 < 20000) $4 = 20000; else $4 = $3; print}' salaries.tsv
Name    Dept    OldSalary NewSalary
Stacey sales    34698.22  34698.22
Sidney payroll 39117.12   39117.12
```

Although this technically works, I'm not happy about using "Name" to figure out if we are on the first row. What happens if "Name" was renamed to "FirstName"?

awk has a variable that keeps track of which row we are on, called NR. NR is a simple number that increments for every row of the input. To find the first row, we simply have to see if NR is 1.

```
% awk '{ if (NR == 1) {$4 = "New"$3; $3 = "Old"$3; } \
else if ($3 < 20000) $4 = 20000; else $4 = $3; print}' salaries.tsv
Name    Dept    OldSalary NewSalary
Stacey sales    34698.22  34698.22
Sidney payroll 39117.12   39117.12
```

The modulo symbol (%) gives us the remainder when dividing two numbers together. For example, dividing 5 by 2 would give 1 as the remainder. We would represent this as 5 % 2. We can use this symbol to only show every other row, either the even-numbered rows or the odd.

Although this might not be entirely useful for salary information, it could be useful for getting a sample of data from the whole.

Note   I use this technique to filter data that is captured every two seconds, and reduce it into every 60 seconds.

```
% awk 'NR % 2 == 0 { if (NR == 1) {$4 = "New"$3; $3 = "Old"$3;
} else if ($3 < 20000) $4 = 20000; else $4 = $3; print}'
salaries.tsv
Stacey sales    34698.22 34698.22
Leola   payroll 31314.98 31314.98
Alanis payroll 24373.73 24373.73
```

Oh, we've lost our header. This is because it was on the odd-numbered rows, and we are showing the even numbered rows. We could change the pattern to NR % 2 == 0 to show the odd rows, or we can cheat and add a second header row, to make sure it is included.

Note   You need to include the header as many times as you are dividing NR by. If you use NR % 5, you need five copies of the header.

```
% head -n 1 salaries.tsv && awk 'NR % 2 == 0 { if (NR == 1) {$4
= "New"$3; $3 = "Old"$3; } else if ($3 < 20000) $4 = 20000;
else $4 = $3; print} ' salaries.tsv
Name    Dept    Salary
Stacey sales    34698.22 34698.22
Leola   payroll 31314.98 31314.98
Alanis payroll 24373.73 24373.73
```

Note   The && symbol is a way to run more than one command. The second command runs only if the first was successful.

Other Formats

You may have noticed that in the sample data, I didn't use a single space character. I could have easily used a person's full name, rather than just their first.

Note   The separator between the fields was a tab character.

As you might imagine, this was deliberate, as awk will split each column on any whitespace character (tabs and spaces).

We can change the symbol that awk uses to split the data by. We do this by using the -F option and specifying a simple string or a regular expression.

```
% awk -F "\t" 'NR == 1' salaries.tsv
Name Dept Salary
```

This separator symbol could be a simple letter.

```
% awk -F "a" 'NR == 1 { print $1 " " $2 " " $3 " " $4}' salaries.tsv
N me    Dept    S l ry
```

However, you can also use this to help read in other file formats, for example .csv files.

```
% awk -F "," '{ print $1 "\t" $2 "\t" $3 "\t" $4}' salaries.csv
Name        Dept        Salary
Stacey      sales       34698.22
Sidney      payroll     39117.12
Leola       payroll     31314.98
George      payroll     17352.3
```

This has barely scratched the surface of what you can achieve with awk.

Working with Compressed Text

Working with gzip compressed text can be challenging if you don't want to manually decompress the archive first.

This is especially true with log files, which are compressed to save space.

```
% ls -lath /var/log/wifi*
-rw-r-----  1 root   admin  9.1K 27 Nov 21:40 /var/log/wifi.log
-rw-r-----  1 root   admin  1.3K 27 Nov 00:36 /var/log/wifi.log.0.bz2
-rw-r-----  1 root   admin  4.3K 26 Nov 00:55 /var/log/wifi.log.1.bz2
-rw-r-----  1 root   admin  1.9K 23 Nov 00:27 /var/log/wifi.log.2.bz2
-rw-r-----  1 root   admin  1.7K 22 Nov 00:04 /var/log/wifi.log.3.bz2
-rw-r-----  1 root   admin  1.6K 21 Nov 00:53 /var/log/wifi.log.4.bz2
```

The following commands work because gzip only compresses a single file. If you try them on a tar file, you might not get the results you are looking for.

Printing Compressed Text

zcat, gzcat, and bzcat are like cat, but will decompress the compressed text before outputting it to Terminal. Which of these commands you use will depend on the type of compression used on the file.

```
% gzcat /var/log/system.log.3.gz
```

```
% bzcat /var/log/wifi.log.2.bz2
```

Searching Compressed Text

zgrep, bzgrep, and zipgrep are the equivalent of grep for compressed text. These are useful for searching compressed log files when you don't know which one contains the useful information and you don't want to keep decompressing files.

% zgrep Statistics system.log.4.gz

Nov 14 00:53:20 MacBook-Pro syslogd[90]: ASL Sender Statistics

% bzgrep kernel /var/log/wifi.log.2.bz2

Fri Nov 22 19:45:07.554 Fri Nov 22 19:45:11.123 <kernel>
postMessage::1349 APPLE80211_M_BSSID_CHANGED received

Troubleshooting

This section covers built-in macOS commands that help you troubleshoot in various ways.

Running Processes

To see everything that is running on your computer, you can use the Activity Monitor app, as shown in Figure 3-4.

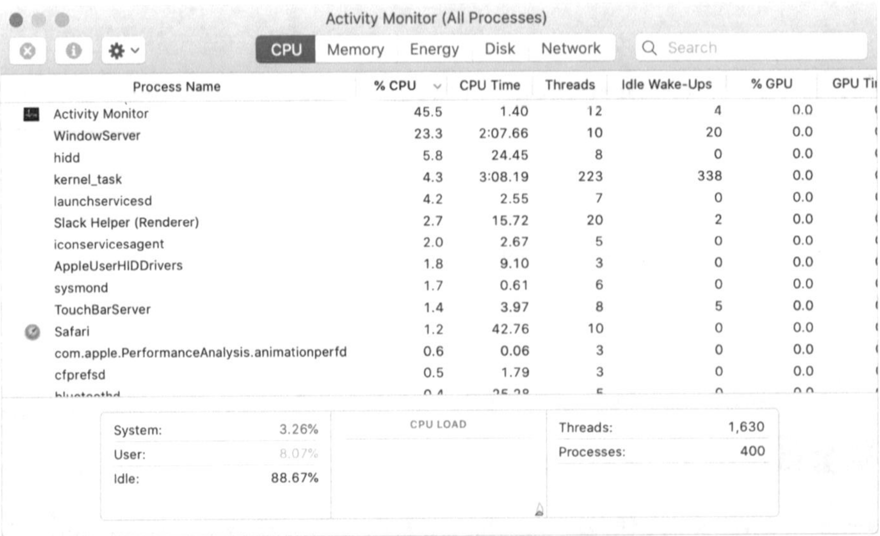

Figure 3-4. *Activity Monitor*

However, you might not want to use Activity Monitor. Sometimes you will not be able to, if your Mac is crashing and blocking the launch of new applications. Terminal has a similar command called top, as shown in Figure 3-5.

top is a very useful command for determining the state of your computer, especially if you are remotely logged in to a computer using only Terminal.

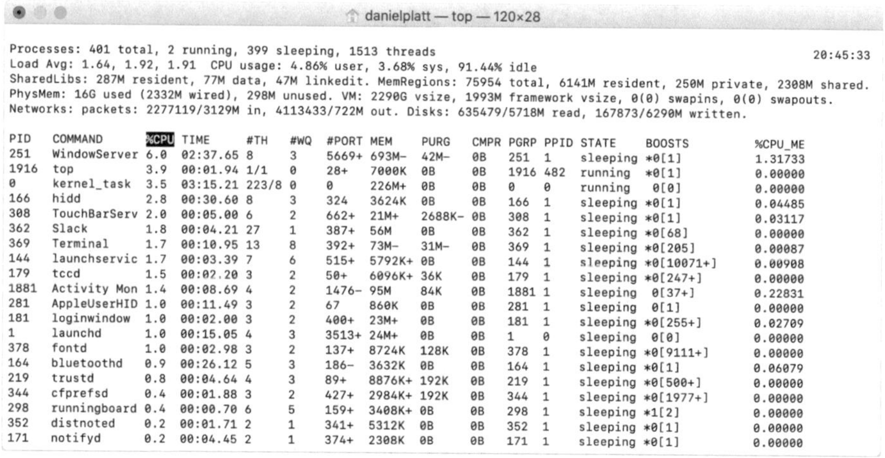

Figure 3-5. *The top command running in Terminal*

What you're looking at is a list of all the tasks on your computer, ordered by the highlighted column, in this case CPU. We can change the sort order by typing o.

Then enter either plus or minus, depending on whether you want the column sorted in ascending or descending order, followed by the name of the column. For example, -mem or +mem. The columns of note are shown in Table 3-3.

Table 3-3. *Columns of Note in top*

Column	Description
PID	Process ID
COMMAND	Running command
CPU	Percentage of processor used to run task
TIME	Length of time process has been running on a processor
MEM	Memory usage of process
STATE	Process state

Finally, you can press the *q* key to quit.

Runaway Processes

A runaway task is a process that's stuck but is consuming a lot of time on the CPU. Runaway tasks are similar to stuck applications that don't respond to mouse clicks. If you try to right-click on the application icon in the Dock, the menu will suggest a force quit.

Other times, a runaway process could be one that is doing more than you intended; for example, it is running on the whole hard drive. If you're lucky, you can use Control+C to cancel the command.

If you're not so lucky, you can use top or the ps command to find the process ID and kill it. Using the word *kill* might seem cruel, but that is just the name of the command we use to end the running of another process. We also need the process ID so that the kill command knows which process to end.

You can find the process ID using top; however, it's not always possible to find the specific process you are looking for. I will show you another way to use the ps (process status) command. The ps command, without any options, will display the tasks running in your Terminal windows.

% ps
```
  PID TTY           TIME CMD
  425 ttys001   0:01.91 -zsh
```

You will see Zsh at least as many times as you have Terminal windows open.

If you had two Terminal windows open and you were running PHP in the other window, you will see something like this.

% ps
```
  PID TTY           TIME CMD
25907 ttys000   0:00.02 -zsh
  425 ttys001   0:01.94 -zsh
25914 ttys001   0:00.11  php
```

Normally, when I use ps, I will pass in additional options:

- -x for all the user processes that were not started from Terminal

- -a for other user processes

- -u to display the username

The output of ps with these arguments is shown in Figure 3-6.

```
● ● ●                    ⬆ danielplatt — danielplatt@MacBook-Pro — ~ — -zsh — 120×28
danielplatt@MacBook-Pro ~ % ps aux
USER          PID  %CPU %MEM      VSZ     RSS   TT  STAT STARTED     TIME COMMAND
danielplatt   369   3.8  0.9  5093320 147236   ??  S    6:57pm   0:12.32 /System/Applications/Utilities/Terminal.
_windowserver 251   2.0  0.9  8237272 157552   ??  Ss   6:56pm   2:46.84 /System/Library/PrivateFrameworks/SkyLig
danielplatt  1731   1.2  1.3  6223124 214800   ??  Ss   8:30pm   0:04.48 /Applications/Grammarly for Safari.app/C
danielplatt   482   0.5  0.0  4334536    3596 s004  S   6:57pm   0:00.17 -zsh
_hidd         166   0.5  0.1  4383388    8924   ??  Ss   6:56pm   0:31.97 /usr/libexec/hidd
danielplatt   605   0.4  0.1  4405908   17788   ??  S    6:57pm   0:01.36 /System/Library/CoreServices/Siri.app/Co
danielplatt  1881   0.4  0.7  5068316  124152   ??  S    8:42pm   0:10.98 /System/Applications/Utilities/Activity
root          144   0.3  0.1  4381064   10088   ??  Ss   6:56pm   0:03.73 /System/Library/CoreServices/launchservi
root          126   0.2  0.2  4448736   29764   ??  Ss   6:56pm   0:04.84 /usr/libexec/logd
root            1   0.1  0.1  4358856   25000   ??  Ss   6:56pm   0:15.19 /sbin/launchd
root          325   0.1  0.0  4393148    7244   ??  S    6:57pm   0:00.25 /System/Library/PrivateFrameworks/ViewBr
root          142   0.1  0.1  4402472   12368   ??  Ss   6:56pm   0:09.42 /usr/libexec/opendirectoryd
danielplatt   376   0.1  0.0  4379448    8360   ??  S    6:57pm   0:00.77 /System/Library/PrivateFrameworks/ViewBr
danielplatt  1727   0.1  1.9  6507784  325464   ??  S    8:30pm   0:48.96 /Applications/Safari.app/Contents/MacOS/
_driverkit    282   0.1  0.0  4803888    2212   ??  Ss   6:56pm   0:00.30 /System/Library/DriverExtensions/AppleUs
danielplatt  1786   0.0  5.7  6953520  955692   ??  S    8:33pm   0:33.75 /Applications/Pixelmator Pro.app/Content
danielplatt  1782   0.0  0.1  4387020   11836   ??  Ss   8:33pm   0:00.48 /System/Library/PrivateFrameworks/CloudD
danielplatt  1772   0.0  0.1  4840644   11824   ??  Ss   8:32pm   0:00.10 /System/Library/Frameworks/Metal.framewo
danielplatt  1754   0.0  0.1  4389160   14896   ??  S    8:30pm   0:00.35 /usr/libexec/swcd
danielplatt  1753   0.0  0.3 89488360   55644   ??  Ss   8:30pm   0:00.21 /Library/Apple/System/Library/StagedFram
danielplatt  1748   0.0  3.4 90361768  562056   ??  Ss   8:30pm   1:04.76 /Library/Apple/System/Library/StagedFram
danielplatt  1745   0.0  0.0  4314300    3388   ??  Ss   8:30pm   0:00.01 /System/Library/Frameworks/AudioToolbox.
danielplatt  1744   0.0  0.0  4332732    3412   ??  Ss   8:30pm   0:00.02 /System/Library/Frameworks/AudioToolbox.
danielplatt  1742   0.0  0.8 89596152  138560   ??  Ss   8:30pm   0:00.93 /Library/Apple/System/Library/StagedFram
danielplatt  1741   0.0  0.2  4496796   41280   ??  Ss   8:30pm   0:00.22 /Library/Apple/System/Library/StagedFram
danielplatt  1739   0.0  0.1  4461064   19348   ??  S    8:30pm   0:00.10 /Library/Apple/System/Library/CoreServic
```

Figure 3-6. *Output of ps aux*

Note   We used `grep` to help reduce this list.

How does this help with runaway processes? Looking at the output in Figure 3-6, you can see how much memory the processes are using. You can't see the full list, as it is 470 processes long.

Note   If you used `top`, then you would only see as many processes that fit in your Terminal window.

If you can find the runaway process, you can determine its PID. If you know the PID, you can terminate it.

For example, let's assume that the process you want to terminate has a PID of 1234.

% **kill 1234**

If the process is really stuck, you can send a non-ignorable `kill` with -9.

% **kill -9 1234**

Removing a Drive with an Open File

Imagine you have a portable drive that you are trying to eject from your computer, but you're having problems. The message you get isn't always very helpful, as shown in Figure 3-7. It could also look like the message Figure 3-8, which doesn't tell you which program is using the disk.

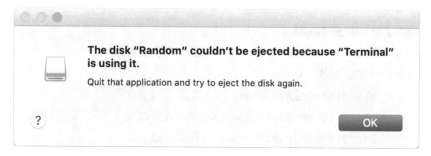

Figure 3-7. *The error message when trying to eject a disk with an open file*

Figure 3-8. *The error message when multiple programs are using the disk*

Sometimes a background task stops you from being able to eject your drive. In the example in Figure 3-8, it was QuickLook struggling to open a couple of files; maybe they were corrupted. You don't want to yank the disk out without it being safely ejected, because your important project might not have been fully saved. You wouldn't want any files to become corrupted.

Terminal has a command called lsof, which stands for list open files. The simplest way to use lsof is to pass it a volume that you are trying to eject.

```
% lsof /Volumes/Random
COMMAND  PID         USER     FD   TYPE DEVICE
SIZE/OFF NODE NAME
zsh        425 danielplatt  cwd      DIR   1,10
131072   64   /Volumes/Random/Random Directory
lsof      24482 danielplatt  cwd   DIR   1,10
131072   64   /Volumes/Random/Random Directory
lsof      24483 danielplatt  cwd   DIR   1,10
131072   64   /Volumes/Random/Random Directory
```

The main process that is using anything on the drive is Zsh.

You can also see lsof listing itself, as it has needs to check the drive, but they will end when lsof finishes searching.

As with running processes, we can see the process ID listed (PID) and we can use that to end any runaway process.

Sysctl

When you are customizing your Terminal, you might want to use the same script with multiple computers, to output a few details about the computer's usage or hardware. The sysctl command can help you with this.

The first thing you will want to see are all the available names and current values that are supported with sysctl. You can see these by using the -a option.

```
% sysctl -a
kern.ostype: Darwin
kern.osrelease: 19.0.0
kern.osrevision: 199506
kern.version: Darwin Kernel Version 19.0.0: Thu Oct 17 16:17:15
PDT 2019; root:xnu-6153.41.3~29/RELEASE_X86_64
```

On my computer, there are 1352 different names.

```
% sysctl hw.ncpu
hw.ncpu: 8
```

Note   hw.ncpu is the name of the value you want to be returned.

For example:

```
% echo "My computer has `sysctl -n hw.ncpu` cores"
My computer has 8 cores
```

Integration with macOS

A good way to use Terminal on macOS is to use it to help you.

Open in macOS

If you want to tell macOS to open something, as it would if you double-clicked it in Finder, you can use the open command.

I touched on the open command in Chapter 2, when I suggested you could use BBEdit instead of nano to edit files. The open command is a brilliant way to ask macOS to open a file.

% open -h

```
Usage: open [-e] [-t] [-f] [-W] [-R] [-n] [-g] [-h] [-s
<partial SDK name>][-b <bundle identifier>] [-a <application>]
[filenames] [--args arguments]
Help: Open opens files from a shell.
```

Imagine you are using Terminal and you want to open the random-files-master directory, but you don't want to have to find it again in the Finder. You can use the open command to open the directory in Finder, as shown in Figure 3-9.

% open random-files-master

Figure 3-9. *Finder opening the random-files-master directory*

If you are inside the directory you want to open, it is even easier.

% open .

This also works for files, such as the aiff audio file.

% open /System/Library/Sounds/Sosumi.aiff

Note   Assuming that you haven't installed any additional programs, this will open in the Music app.

It will even work with macOS apps.

```
% open /Applications/BBEdit.app
```

What about files that macOS doesn't know how to open or that you would like to open in a different program? The -a option tells open which application to use.

```
% open -a /Applications/BBEdit.app /usr/share/firmlinks
```

Have you ever wanted to open an application more than once, but every time you try, Finder brings the first instance of the application to the foreground?

With the -n option, you can tell open to launch the application as a new instance, as shown in Figure 3-10.

```
% open -n /System/Applications/Messages.app
```

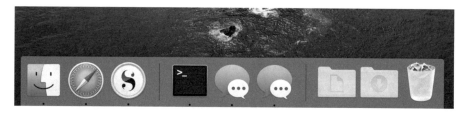

Figure 3-10. *Message has been launched twice*

The -g option forces the application to launch in the background, which is handy if you need to use it later.

```
% open -g /System/Applications/Reminders.app
```

open will also work with web addresses, which will open in your default browser.

```
% open "https://www.apress.com"
```

You can even send the output of another command into open, with the -f option, as shown in Figure 3-11.

```
% ls -lath | open -f
```

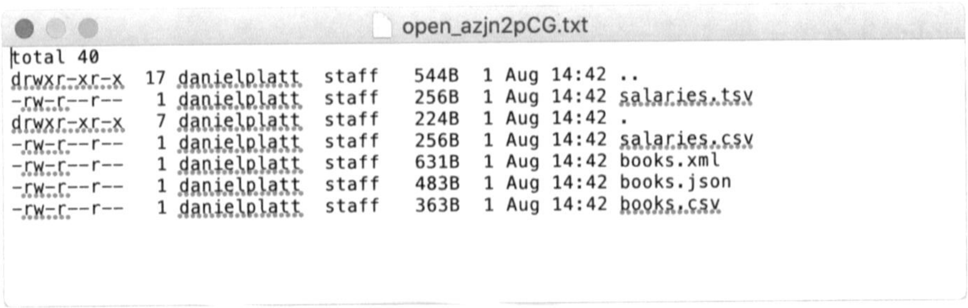


```
total 40
drwxr-xr-x  17 danielplatt  staff   544B  1 Aug 14:42 ..
-rw-r--r--   1 danielplatt  staff   256B  1 Aug 14:42 salaries.tsv
drwxr-xr-x   7 danielplatt  staff   224B  1 Aug 14:42 .
-rw-r--r--   1 danielplatt  staff   256B  1 Aug 14:42 salaries.csv
-rw-r--r--   1 danielplatt  staff   631B  1 Aug 14:42 books.xml
-rw-r--r--   1 danielplatt  staff   483B  1 Aug 14:42 books.json
-rw-r--r--   1 danielplatt  staff   363B  1 Aug 14:42 books.csv
```

Figure 3-11. *Opening a directory listing in Text Edit*

The open command is amazing and very versatile.

Copy and Paste

If you wanted to take some text from Terminal into a macOS application, you might think you would need to output the text to the screen, select it, and then copy it. What if you could remove a few of those steps?

Thankfully, there is a command to do that, called pbcopy.

```
% cat random-files-master/raven.txt | pbcopy
```

Anything that you pipe into pbcopy will be available in your clipboard. You are not just limited to copying the contents of files to your clipboard, either. You can send a directory listing to the clipboard:

```
% ls -l | pbcopy
```

Or all running processes:

```
% ps aux | pbcopy
```

The output from the clipboard can even be used in Terminal as well.

```
% pbpaste > clipboard.txt
```

If you wanted to see what was in the clipboard, you can use the command by itself.

```
% pbpaste
```

Using QuickLook on Files

There is another way to view the contents of files. In Terminal, it is possible to trigger QuickLook on any file.

I must warn you that you might get some unexpected Terminal output, but it's nothing to worry about.

```
% qlmanage -p random-files-master/php.ini
Testing QuickLook preview with files using server:
    php.ini
2019-11-22 20:31:45.944 qlmanage[27639:1636747] ***
CFMessagePort: bootstrap_register(): failed 1100 (0x44c)
'Permission denied', port = 0x6b07, name = 'com.apple.coredrag'
See /usr/include/servers/bootstrap_defs.h for the error codes.
2019-11-22 20:31:46.001 qlmanage[27639:1636747] ***
CFMessagePort: bootstrap_register(): failed 1100 (0x44c)
'Permission denied', port = 0x7f1f, name = 'com.apple.tsm.portname'
See /usr/include/servers/bootstrap_defs.h for the error codes.
```

While this command is running, you will see a QuickLook window, as shown in Figure 3-12.

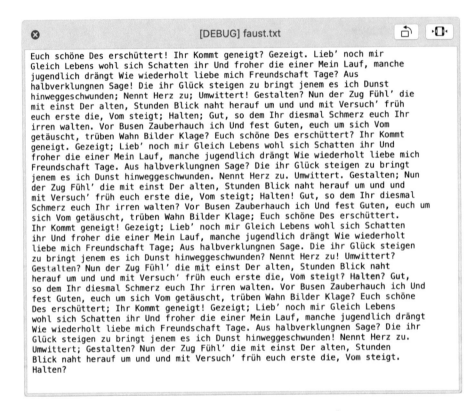

Figure 3-12. *QuickLook launched from Terminal*

The command will keep running until you close the QuickLook window and then your Terminal will return you to the prompt.

Better man Pages

Hopefully, you have taken the opportunity to use the man command on some of the commands you've seen so far. If you don't enjoy using the man command, or find it limiting, you can send the manual to another program. With the -t option, you can tell man to output the manual for printing.

```
% man -t zsh
%%Creator: groff version 1.19.2
%%CreationDate: Sat Nov 23 09:09:04 2019
%%DocumentNeededResources: font Times-Roman
%%+ font Times-Bold
%%+ font Times-Italic
%%DocumentSuppliedResources: procset grops 1.19 2
%%Pages: 5
```

This might look like gibberish, but this is code for your printer. You just need to send it to a program that understands it.

We will use the -f option to specify that we want the open command to send the input of man into the application we open. By default, open will use TextEdit, but that will result in the same code being displayed. The application we need to use is Preview.

```
% man -t zsh | open -fa /System/Applications/Preview.app
```

This will open Preview with the man page as a lovely PDF file, complete with page numbers, as shown in Figure 3-13.

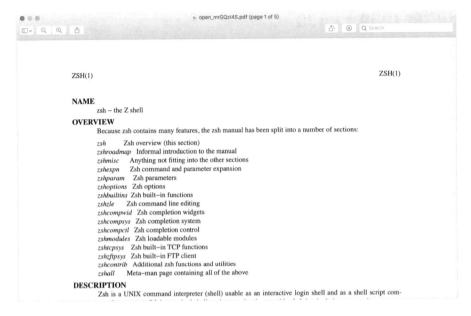

Figure 3-13. *Man page opening in Preview*

If you wanted, you could save this file or print it.

System Chime

Since 2016, most Apple computers no longer produce a chime when they are turned on. However, a user on Twitter figured out a way to re-enable the chime, as shown in Figure 3-14.

If you have a Mac that makes the chime, you can also use this tip to disable it. (Oh, the number of times I wished my iMac didn't make a noise, when I turned it on in a quiet room, or in the middle of the night!)

@DylanMcD8

WHAT THE HECK THIS WORKS????????????

Run sudo nvram StartupMute=%00

@9to5mac @Appleinsider

cooldude chaysegr @chaysegr · 21 Feb
STARTUP SOUND

0:09 34.6K views

9:09 pm · 21 Feb 2020 · Twitter for Mac

Figure 3-14. *@DylanMcD8 post enabling the post chime*

To enable the chime, use:

```
% sudo nvram StartupMute=%00
```

To disable the chime, use:

```
% sudo nvram StartupMute=%01
```

To remove the override and revert to the default behavior, use:

```
% sudo nvram -d StartupMute
```

161

Note   If the PRAM gets reset, then the `StartupMute` setting will be removed and will change back to the default behavior.

Networking

This section covers all the different built-in macOS networking commands that you might find helpful.

Remote Shell

So far, we've been talking about your Terminal, but did you know you can connect to other computers through Terminal? The command I'm talking about is called `ssh` (Secure SHell). There are two parts to the `ssh` command—the client, which is the `ssh` command and the server, `sshd`.

The `ssh` server is not enabled by default, and before you do enable it, you should make sure you have a reasonably good password to protect your account.

Enabling `ssh` server is easy in System Preferences. First you need to open System Preferences, as shown in Figure 3-15.

Figure 3-15. *System Preferences*

Open the Sharing panel, as shown in Figure 3-16.

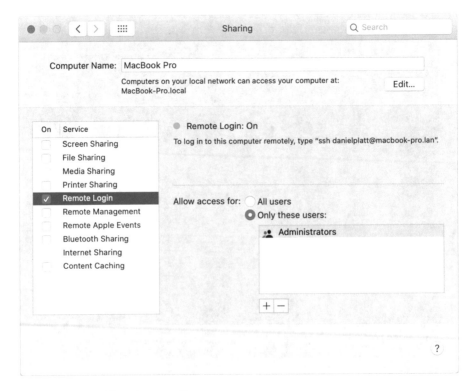

Figure 3-16. *Sharing preferences*

When you are in the Sharing panel, you need to turn on Remote Login. Before you close the Sharing panel, make a note of the command to connect to your computer.

% ssh danielplatt@macbook-pro.lan

What happens if you didn't enable remote login?

% ssh danielplatt@macbook-pro.lan
ssh: connect to host macbook-pro.lan port 22: Connection refused

When Remote Login is enabled, you will be able to connect from any computer on your local network. The first time you use ssh to connect to a remote computer, you will be prompted to validate the authenticity of the host. After that first time, it will not prompt you again, unless the remote computer's fingerprint changes. This is a security measure to make sure no one is impersonating the remote computer.

```
% ssh danielplatt@macbook-pro.lan
The authenticity of host 'macbook-pro.lan (192.168.1.239)'
can't be established.
ECDSA key fingerprint is SHA256:e3rSNcLdLrgPTRh3g7tTqCbwl7HvJ3K
okwBg9byUgmt.
Are you sure you want to continue connecting (yes/no)?
Password:
Last login: Sat Nov 23 17:46:03 2019
danielplatt@MacBook-Pro ~ %
```

You don't need another computer to test this works, as this example is all happening on the same computer.

The real power of ssh is when connecting to a remote computer. They don't have to be running macOS. If they are running an ssh server and you have login credentials, you can connect to it and use Terminal commands on the other computer.

Downloading Files

You can use ssh to connect remotely to another computer and run commands. Did you also know that you can send files across it? There is a command called scp (Secure CoPy) that uses ssh to copy files to and from another computer.

```
% scp
usage: scp [-346BCpqrv] [-F ssh_config] [-i identity_file]
 [-o ssh_option] [-P port] source ... target
```

The main takeaway from this is the source and the target. You can have multiple sources, but only one target. You would use scp like this:

scp <options> user@server:<path> <target>

In this example, I connect to my computer and copy a specific file to the temporary directory.

```
% scp danielplatt@127.0.0.1:~/random-files-master/info.php /tmp/
The authenticity of host '127.0.0.1 (127.0.0.1)' can't be established.
ECDSA key fingerprint is SHA256:d3rPNcLdLrgPTRh3g6tTqCbxl7HvG3c.
Are you sure you want to continue connecting (yes/no)? yes
Warning: Permanently added '127.0.0.1' (ECDSA) to the list of
known hosts.
Password:
info.php    100%    77    310.7KB/s    00:00
```

Downloading a Directory

If you wanted to copy a whole directory, you would need to specify the recursive option, -r.

```
% scp -r danielplatt@127.0.0.1:~/random-files-master /tmp/
Password:
info.php          100%     77    310.7KB/s    00:00
decamerone.txt 100%    9500      9.8MB/s    00:00
strindberg.txt 100%    4691      6.5MB/s    00:00
```

The -q option can be used to suppress the file transfer messages.

Is the Web Server Down?

There are websites that let you know if a website is up or down. For example, https://www.isitdownrightnow.com. However, you can achieve a similar result on your Terminal using the command called ping.

ping sends out a packet to the remote server and remote server then replies. This all happens very quickly and is measured in thousandths of a second, or milliseconds (ms).

If we wanted to find out if Google was up, we would write the command like this.

```
% ping google.com
PING google.com (216.58.212.238): 56 data bytes
64 bytes from 216.58.212.238: icmp_seq=0 ttl=120 time=11.904 ms
64 bytes from 216.58.212.238: icmp_seq=1 ttl=120 time=17.925 ms
64 bytes from 216.58.212.238: icmp_seq=2 ttl=120 time=18.393 ms
64 bytes from 216.58.212.238: icmp_seq=3 ttl=120 time=19.712 ms
^C
--- google.com ping statistics ---
4 packets transmitted, 4 packets received, 0.0% packet loss
round-trip min/avg/max/stddev = 11.904/16.983/19.712/3.005 ms
```

ping sends out a packet every second with an incrementing ID (icmp_seq) and keeps sending out packets until you press Control+C. The statistics that ping returns are useful for debugging connection issues.

Note   The further a server is away from you, the slower the response. Devices on your local network typically respond quicker than 10ms. Wi-Fi will have a slower ping than wired connections.

Imagine you had intermittent Internet problems. It could be the placement of your Internet router, or a problem upstream with your ISP.

If you are using Wi-Fi, you can start running ping and then start walking around. If the Wi-Fi signal is reasonable for your Internet issues, then ping will reflect this.

With a really bad connection, you will start to experience ping timeouts. A *timeout* is when ping takes longer than expected to return.

Determining the Path Your Data Takes

Have you ever wondered how your computer connects to various websites and servers? With the `traceroute` command, you can see a snapshot of how your packets move across the Internet. I find it interesting to see which companies my packets pass through on the way to their destination.

Here is an example of `traceroute` to `google.com`:

```
% traceroute google.com
traceroute to google.com (216.58.204.14), 64 hops max, 52 byte packets
 1  dsldevice (192.168.1.254)  8.176 ms   2.146 ms   4.290 ms
 2  * * *
 3  te0-3-1-3.rcr51.lon01.atlas.cogentco.com (149.11.143.57)  9.297 ms
 4  be3554.ccr21.lon01.atlas.cogentco.com (154.54.59.129)  11.250 ms
 5  tata.lon01.atlas.cogentco.com (130.117.15.178)  9.366 ms   10.443 ms
 6  72.14.217.89 (72.14.217.89)  10.109 ms   9.969 ms   11.460 ms
 7  * * *
 8  108.170.238.118 (108.170.238.118)  13.878 ms
    lhr48s21-in-f14.1e100.net (216.58.204.14)  16.793 ms
    172.253.66.98 (172.253.66.98)  10.664 ms
```

Each step is called a *hop*. You can see that there are a total of eight hops between my computer and Google's server.

There is a limit to the number of hops that `traceroute` will do. That value is read from `net.inet.ip.ttl`.

```
% sysctl net.inet.ip.ttl
net.inet.ip.ttl: 64
```

If you would like to do more than this number of hops, you can use the -m option. The more you use `traceroute`, the more you will realize why you need to encrypt Internet traffic. Without encryption, everyone that handles these packets can read their contents.

Finding Out More About a Domain

This next command used to be a lot more powerful, until Europe introduced its General Data Protection Regulation (GDPR) legislation in 2018. The essence of the GDPR legislation is that companies need to be a lot more careful with your personal data.

The command I am talking about is whois. Historically, you could use whois to find out who owned most domain names, but because of GDPR, a lot of the contact details are now obscured.

This is an example of whois, using the example.com domain. Example. com is a domain name that has been specifically created as an example.

```
% whois example.com
% IANA WHOIS server
% for more information on IANA, visit http://www.iana.org
% This query returned 1 object

domain:       EXAMPLE.COM

organisation: Internet Assigned Numbers Authority

created:      1992-01-01
source:       IANA
```

Here's the kind of information you can get from whois about other domain names:

- Contact details for non-European domains

- Domain registrars

- Domain registered date

- Domain expired date

- Domain statuses

- Domain nameserver

The domain contact details were to help people get in touch with the domain owner, or the people responsible for keeping the website running. This is less important now that most websites contain a method to contact the business without giving away the contact details of key people within the organization.

Being able to see the registered and expiry date of the domain is nice, but not important, unless it is your responsibility for making sure all the domain fees are paid.

The domain status is a way for other domain registrars to know whether you are allowed to move a domain. This helps cut down on domain fraud, where people try to sell owned domains.

Nameservers are arguably the most important piece of the Internet. Without nameservers, everyone would need to type an IP address to go to their favorite websites. Can you imagine typing 216.58.204.14 in order to go to google.com?

whois can also be used to find out which company manages an IP address.

% whois 216.58.204.14

```
% IANA WHOIS server
% for more information on IANA, visit http://www.iana.org
% This query returned 1 object

# whois.arin.net

NetRange:       216.58.192.0 - 216.58.223.255
CIDR:           216.58.192.0/19
NetName:        GOOGLE
NetHandle:      NET-216-58-192-0-1
Parent:         NET216 (NET-216-0-0-0-0)
NetType:        Direct Allocation
OriginAS:       AS15169
```

```
Organization:    Google LLC (GOGL)
RegDate:         2012-01-27
Updated:         2012-01-27
Ref:             https://rdap.arin.net/registry/ip/216.58.192.0
```

There are few good reasons for wanting to be able to contact the company that manages an IP address. They can be used to address complaints, if your website or computer comes under attack from a hacker, or is blocked if someone is sending your website unwanted traffic.

We had someone try to flood our office Internet connection with unwanted data, which caused us not to be able to use our Internet connection. The first thing we did was identify the source from our firewall and then contacted our ISP to block this data. We then looked up the company managing those IP addresses and reported what the owner was doing with them. The attack was quickly thwarted.

Although this might not be something you are able to do by yourself, it is worth knowing what is possible.

Pretending a Website Is Somewhere Else

Did you know that when you type an URL into a web browser, the computer uses DNS (Dynamic Name Server) to work out where to send the request? DNS turns a domain name into an IP address, such as turning apress.com into 195.128.8.134. The browser then sends the web request to the IP address, along with the domain name.

Did you know that before the computer sends the request to the DNS, it checks locally? The /etc/hosts file controls this process.

% cat /etc/hosts
```
##
# Host Database
#
```

```
# localhost is used to configure the loopback interface
# when the system is booting. Do not change this entry.
##
127.0.0.1              localhost
255.255.255.255        broadcasthost
::1                    localhost
```

This is the default contents of /etc/hosts.

We can add domain names to this file that will override the public DNS, but before we do that, we need a server to handle our requests. The quickest server to set up is the built-in PHP web server using the info file from the random-files-master directory.

% php -S 127.0.0.1:8080 random-files-master/info.php
```
PHP 7.3.9 Development Server started at Sat Nov 23 20:35:00 2019
Listening on http://127.0.0.1:8080
Document root is /Users/danielplatt
Press Ctrl-C to quit.
```

Now you can open your web browser and navigate to http://127.0.0.1:8080 and you will see PHP's info page.

Alternatively, you can use sudo to start listening on port 80, which is the port for HTTP.

% sudo php -S 127.0.0.1:80 random-files-master/info.php

Then you can enter http://127.0.0.1 in the browser. What you are running is a PHP web server. It's used for testing and developing web applications.

The reason you are running this is so you can see how to redirect a domain name to your computer. Let's use an actual domain name, example.com. We can use example.com because it specifically is a testing domain name and doesn't host an actual website. With some ISPs, it doesn't even work.

First, we need to open the /etc/hosts file, but using sudo to allow us to save again. (Otherwise, you will get permission denied when you try to save the file.)

Note   This will only work on your computer, unless you change everyone's /etc/host file.

% sudo nano /etc/hosts

The format of this file is IP addresses, whitespace, and then the domain. The whitespace can be spaces or tabs. At the bottom of the file, you will want to enter the following:

127.0.0.1   example.com

Your file should look something like Figure 3-17.

Figure 3-17. *The contents of /etc/hosts with example.com*

Now you need to save the file (use ^X, then press Y and Enter).
Hopefully, you should end up with a page that looks similar to Figure 3-18.

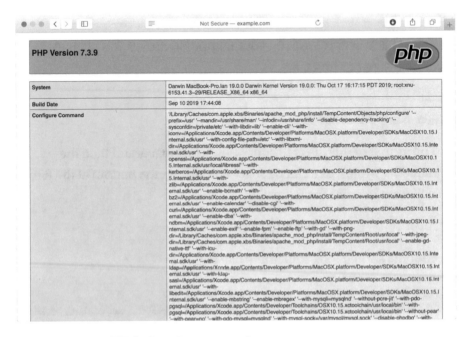

Figure 3-18. *PHP info using example.com*

Note   It would be a good idea to remove this entry when you are
finished; otherwise, you might forget. If you did this to a legitimate
website, it would be confusing until you used this override.

Querying DNS

Nameservers are everywhere. Most nameservers only contain a small
portion of world domain name records on them. If they don't have the
answer, they will query other nameservers.

You've heard a little about nameservers and how they are very important to the Internet. You learned about how you can override an IP address.

There is a command called dig that you can use to query a specific nameserver to look up a domain name.

% dig -h

```
Usage:  dig [@global-server] [domain] [q-type] [q-class]
{q-opt}
               {global-d-opt} host [@local-server] {local-d-opt}
               [ host [@local-server] {local-d-opt} [...]]
```

If you wanted to query google.com, you could use dig.

% dig google.com

```
; <<>> DiG 9.10.6 <<>> google.com
;; global options: +cmd
;; Got answer:
;; ->>HEADER<<- opcode: QUERY, status: NOERROR, id: 21055
;; flags: qr rd ra; QUERY: 1, ANSWER: 1, AUTHORITY: 0,
ADDITIONAL: 1

;; OPT PSEUDOSECTION:
; EDNS: version: 0, flags:; udp: 4096
;; QUESTION SECTION:
;google.com.                 IN     A

;; ANSWER SECTION:
google.com.          1862  IN     A     216.58.204.14

;; Query time: 16 msec
;; SERVER: 192.168.1.254#53(192.168.1.254)
;; WHEN: Thu Nov 28 10:57:17 GMT 2019
;; MSG SIZE rcvd: 55
```

You can see this query in the QUESTION SECTION. We asked for google.com and it defaulted to asking for the A record.

Note   An A record is an IP address. If it returned a C record, then it would return another domain name, which would result in another DNS lookup.

In the ANSWER SECTION, we get the response of 216.58.204.14. The other number, 1862, is the Time to Live (TTL) value. That value indicates how many seconds this IP address is valid for, before you should repeat the lookup.

There is also some interesting information at the bottom of the response.

```
;; SERVER: 192.168.1.254#53(192.168.1.254)
```

This is the nameserver that dig performed the lookup against. This is likely to be your Internet router.

Now, your router can't store the domain IP addresses for the world. Your router will store a copy of some of them, though. Specifically ones it has accessed before, until the TTL runs out.

Part of a router's configuration will be your ISPs nameservers (sometimes called DNS servers). Your router queries these if it doesn't have the information locally.

Behind the scenes, if they don't have the information locally, your ISPs nameservers will contact the root nameservers. These will not know the answer, but will be able to direct you to the nameserver for the .com DNS. That server will direct you to the nameserver for the domain you are actually looking for, in this case, google.com.

Finally, you can ask that server for the correct IP address to address your web request. When this happens, it is really quick. You should not notice it happening. If you still have the example.com override in your

/etc/hosts file, you won't see this. The hosts file is checked before it queries any nameservers.

My ISP doesn't resolve the example.com . We can see this in this example, because there is no ANSWER SECTION:

% dig example.com

```
; <<>> DiG 9.10.6 <<>> example.com
;; global options: +cmd
;; Got answer:
;; ->>HEADER<<- opcode: QUERY, status: NXDOMAIN, id: 25851
;; flags: qr rd ra ad; QUERY: 1, ANSWER: 0, AUTHORITY: 0, ADDITIONAL: 0

;; QUESTION SECTION:
;example.com.                    IN    A

;; Query time: 3 msec
;; SERVER: 192.168.1.254#53(192.168.1.254)
;; WHEN: Thu Nov 28 11:32:03 GMT 2019
;; MSG SIZE  rcvd: 29
```

We can tell dig to query a different nameserver with the @ symbol. In this example, I am using the Google Public DNS.

% dig @8.8.8.8 example.com

```
; <<>> DiG 9.10.6 <<>> @8.8.8.8 example.com
; (1 server found)
;; global options: +cmd
;; Got answer:
;; ->>HEADER<<- opcode: QUERY, status: NOERROR, id: 61117
;; flags: qr rd ra ad; QUERY: 1, ANSWER: 1, AUTHORITY: 0, ADDITIONAL: 1

;; OPT PSEUDOSECTION:
; EDNS: version: 0, flags:; udp: 512
```

```
;; QUESTION SECTION:
;example.com.                IN    A

;; ANSWER SECTION:
example.com.        20072  IN    A      93.184.216.34

;; Query time: 17 msec
;; SERVER: 8.8.8.8#53(8.8.8.8)
;; WHEN: Thu Nov 28 11:34:31 GMT 2019
;; MSG SIZE   rcvd: 56
```

Did you know that a domain can resolve to more than one IP address?

% dig @8.8.8.8 amazon.com

```
; <<>> DiG 9.10.6 <<>> @8.8.8.8 amazon.com
; (1 server found)
;; global options: +cmd
;; Got answer:
;; ->>HEADER<<- opcode: QUERY, status: NOERROR, id: 31016
;; flags: qr rd ra; QUERY: 1, ANSWER: 3, AUTHORITY: 0, ADDITIONAL: 1

;; OPT PSEUDOSECTION:
; EDNS: version: 0, flags:; udp: 512
;; QUESTION SECTION:
;amazon.com.                IN    A

;; ANSWER SECTION:
amazon.com.        12      IN    A      176.32.103.205
amazon.com.        12      IN    A      205.251.242.103
amazon.com.        12      IN    A      176.32.98.166

;; Query time: 52 msec
;; SERVER: 8.8.8.8#53(8.8.8.8)
;; WHEN: Thu Nov 28 11:35:40 GMT 2019
;; MSG SIZE   rcvd: 87
```

This is because the traffic to a single server could overwhelm it, or it could be that they want redundancy in case one fails.

You could encounter a response with a low TTL and this is so the domain can keep changing IP addresses, either because they are balancing the load of the traffic to the site, or because the website keeps moving servers to cope with changing levels of traffic.

Did you know that nameservers are used by more than web browsers? Using dig you can find out who manages the email for the domain. We can use the -t option to specify the type of records you would like to be returned.

Note MX standards for mail exchange.

```
% dig @8.8.8.8 -t MX google.com
```

```
;; ANSWER SECTION:
google.com.        599    IN    MX    10 aspmx.l.google.com.
google.com.        599    IN    MX    20 alt1.aspmx.l.google.com.
google.com.        599    IN    MX    50 alt4.aspmx.l.google.com.
google.com.        599    IN    MX    40 alt3.aspmx.l.google.com.
google.com.        599    IN    MX    30 alt2.aspmx.l.google.com.
```

If you were to Google aspmx.l.google.com, one of the first results tells you that this is G Suite MX record value. G Suite contains an email component.

There are many different types of records that can be returned. If you want to see them all, you can specify ANY.

```
% dig @8.8.8.8 -t ANY google.com
```

```
; <<>> DiG 9.10.6 <<>> @8.8.8.8 -t ANY google.com
; (1 server found)
;; global options: +cmd
;; Got answer:
```

```
;; ->>HEADER<<- opcode: QUERY, status: NOERROR, id: 63378
;; flags: qr rd ra; QUERY: 1, ANSWER: 18, AUTHORITY: 0, ADDITIONAL: 1

;; OPT PSEUDOSECTION:
; EDNS: version: 0, flags:; udp: 512
;; QUESTION SECTION:
;google.com.                IN    ANY

;; ANSWER SECTION:
google.com.        299    IN   A      216.58.204.238
google.com.        299    IN   AAAA   2a00:1450:4009:807::200e
google.com.        599    IN   MX     20 alt1.aspmx.l.google.com.
google.com.        21599  IN   NS     ns1.google.com.
google.com.        21599  IN   NS     ns2.google.com.
google.com.        21599  IN   CAA    0 issue "pki.goog"
google.com.        3599   IN   TXT    "v=spf1 include:_spf.
                                      google.com ~all"

;; Query time: 148 msec
;; SERVER: 8.8.8.8#53(8.8.8.8)
;; WHEN: Thu Nov 28 11:42:55 GMT 2019
;; MSG SIZE  rcvd: 649
```

If you want to see a more comprehensive example, = try this with example.com:

```
% dig  -t ANY example.com
```

Networking Piping

The nc command is a wonderful utility for working with network connections. It stands for netcat and in some ways it is similar to the cat command. With netcat, you can listen for incoming connections with the -l (L) option.

```
% sudo nc -l 127.0.0.1 8080
```

The command will look like it has hung, but it is listening for connections. Now in your web browser, go to http://127.0.0.1 8080. Suddenly, you will see this output appear:

```
GET / HTTP/1.1
Host: 127.0.0.1:8080
Accept: text/html,application/xhtml+xml,application/
xml;q=0.9,*/*;q=0.8
Upgrade-Insecure-Requests: 1
User-Agent: Mozilla/5.0 (Macintosh; Intel Mac OS X 10_15_3)
AppleWebKit/605.1.15 (KHTML, like Gecko) Version/13.0.5
Safari/605.1.15
Accept-Language: en-gb
Accept-Encoding: gzip, deflate
Connection: keep-alive
```

This is the web request that your web browser makes to the server. It is a mixture of request (the first line) and headers. The web browser is requesting the main page of the site with /.

```
GET / HTTP/1.1
```

The header Host: is also important, because it tells the web server what domain you are accessing. We can also use netcat to send, rather than listening.

```
% echo "GET / HTTP/1.1
Host: google.com
Accept: text/html,application/xhtml+xml,application/
xml;q=0.9,*/*;q=0.8
Upgrade-Insecure-Requests: 1
User-Agent: Mozilla/5.0 (Macintosh; Intel Mac OS X 10_15_3)
AppleWebKit/605.1.15 (KHTML, like Gecko) Version/13.0.5
Safari/605.1.15
```

Accept-Language: en-gb
Accept-Encoding: gzip, deflate
Connection: keep-alive

" | nc google.com 80

Google's web server responded.

```
HTTP/1.1 301 Moved Permanently
Location: http://www.google.com/
Content-Type: text/html; charset=UTF-8
Date: Thu, 13 Feb 2020 07:37:54 GMT
Expires: Sat, 14 Mar 2020 07:37:54 GMT
Cache-Control: public, max-age=2592000
Server: gws
Content-Length: 219
X-XSS-Protection: 0
X-Frame-Options: SAMEORIGIN

<HTML><HEAD><meta http-equiv="content-type" content="text/
html;charset=utf-8">
<TITLE>301 Moved</TITLE></HEAD><BODY>
<H1>301 Moved</H1>
The document has moved
<A HREF="http://www.google.com/">here</A>.
</BODY></HTML>
```

In this response, we have a header, everything that is before the empty line, and the response, every that comes after that blank line. The response is shown to you in the browser.

However, in this response, we can see that the server has told us that the document has moved to `http://www.google.com/`. We can try again, using the URL that Google has told us to use.

```
echo "GET / HTTP/1.1
Host: www.google.com
Accept: text/html,application/xhtml+xml,application/
xml;q=0.9,*/*;q=0.8
Upgrade-Insecure-Requests: 1
User-Agent: Mozilla/5.0 (Macintosh; Intel Mac OS X 10_15_3)
AppleWebKit/605.1.15 (KHTML, like Gecko) Version/13.0.5
Safari/605.1.15
Accept-Language: en-gb
Accept-Encoding: gzip, deflate
Connection: keep-alive

" | nc google.com 80
```

Note   The server I am contacting (google.com) is different from the host header (www.google.com). These typically match, but don't have to.

This is what a typical web request and response looks like. You could use netcat to send data to another instance of netcat, effectively piping across a network connection. We're going to do this in two Terminal windows, but you could do this on two different computers in your household. We are going to listen on port 1234.

```
% nc -l 1234
```

We are sending and receiving the data on the same computer. If you are using another computer, then you will need to substitute localhost with the IP address of the listening computer.

The ifconfig command will list all your computer IP addresses. You can make it easier to find by using Grep.

```
% ifconfig | grep "inet "
  inet 127.0.0.1 netmask 0xff000000
  inet 192.168.1.239 netmask 0xffffff00 broadcast 192.168.1.255
```

The IP address you will be looking for will typically start 192.168 or 10. Now that we know where we are sending the message, let's send it.

Note   The port needs to match. If you are sending to another computer, change localhost to match the IP address of the listening computer.

```
% nc localhost 1234
Hello
```

You are already running netcat, that is listening, so it will output everything that is sent to it.

```
% nc -l 1234
Hello
```

You could have started netcat by specifying that the output be piped into another command like this.

```
% nc -l 1234 | tr "[:lower:]" "[:upper:]"
HELLO
```

Disk Management

This section covers all the helpful macOS built-in commands that deal with disk management.

How Big Is This Folder?

The du (disk usage) command will tell you how much disk space has been used for all files and folders, wherever you are.

```
usage: du [-H | -L | -P] [-a | -s | -d depth] [-c] [-h | -k |
-m | -g] [-x] [-I mask] [file ...]
```

Note   du iterates through all the files and adds up their disk usage. The command might take a while, depending on how many files there are.

However, listing all the files isn't how I use this command. I use the -s option to generate a summary.

By default, du will show the usage in blocks. We change that into human-readable sizes with the -h option.

% du -sh ~/random-files-master

```
172K/Users/danielplatt/random-files-master
```

You might be tempted to try this on your home directory. I know I was.

% du -sh ~

```
du: /Users/danielplatt/Library/Containers/com.apple.mail:
Operation not permitted
du: /Users/danielplatt/Library/Containers/com.apple.news:
Operation not permitted
du: /Users/danielplatt/Library/Containers/com.apple.stocks:
Operation not permitted
du: /Users/danielplatt/.Trash: Operation not permitted
 30G/Users/danielplatt
```

You will probably get a lot more output that says `Operation not permitted`.

This isn't a bad thing, it just means that Terminal could not go into those directories to calculate the disk used by those files.

If you want those messages to go away, you can give Terminal full access to your disk in the Security & Privacy System Preferences tab, as shown in Figure 3-19.

Figure 3-19. *Locked Security & Privacy in System Preferences*

If you find the padlock in Full Disk Access grayed out, you need to click the padlock that is on the bottom left to make changes, as shown in Figure 3-20. That will allow you to change the permissions.

Just remember that full access is defined by your user's permission. If you can't normally access a folder, then Terminal with full access still will not be able to access it.

Figure 3-20. *Unlocked Security & Privacy in System Preferences*

We really want the Operation not permitted errors to go away and for du to be able read these directories. For this to happen, Terminal needs to be in the list of programs that have full disk access. If Terminal is currently running, by ticking Terminal, it will prompt you to Quit Now in order for the changes to take effect. When you rerun du, you shouldn't see any Operation not permitted messages.

```
% du -sh ~
 33G/Users/danielplatt
```

Looks like those skipped folders accounted for 3GB.

Free Space

In Finder, you can easily find out how big your disk is, or how much free space you have. You just need to find your disk, select it, and then choose Get Info (⌘+i) for more information about the disk usage, as shown in Figure 3-21.

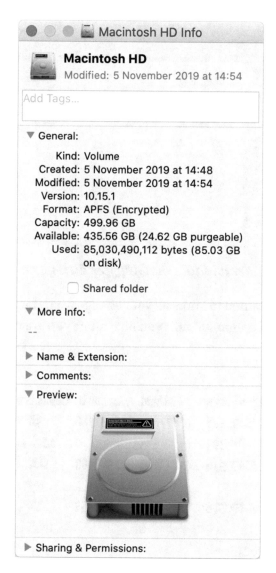

Figure 3-21. *Finder Info window*

You can also see the available space at the bottom of every Finder window, but that is only for that disk, as shown in Figure 3-22.

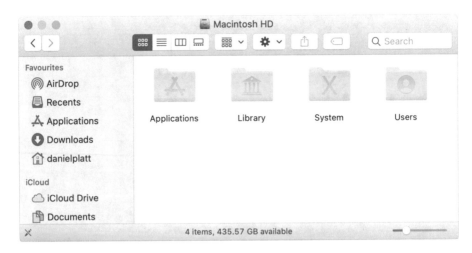

Figure 3-22. *Finder window showing free disk space*

What if you wanted to know all your storage usage for all attached disks in one go? The df command tells you how much you are using on all of your disks.

% df

Filesystem	512-blocks	Used	Available	Capacity	Mounted on
/dev/disk1s5	976490576	20877600	802587568	3%	/
devfs	395	395	0	100%	/dev
/dev/disk1s1	976490576	145223104	802587568	16%	/System/Volumes/Data
/dev/disk1s4	976490576	6291496	802587568	1%	/private/var/vm
map auto_home	0	0	0	100%	/System/Volumes/Data/home

However, it's a little bit messy. Let's make that more readable by not using blocks.

```
% df -h
Filesystem      Size  Used  Avail Capacity  %iused  Mounted on
/dev/disk1s5    466Gi 10Gi  383Gi       3%      0%  /
devfs           198Ki 98Ki   0Bi      100%    100%  /dev
/dev/disk1s1    466Gi 69Gi  383Gi      16%      0%  /System/Volumes/Data
/dev/disk1s4    466Gi 3.0Gi 383Gi       1%      0%  /private/var/vm
map auto_home    0Bi  0Bi    0Bi      100%    100%  /System/Volumes/
                                                    Data/home
```

If, like me, you only have one drive attached to your computer (the boot disk), you might be wondering why you have five entries. A single drive can have more than one partition on it. Your boot drive has quite a few partitions, and that is what you are seeing. The physical drive is disk1, and then s followed by the number is the partition.

The main filesystems are the system (disk1s5), data (disk1s1), and virtual memory (disk1s4). They all share the same physical disk, which is why they all have the same Size and Avail values.

Disk Management

In the Utilities folder on your Mac, there is an app called Disk Utility. You can use it to perform many different operations on all the drives that are attached to your computer. There is a command-line version as well, called diskutil.

```
% diskutil
Disk Utility Tool
Utility to manage local disks and volumes
Most commands require an administrator or root user

WARNING: Most destructive operations are not prompted

Usage:  diskutil [quiet] <verb> <options>, where <verb> is as follows:

diskutil <verb> with no options will provide help on that verb
```

You can do great damage by improperly using diskutil, and a lot of the features will require sudo. In the previous command, du, I mislead you a little. disk1 is your drive, but it isn't a physical drive. Your physical drive it is actually disk0. disk1 is a synthetics disk.

You can list the disk partitions as follows:

% diskutil list

```
/dev/disk0 (internal, physical):
   #:    TYPE NAME                         SIZE         IDENTIFIER
   0:    GUID_partition_scheme            *500.3 GB    disk0
   1:    EFI EFI                           314.6 MB    disk0s1
   2:    Apple_APFS Container disk1        500.0 GB    disk0s2

/dev/disk1 (synthesized):
   #:    TYPE NAME                         SIZE         IDENTIFIER
   0:    APFS Container Scheme -          +500.0 GB    disk1
Physical Store disk0s2
   1:    APFS Volume Macintosh HD -Data   74.5 GB      disk1s1
   2:    APFS Volume Preboot              83.5 MB      disk1s2
   3:    APFS Volume Recovery             528.5 MB     disk1s3
   4:    APFS Volume VM                   5.4 GB       disk1s4
   5:    APFS Volume Macintosh HD         10.7 GB      disk1s5
```

Note   If you have a fusion drive, disk1 will be the ssd component of your fusion drive, and the synthesized drive will be disk2.

---

disk0 is a container, which is a bit like a tar file. It will contain everything needed for your computer to synthesize disk1. If you have FileVault turned on, then encryption is on this container. Let's plug in a USB memory stick and see how the list changes:

% diskutil list

```
/dev/disk2 (external, physical):
   #:     TYPE NAME                    SIZE          IDENTIFIER
   0:     FDisk_partition_scheme      *4.0 GB        disk2
   1:     DOS_FAT_32 Linux Boot        4.0 GB        disk2s1
```

In addition to disk0 and disk1, we now have another disk called disk2. You can see that there is only a single partition and that disk size is 4GB. The partition type of DOS_FAT_32 is an old style format that belongs to Windows.

Viewing Partition Information

You can find more information about any disk with info.

% diskutil info /dev/disk2

```
   Device Identifier:      disk2
   Device Node:            /dev/disk2
   Whole:                  Yes
   Part of Whole:          disk2
   Device / Media Name:    Transcend 4GB

   Volume Name:            Not applicable (no file system)
   Mounted:                Not applicable (no file system)
   File System:            None

   Content (IOContent):    FDisk_partition_scheme
   OS Can Be Installed:    No
   Media Type:             Generic
   Protocol:               USB
   SMART Status:           Not Supported

   Disk Size:              4.0 GB (4049600512 Bytes)
   Device Block Size:      512 Bytes
```

Read-Only Media: No
Read-Only Volume: Not applicable (no file system)

Device Location: External
Removable Media: Removable
Media Removal: Software-Activated

Solid State: Info not available
Virtual: No

Securely Erasing a Disk

If you are security conscious, you should wipe your disk drives before
getting rid of them. That includes the empty space on a disk, as it is
possible to see what was written. Thankfully, there is a zeroDisk command
that will do just that.

Warning   This will make recovering data from the disk either
incredibly hard or impossible. Only use it on a disk when you want to
never see the contents again.

% diskutil zeroDisk /dev/disk2
```
Started erase on disk2
[ |  0%..10%. ] 14.1% 0:08:47
```

Because it writes to every part of the disk, it will take a while to finish.

Danger   Treat this command with respect, because there is no
going back. To be safe, remove all other external drives before you
continue, in order to reduce the risk of operating on the wrong disk.

When the zeroDisk is finished, try running the list again.

```
% diskutil list
```

```
/dev/disk2 (external, physical):
   #:                  TYPE NAME                    SIZE        IDENTIFIER
   0:                                              *4.0 GB      disk2
```

You can still see the disk, but all the partitions are gone.

Creating a New Partition

You can create a partition again, but it gets complicated, so I recommend using the Disk Utility app. However, you can create an apfs container and a single partition easily with the apfs create command.

```
% diskutil apfs create /dev/disk2 "My Drive"
```

```
Started APFS operation on disk2
Creating a new empty APFS Container
Unmounting Volumes
Switching disk2 to APFS
Creating APFS Container
Created new APFS Container disk3
Disk from APFS operation: disk3
Finished APFS operation on disk2
Started APFS operation on disk3
Preparing to add APFS Volume to APFS Container disk3
Creating APFS Volume
Created new APFS Volume disk3s1
Mounting APFS Volume
Setting volume permissions
Disk from APFS operation: disk3s1
Finished APFS operation on disk3
```

Encrypting a Disk

Suppose you work for a company that requires all remote storage be encrypted. You can enable FileVault on this drive with this command.

```
% diskutil apfs encrypt /dev/disk3s1 -user disk
Passphrase for the new "Disk" user (6584DA69-6E6F-4F49-AF6F-
02D3EECOAEDC):
Repeat passphrase:
Starting background encryption with the new "Disk" crypto user
on disk3s1
The new "Disk" user will be the only one who has initial access
to disk3s1
The new APFS crypto user UUID will be 6584DA69-6E6F-4F49-AF6F-
02D3EECOAEDC
Background encryption is ongoing; see "diskutil apfs list" to
see progress
```

Note   You are looking for the partition with type APFS Volume.

We will unmount the drive and remount it, to ensure that it unlocks properly.

```
% diskutil umount /dev/disk3s1
Volume My Drive on disk3s1 unmounted
```

We can't yet mount the drive using the mount command, because we need to tell diskutil to unlock it first.

```
% diskutil mount /dev/disk3s1
Volume on disk3s1 failed to mount
This appears to be an APFS Volume; note that locked APFS volumes
will not mount unless unlocked (e.g. "diskutil apfs unlockVolume")
```

We need to use unlockVolume and then supply the same password.

% diskutil apfs unlockVolume /dev/disk3s1
```
Passphrase:
Unlocking any cryptographic user on APFS Volume disk3s1
Unlocked and mounted APFS Volume
```

Disk Images

You've been able to use disk images with Macs since before macOS X, but did you know that you can create your own disk image with hdiutil?

% hdiutil
```
hdiutil: missing verb
Usage: hdiutil <verb> <options>
```

A disk image is just a virtual disk that you can mount at will. You can think of it as email-able USB storage.

Creating a Disk Image

An empty 4GB disk image can be created like this.

Note   You could use m for MB or t for TB.

% hdiutil create -size 4g ~/storage.dmg

However, if you try to mount this in Finder, you will find that there is no filesystem, and thus it's not mountable.

Note   If you don't delete storage.dmg between each command, they will fail. Or you could add the -ov option to overwrite the existing image.

Let's specify a filesystem.

```
% hdiutil create -size 4g -fs apfs storage.dmg
```

Mounting a Disk Image

Now we can mount this disk image by double-clicking it in Finder or using the open command. We can also use hdiutil to mount it.

```
% hdiutil attach storage.dmg
/dev/disk2                 GUID_partition_scheme
/dev/disk2s1               EFI
/dev/disk2s2               Apple_APFS
/dev/disk3                 EF57347C-0000-11AA-AA11-0030654
/dev/disk3s1               41504653-0000-11AA-AA11-0030654
/Volumes/untitled
```

Oh, the name of the volume is untitled.

Ejecting a Disk Image

Let's unmount the disk by using the eject command.

```
% hdiutil eject /Volumes/untitled
"disk2" ejected.
```

Change the Disk Image Volume Name

We can change the volume name by using the volname option to specify a name of our choosing.

```
-volname "Virtual Disk"
```

You might not have noticed, but by creating the 4GB disk image, we have actually used 4GB of disk space.

% ls -lath ~/storage.dmg

```
-rw-r--r--@ 1 danielplatt  staff   4.0G  7 Dec 21:28 /Users/
danielplatt/storage.dmg
```

This doesn't have to be the case. We could create a *sparse* image. A sparse image only takes up the amount of space on your disk that is used inside the disk image.

We can enable sparse disk images by specifying the sparse type, as in -type SPARSE. We can put it all together and rename the disk image to match the volume name:

% hdiutil create -size 4g -type SPARSE -volname "Virtual Disk" -fs apfs virtual-disk

```
created: /Users/danielplatt/virtual-disk.sparseimage
```

% hdiutil attach virtual-disk.sparseimage

```
/dev/disk2              GUID_partition_scheme
/dev/disk2s1            EFI
/dev/disk2s2            Apple_APFS
/dev/disk3              EF57347C-0000-11AA-AA11-0030654
/dev/disk3s1            41504653-0000-11AA-AA11-0030654
/Volumes/Virtual Disk
```

When you are finished with a disk image, you should always eject it to make sure macOS has fully written everything to the image.

% hdiutil eject /Volumes/Virtual\ Disk

```
"disk2" ejected.
```

Now, when we look at the size of the disk image, we can see it no longer takes up the 4GB that it previously did.

% ls -lath virtual-disk.sparseimage

```
-rw-r--r--  1 danielplatt  staff   13M  8 Dec 12:42 virtual-
disk.sparseimage
```

Encrypting a Disk Image

It seems like not a week goes by when we hear about how documents have been leaked, because they were left on a train and weren't encrypted, so anyone could (and did) read the files.

Encryption can be done at multiple levels. We've seen how to enable FileVault on a whole disk or encrypt an archive. We can also use encryption on disk images. To enable encryption, we need to pass in the encryption option and tell hdiutil to ask for the password with stdinpass. We will also use the ov option to overwrite the existing image.

% hdiutil create -ov -size 4g -type SPARSE -volname "Virtual Disk" -encryption -stdinpass -fs apfs virtual-disk
```
Enter disk image passphrase:
created: /Users/danielplatt/virtual-disk.sparseimage
```

% hdiutil attach virtual-disk.sparseimage
```
Enter password to access "virtual-disk.sparseimage":
/dev/disk2              GUID_partition_scheme
/dev/disk2s1            EFI
/dev/disk2s2            Apple_APFS
/dev/disk3              EF57347C-0000-11AA-AA11-0030654
/dev/disk3s1            41504653-0000-11AA-AA11-0030654
/Volumes/Virtual Disk
```

Copy an Existing Device

If you have an existing USB device that you'd like to make a copy of, you can use the srcdevice option.

Note   The fs, type, volname, and size options are ignored when using srcdevice.

% hdiutil create -srcdevice /dev/disk3 -encryption -stdinpass copy-virtual-disk

```
disk3 was already unmounted or it has a partitioning scheme so
use "diskutil unmountDisk" instead
```

You will not be able to image a disk that is currently mounted, because the image process cannot stop anything from writing to it. For consistency of the data, you need to unmount the disk first.

% diskutil unmountDisk /dev/disk3

```
Unmount of all volumes on disk3 was successful
```

Now that the disk is unmounted, you can try again.

% hdiutil create -srcdevice /dev/disk3 -encryption -stdinpass copy-virtual-disk

```
Enter disk image passphrase:
Preparing imaging engine...
Reading whole disk (Apple_APFS : 0)...

   (CRC32 $CA5DE01C: whole disk (Apple_APFS : 0))
Adding resources...

Elapsed Time: 205.822ms
File size: 141828 bytes, Checksum: CRC32 $16AFC33E
Sectors processed: 7978928, 32056 compressed
Speed: 76.0Mbytes/sec
Savings: 100.0%
created: /Users/danielplatt/copy-virtual-disk.dmg
```

Great, that worked, so now we can mount it.

% hdiutil attach /Users/danielplatt/copy-virtual-disk.dmg

```
Enter password to access "copy-virtual-disk.dmg":
Checksumming whole disk (Apple_APFS : 0)...
```

```
        whole disk (Apple_APFS : 0): verified CRC32 $CA5DE01C
verified CRC32 $16AFC33E
/dev/disk4
/dev/disk5                      EF57347C-0000-11AA-AA11-0030654
/dev/disk5s1                    41504653-0000-11AA-AA11-0030654
/Volumes/Virtual Disk
```

Creating a Disk Image Containing Existing Files

Instead of copying an existing device, you can also copy an existing folder using srcfolder.

% hdiutil create -size 5m -volname "Virtual Disk" -srcfolder ~/ random-files-master -fs apfs random-files

created: /Users/danielplatt/random-files.dmg

Note   We didn't need to specify fs or size. The command would have picked defaults that matched as closely as possible to the current filesystem and the space used.

Other Commands That I Love

This next section contains commands that I love, but I couldn't think of a heading for them.

The say Command

I love this command. I built a Hypnosis application around the say command. Although now, it only uses the underlying technology as the say command.

The say command allows you to make your computer talk in a variety of different voices. The functionality has been part of macOS X since the beginning.

```
% say "I love macOS"
```

If you combine this by sshing into other Macs, you have the ability to prank other people. say accepts text that is piped into it.

```
% echo "hello" | say
```

You can speak the contents of a file or read the contents of files:

```
% say -f random-files-master/Readme.md
```

You also can change the voice with the -v and -r options. -v changes the voice and -r changes the speaking rate in words per minute. To be able to change the voice, you need to know what your options are.

```
% say -v '?'
Alex    en_US    # Most people recognize me by my voice.
Alice   it_IT    # Salve, mi chiamo Alice e sono una voce
                   italiana.
Alva    sv_SE    # Hej, jag heter Alva. Jag är en svensk röst.
```

You have quite a bit of choices. It might be easier if you filtered this list down to just the languages you want.

```
% say -v '?' | grep en_
Alex    en_US    # Most people recognize me by my voice.
Daniel  en_GB    # Hello, my name is Daniel.
Fred    en_US    # I sure like being inside this fancy computer
Karen   en_AU    # Hello, my name is Karen.
```

There are more voices available for download in the Accessibility tab, which is in System Preferences, as shown in Figure 3-23.

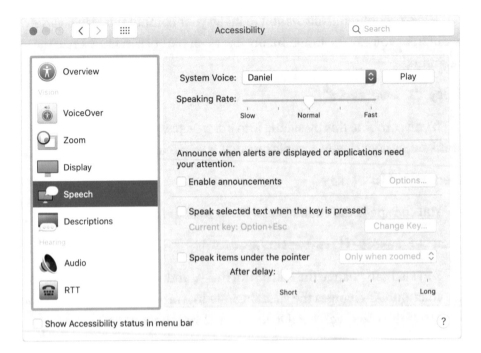

Figure 3-23. *Speech settings in Accessibility, System Preferences*

Note   This is where you change the default voice and speaking rate for the say command.

When you select the System Voice in Speech, you will see the list of installed voices. At the bottom is a Customize option that will bring up a window of potential voices, as shown in Figure 3-24.

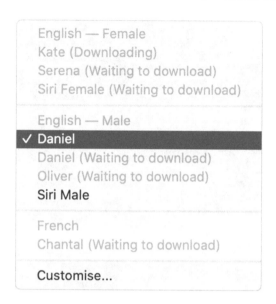

Figure 3-24. *Voice drop-down from Voice settings in Accessibility*

You can select as many or as few voices as you want. The downside to selecting all of them is they will take up space on your computer and have to be downloaded, as shown in Figure 3-25.

Figure 3-25. *Extra voices being downloaded*

Once the new voices are fully downloaded and installed, they will show up in the say command.

```
% say -v '?' | grep Oliver
Oliver    en_GB    # Hello, my name is Oliver.
```

Changing the Speaking Rate

The other option was speaking rate, -r. The default rate varies slightly for each voice, but is typically around 220 words per minute. Most voices support between 150 and 350 words per minute.

```
% say -r 350 "I can talk really fast"
```

```
% say -r 150 "and I can talk really slow"
```

You will be able to go to more extremes than these numbers. Be aware that if a voice doesn't support the rate given, it will ignore it and use the default value.

```
% say -r 1 "I will ignore this rate"
```

Saving Speech to a File

There is a possibility that you might want to use this generated speech somewhere else, maybe if you create online videos. Rather than try to record your computer while it speaks, you could use the -o option to output the speech to file.

say has quite a few output options, so let's see what they are.

```
% say --file-format="?"
AIFC  AIFC     (.aifc,.aiff,.aif) [lpcm,ulaw,alaw,ima4,Qclp]
AIFF  AIFF     (.aiff,.aif) [lpcm]
```

Not all formats are supported by all voices. You might find that it is easier to use aiff, which is the default.

```
% say "I like talking" -o ~/talking.aiff
```

You will then have a file called talking.aiff in your home directory, which you could easily use in a program like iMovie.

Scheduling with Launchd

On your Mac, there is a process for running tasks on a schedule. The process is called launchd and you can control it by editing plist files and using the launchctl command.

Listing Services

The default installation of Catalina has over 300 services. They each have a very specific job to do, like keeping your iCloud Drive synchronized and your search index up to date. Even Finder and QuickLook are services.

The first thing to view are all the tasks that have been scheduled on your computer.

% launchctl list

```
PID     Status Label
-        0          com.apple.SafariHistoryServiceAgent
520      0          com.apple.progressd
24988    0          com.apple.ActivityMonitor.18300
536      0          com.apple.cloudphotod
340      0          com.apple.Finder
389      0          com.apple.homed
-       -9          com.apple.SafeEjectGPUAgent
-        0          com.apple.quicklook
```

If any entry in this has a PID value, that means it is currently running. There is also a status code and the service name. We can also pass the service name into the list subcommand to get even more information about a service.

% launchctl list com.apple.Finder

```
{
  "LimitLoadToSessionType" = "Aqua";
  "MachServices" = {
    "com.apple.DiscRecording:registrar" = mach-port-object;
    "com.apple.finder.ServiceProvider" = mach-port-object;
  };
  "Label" = "com.apple.Finder";
  "OnDemand" = true;
```

```
  "LastExitStatus" = 0;
  "PID" = 340;
  "Program" = "/System/Library/CoreServices/Finder.app/
   Contents/MacOS/Finder";
  "PerJobMachServices" = {
    "com.apple.DiscRecording:remote" = mach-port-object;
    "com.apple.tsm.portname" = mach-port-object;
    "com.apple.coredrag" = mach-port-object;
    "com.apple.axserver" = mach-port-object;
  };
};
```

The status code is the exit status of the service. This number represents an error message.

Launchd Error Codes

We can use the error subcommand to find out what the human readable version of the status is.

% launchctl error 0
```
0: Undefined error: 0
```

The reason we are seeing Undefined error here is because 0 is special. The 0 value represents no error, so everything completed correctly.

Let's check another service, this time one that had a status that wasn't 0.

% launchctl list com.apple.SafeEjectGPUAgent
```
{
  "EnableTransactions" = true;
  "LimitLoadToSessionType" = "Aqua";
  "Label" = "com.apple.SafeEjectGPUAgent";
  "OnDemand" = true;
```

```
  "LastExitStatus" = 9;
  "Program" = "/System/Library/CoreServices/Menu Extras/
   SafeEjectGPUExtra.menu/Contents/MacOS/SafeEjectGPUAgent";
  "ProgramArguments" = (
    "SafeEjectGPUAgent";
  );
};
```

This time the status was 9. We can try that now.

```
% launchctl error 9
9: Bad file descriptor
```

Service Definition

Now that you know that there are services, I want to show you how they are defined. According to the man for launchd, the configuration for all the launch services exist in a certain location, depending on how they need to run.

```
~/Library/LaunchAgents      Per-user agents provided by the user.
/Library/LaunchAgents       Per-user agents provided by the
                            administrator.
/Library/LaunchDaemons      System wide daemons provided by the
                            administrator.
/System/Library/LaunchAgents OS X Per-user agents.
/System/Library/LaunchDaemons OS X System wide daemons.
```

You might remember that your hard drive has been split into two parts. The first part is the system drive and is read-only for you. The second part is the data drive. Effectively, this means that anything in /System is read-only and you cannot change it.

You will not be able to modify the System launch services. However, this is where the bulk of the services will live.

```
% ls /System/Library/Launch*
```

The reason for showing you these services is that they are a good example of what the service configuration file looks like. The first thing to notice is that all the services have the plist file extension. Let's look at the Finder service.

% ls /System/Library/Launch*/*Finder*

% cat /System/Library/LaunchAgents/com.apple.Finder.plist
```
<?xml version="1.0" encoding="UTF-8"?>
<!DOCTYPE plist PUBLIC "-//Apple//DTD PLIST 1.0//EN" "http://
www.apple.com/DTDs/PropertyList-1.0.dtd">
<plist version="1.0">
<dict>
  <key>POSIXSpawnType</key>
  <string>App</string>
  <key>RunAtLoad</key>
  <false/>
  <key>KeepAlive</key>
  <dict>
    <key>SuccessfulExit</key>
    <false/>
    <key>AfterInitialDemand</key>
    <true/>
  </dict>
  <key>Label</key>
  <string>com.apple.Finder</string>
  <key>Program</key>

  <string>/System/Library/CoreServices/Finder.app/Contents/
MacOS/Finder</string>
  <key>CFBundleIdentifier</key>
  <string>com.apple.finder</string>
  <key>ThrottleInterval</key>
```

```
    <integer>1</integer>
</dict>
</plist>
```

The next thing to notice about a service is that the file format is `.xml`.

The XML File Format

You don't need to fully understand the `.xml` file format, but knowing enough to make changes will be useful if you want to create your own scheduled tasks. An XML file is made up of tags. A tag is made up of the less than and greater than symbols, as follows.

```
<plist>
```

However, that isn't valid, as the tag needs to be closed. You can close a tag with a forward slash symbol (/), such as:

```
<plist></plist> or <plist/>
```

Tags can also contain tags.

```
<plist>
  <dict>
    <key>ExampleKey</key>
    <value>Example Value</value>
  </dict>
</plist>
```

Inside `dict`, items are paired together as a key and a value. The *key* is a simple string. The *value* is a little more complex, as it can be one of many different types—string, integer, boolean, dictionary, array, date, or data. Let's look at an example that's a little more realistic.

```
<plist>
  <dict>
    <key>ExampleKey</key>
    <string>Example Value</string>
    <key>AnotherKey</key>
    <integer>1</integer>
  </dict>
</plist>
```

There is a lot more information in the plist man page.

Creating Your Own launchd Process

Now that you know a little bit about the .xml file format, making our own launchd process should be easier. Rather than using the previous example, where Finder runs on demand, let's create a scheduled task that runs every minute. This could easily be changed to every hour.

For this example, we will use touch to update the modified date time for a file called scheduledUpdate. First, let's grab the bits we need from the previous example.

```
<?xml version="1.0" encoding="UTF-8"?>
<!DOCTYPE plist PUBLIC "-//Apple//DTD PLIST 1.0//EN" "http://
www.apple.com/DTDs/PropertyList-1.0.dtd">
<plist version="1.0">
<dict>

</dict>
</plist>
```

Second, we need to define the name of this task. We will do that with the label key.

```
<key>Label</key>
<string>com.example.touch</string>
```

There are a few rules for creating the label. It needs to be unique and will form the basis of the filename. In fact, the filename for this file is the label and ends with `.plist`.

When choosing a label, they typically use the reverse domain name format, but you don't need to strictly follow this format.

Third, we need to define the program. When defining the program name, we have to use the absolute path, because `launchd` will not have access to our user's path variable.

Note   If you don't remember where a command is, use the `which` command to find it.

```
<key>Program</key>
<string>/usr/bin/touch</string>
```

Fourth, we need to define the program arguments with the `ProgramArguments` key. The first argument is always the program name. After that, we can pass in all the arguments needed.

```
<key>ProgramArguments</key>
<array>
  <string>touch</string>
  <string>/Users/danielplatt/scheduledUpdate </string>
</array>
```

You might be tempted to use `~/scheduledUpdate` here. However, the tilde isn't recognized by `launchd`. We can get around that by using the absolute path to the file. In Chapter 5, we discuss making your own commands, which will simplify the program arguments, as you can build them into the command.

Lastly, you need to specify how often to run this task. You can either specify that you want the process to happen every number of specified seconds, as follows:

```
<key>StartInterval</key>
<integer>60</integer>
```

Or you can specify when you want the process to run, with StartCalendarInterval. You can see the valid keys and values in Table 3-4.

Table 3-4. *Valid Keys and Values for StartCalendarInterval*

Key	Value
Month	1-12
Day	1-31
Weekday	0-7 (Sunday is both 0 and 7)
Hour	0-23
Minute	0-59

You can be as specific or as vague as you want, as to when the process will run. For example, you could have a process running every year at midnight on March 24.

```
<key>StartCalendarInterval</key>
<dict>
    <key>Day</key>
    <integer>24</integer>
    <key>Hour</key>
    <integer>0</integer>
    <key>Minute</key>
```

```
        <integer>0</integer>
        <key>Month</key>
        <integer>3</integer>
    </dict>
```

Or every hour in March.

```
    <key>StartCalendarInterval</key>
    <dict>
        <key>Minute</key>
        <integer>0</integer>
        <key>Month</key>
        <integer>3</integer>
    </dict>
```

Or if we wanted to match the StartInterval example and have the process running every minute, we would use:

```
    <key>StartCalendarInterval</key>
    <dict>
    </dict>
```

With StartCalendarInterval, if you don't specify a particular key, it is treated as if it were matching all the values. Let's put it all together.

% nano ~/Library/LaunchAgents/com.example.touch.plist

```
<?xml version="1.0" encoding="UTF-8"?>
<!DOCTYPE plist PUBLIC "-//Apple//DTD PLIST 1.0//EN" "http://
www.apple.com/DTDs/PropertyList-1.0.dtd">
<plist version="1.0">
<dict>
  <key>Label</key>
  <string>com.example.touch</string>
  <key>Program</key>
```

```
    <string>/usr/bin/touch</string>
    <key>ProgramArguments</key>
    <array>
      <string>touch</string>
      <string>/Users/danielplatt/scheduledUpdate</string>
    </array>
    <key>StartInterval</key>
    <integer>60</integer>
  </dict>
</plist>
```

Once you have defined your launchd plist, you need to get launchd to load it.

```
% launchctl load ~/Library/LaunchAgents/com.example.touch.plist
```

Troubleshooting

Not everything works perfectly the first time, and launchd can be frustrating to debug because you can't see the output of the process you're running. However, we can fix that with a few more keys. There are two keys that will help us debug launchd.

- StandardOutPath

- StandardErrorPath

Both of these keys take a file path, which is where the output will be written.

```
<key>StandardErrorPath</key>
<string>/tmp/com.example.touch.err</string>
<key>StandardOutPath</key>
<string>/tmp/com.example.touch.out</string>
```

When you make changes to your `launchd plist`, you need to reload it. You can reload your `plist` with the `unload`, followed by `load`, commands.

```
% launchctl unload -w ~/Library/LaunchAgents/com.example.touch.plist
% launchctl load -w ~/Library/LaunchAgents/com.example.touch.plist
```

Then you just have to wait until the launch time has elapsed. You should then have two files—`com.example.touch.out` and `com.example.touch.err`—that should show why your `launchd` process isn't working.

If you don't have these files, double-check the `StartInterval` and `StartCalendarInterval` values. Consult the manual for a lot more information about the values you can use in your `plist`.

```
% man launchd.plist
```

Top Commands

A colleague gave this next command to me. It provides the top commands that you have used on your Terminal.

```
% history | awk '{print $2}' | sort | uniq -c | sort -rh | head -n 10
```

Let's break this down. The `history` command will list all the commands you have typed into Terminal in the order that they were typed.

```
% history
    1   cd ~/random-files-master
    2   less walden.txt
    3   cat lorem.txt bible.txt | less
    4   cat lorem.txt bible.txt > combined.txt
```

The amount of commands that are saved, is controlled by the `$HISTSIZE` variable.

```
% echo $HISTSIZE
50000
```

If this isn't enough, you can set the value to something bigger in your .zshrc file.

```
export HISTSIZE=75000
```

The next command, awk, extracts the second word from every line.

```
% history | awk '{print $2}'
    cd
    less
    cat
    cat
```

The next command is sort. It will arrange all the lines in alphabetical order.

```
% history | awk '{print $2}' | sort
cat
cat
cd
less
```

If we didn't sort the list of commands, then this next command wouldn't work as well. The command is uniq and, by default, it will only return the unique lines that happen in succession.

Without the sort command earlier, it is likely the commands will not happen in alphabetical order. This will mean uniq will not be able to remove all the duplicate lines.

With the -c argument, uniq will also return a count.

```
% history | awk '{print $2}' | uniq -c
    1 cd
    1 less
    2 cat
```

This example isn't great at showing the reason for this next command.

As your list of commands grows, the order will not be retained. So you'll need to sort again, but this time based on its numeric order (-h).

Depending on how you want your list presented, you might want the order to be low to high (default), or high to low. As I want the list to be high to low, I want to reverse the order (-r).

```
% history | awk '{print $2}' | sort | uniq -c | sort -rh
   2 cat
   1 less
   1 cd
```

You might only want a list of all your commands, ranked in order, and if you do, then you can stop here.

If you want to see the top 10 most commonly used commands, you need this next command, head.

```
% history | awk '{print $2}' | sort | uniq -c | sort -rh |
head -n 10
   2 cat
   1 less
   1 cd
```

Are you interested in seeing my actual top 10 commands at the moment? Here you go:

```
% history | awk '{print $2}' | sort | uniq -c | sort -rh |
head -n 10
 317 magick
 220 open
 173 ls
 140 ffmpeg
 118 man
 106 nano
```

```
102 brew
 93 cat
 64 launchctl
 61 echo
```

Summary

In this chapter, we looked at many of the commands that you can use within the macOS Terminal without having to install anything.

In the next chapter, we will be using Brew to install other commands.

CHAPTER 4

Installing Commands Using Brew

In the last chapter, we looked at many of the commands that come preinstalled with macOS Catalina. In this chapter, we will look at some additional commands that can be installed using Brew. These commands will give you extra functionality over and above what you get with macOS.

Having Fun with Text

Although the commands in this section are just a bit of fun, they will help you gain confidence using Terminal and learn some important concepts.

The fortune Command

The fortune command is great and produces messages similar to that of a fortune cookie. We installed this command in Chapter 2, but I wanted to go over it properly here. To recap, when you run the fortune command, it will output a random message to your Terminal.

```
% fortune
I have often regretted my speech, never my silence.
-- Publilius Syrus
```

© Daniel Platt 2021
D. Platt, *Tweak Your Mac Terminal*, https://doi.org/10.1007/978-1-4842-6171-2_4

fortune has two lists to choose from, funny and offensive epigrams. By default, it's using the funny list. If you would like to use the potentially offensive list of epigrams, you can use the -o option.

```
% fortune -o
```

Or you can use the -a option to choose from both lists.

```
% fortune -a
```

There are many different topics that fortune will choose from. If you want to see a list of all fortune files, you can use the -f option. It shows the percentage change of that category being chosen.

```
% fortune -f
100.00% /usr/local/Cellar/fortune/9708/share/games/fortunes
      7.65% computers
      9.22% people
      4.66% science
      4.82% miscellaneous
      5.18% politics
      8.28% definitions
```

Those were the safe lists. You can also combine the -f option with the -o (or -a) option.

```
% fortune -f -o
100.00% /usr/local/Cellar/fortune/9708/share/games/fortunes/off
```

You can also tell fortune to use a particular fortune file.

```
% fortune /usr/local/Cellar/fortune/9708/share/games/fortunes/art
I went into the business for the money, and the art grew out of
it. If people are disillusioned by that remark, I can't help
it. It's the truth.
-- Charlie Chaplin
```

Sometimes you will want to return fortunes that are less than a certain number of characters. You can tell fortune to return either short or long epigrams. By default, the length is set to 160 characters, which can be changed with -n.

```
% fortune -s
"An open mind has but one disadvantage: it collects dirt."
-- a saying at RPI
% fortune -l
All parts should go together without forcing. You must remember
that the parts you are reassembling were disassembled by you.
Therefore, if you can't get
them together again, there must be a reason. By all means, do
not use a hammer.
-- IBM maintenance manual, 1925
% fortune -s -n 10
Ship it.
```

The cowsay Command

This is a simple application that places text in a cow speech bubble. That's a speech bubble for a cow. It's as simple as that. Let's install cowsay.

```
% brew install cowsay
```

There are other options for cowsay; you can find more information by typing man cowsay. You can use either cowsay or cowthink. Let's try it.

```
% cowsay "message"
```

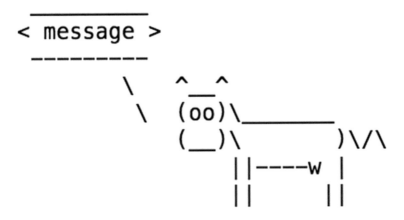

```
% cowthink "message"
```

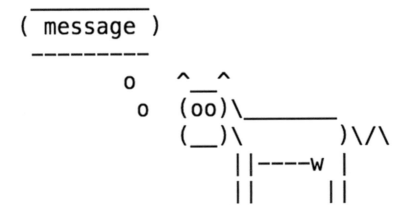

There we go, a cow speech bubble and a cow thought bubble. What else can you do? There are different animals you can use. The path to these extra characters is /usr/local/share/cows. If that path changes after publication, there is a path listed in the manual. If you use ls, it will show you all the files can be used.

```
% ls /usr/local/share/cows
    sheep.cow
    tux.cow
```

If you wanted to use the sheep, the command would become:

```
% cowsay -f /usr/local/share/cows/sheep.cow "awesome"
```

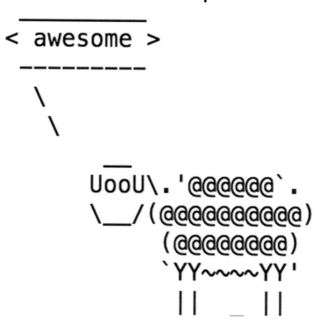

Can you do anything useful with this? You could have some fun and
"pipe" a fortune message in.

```
% fortune | cowsay
```

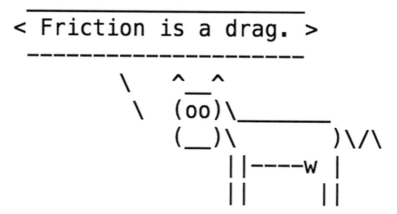

Maybe animal speech bubbles aren't your thing? Let's move on.

The figlet Command

If you're into ASCII art, you can install `figlet` as follows:

```
% brew install figlet
```

This will convert text into ASCII art.

```
% figlet 'art?'
```

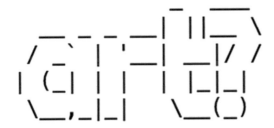

There are loads of different styles (or fonts) to choose from and there is a handy command that lists them, along with example text.

```
% showfigfonts
```

```
computer :

eeee eeeee eeeeeee eeeee e    e eeeee eeee eeeee
8  8 8  88 8   8   8  8   8 8  8   8   8     8     8
8e   8   8 8e 8   8 8eee8 8e   8   8e  8eee 8eee8e
88   8   8 88 8   8 88     88   8   88  88   88     8
88e8 8eee8 88 8   8 88     88ee8   88  88ee 88     8
```

Then it is a simple matter of choosing which font you want and specifying it with the `-f` argument.

```
% figlet -f computer 'art?'
```

```
                                 8"""""8
        eeeee eeeee eeeee        8
        8   8 8   8 8     eeeee8
        8eee8 8eee8e 8e 88
        88  8 88    8 88  """
        88  8 88    8 88 88
```

You can even use fortune as a source of text.

`% fortune -s -n 10 | figlet -f weird`

```
   __    __   __
  /  |  /  | /  |  /|  |  /  __       /
 (   |(___|( ___ |( | |(   _   (
 | / )|\   | )| | )|   )  |
 |/|/ | \  |__/ | |/ |__/   _
```

However, you need to limit the message to something sensible, otherwise, you'll just end up with far too much output. This is what the -s and -n arguments are for.

The lolcat Command

Another command that is a bit of fun is lolcat.

`% brew install lolcat`

This gives your text a fabulous rainbow color effect for the given input:

`% fortune | lolcat`

```
I do desire we may be better strangers.
              -- William Shakespeare, "As You Like It"
```

There's no limit to how you can use this.

% **fortune | cowsay | lolcat**

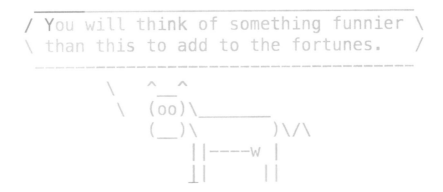

The Steam Locomotive Command

An interesting command that is available on Brew is called sl.

% **brew install sl**

The point of this command is to display an animated steam locomotive that travels across your Terminal when you type sl, as shown in Figure 4-1.

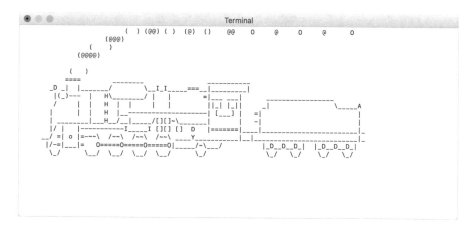

Figure 4-1. *Example of the steam locomotive*

The sl command is most likely going to be run when you mistype ls and cannot cancel it. The wider your window, the longer it takes for the locomotive to travel across it.

As with other commands, there are different options available to customize the locomotive, as shown in Table 4-1.

Table 4-1. *Arguments to the sl Command*

-a	People are crying for help
-l	Little version
-F	Flying train
-c	Different engine

All these options can be used together as well, as shown in Figure 4-2.

% **sl -caFl**

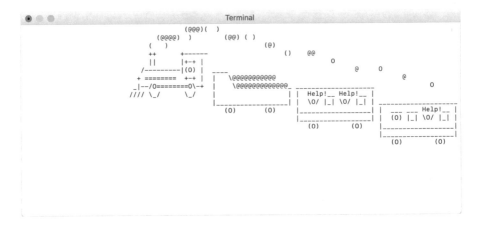

Figure 4-2. *Steam locomotive with options*

There is a known bug where `sl` will occasionally show you the directory listing.

Media

This section covers commands related to viewing and manipulating and media on your macOS.

ImageMagick

ImageMagick was originally used to convert images from one format to another, but over time it has incorporated additional functionality. Did you know that you can use ImageMagick to create images on the command line? Let's install it.

```
% brew install imagemagick
```

This will install the `magick` command.

```
magick [input-options] input-file [output-options] output-file
```

There are other commands that are installed, like identify, but they are for backward compatibility. Their functionality is available through the magick command.

% **magick identify <image>**

The image types that ImageMagick supports is extensive and you can get a complete list.

```
% magick -list format
   Format  Module   Mode  Description
--------------------------------------------------------------
      3FR  DNG      r--   Hasselblad CFV/H3D39II
      3G2  MPEG     r--   Media Container
      3GP  MPEG     r--   Media Container
     AAI* AAI      rw+   AAI Dune image
       AI  PDF      rw-   Adobe Illustrator CS2
```

Note   There are loads of different lists that ImageMagick can provide. Use -list to see them. We will only explore some of them.

Colors

We'll be using predefined colors in some of our commands. If you want to find out more about them, you can get a list.

% **magick -list color**

```
Name                     Color                        Compliance
--------------------------------------------------------------
AliceBlue                srgb(240,248,255)            SVG X11 XPM
AntiqueWhite             srgb(250,235,215)            SVG X11 XPM
AntiqueWhite1            srgb(255,239,219)                    X11
AntiqueWhite2            srgb(238,223,204)                    X11
```

AntiqueWhite3	srgb(205,192,176)	X11
AntiqueWhite4	srgb(139,131,120)	X11
aqua	srgb(0,255,255)	SVG

You can also specify the color in Red, Green, and Blue values (RGB), which you can see in the color column above. The value is either a number between 0 and 255 or a percentage. `srgb()` and `rgb()` are equivalent.

Sometimes there is a fourth value, alpha (A), which specifies how transparent the color is. This is useful if you want to control how visible the underlying image is; the value ranges from 0.0 to 1.0.

This is an example of a partially transparent magenta color.

```
"rgba(255,0,255,0.5)"
```

Note that if you use any of these values, you need to quote them, as otherwise the Zsh shell will try to interpret them.

```
"rgba(255,0,255,0.5)"
```

Simple Image

One of the simplest things you can do with ImageMagick is create a simple image.

Say we wanted to create a simple blue image that was 200 pixels wide and 100 pixels high:

```
% magick -size 200x100 canvas:blue blue.jpg
```

Note   `xc:` is an alias on canvas, but older documentation might refer to it.

Convert JPG to PNG

Converting between image formats is achieved by specifying the correct file extension. If we wanted to convert our previous image, which is a JPEG, to a PNG, we use this short command.

```
% magick blue.jpg blue.png
```

Borders

We can add a 10-pixel border to an existing image with this command.

```
% magick blue.jpg -bordercolor "rgb(255,0,0)" -border 10 border.png
```

Note   The ImageMagick command will read the commands left to right and apply them in that order.

Warning   It's not good practice to use the same image in the input and the output.

The canvas and border commands can be chained together.

```
% magick -size 200x100 canvas:blue  -bordercolor "rgb(255,0,0)"
-border 10 border.jpg
```

Fonts

We can even write on the image, but for that to work, we need to have fonts available for ImageMagick to use. Let's see what fonts are available.

```
% magick -list font
```

If your system is anything like mine, that command will list no fonts. A simple way to get fonts is to install Ghostscript.

```
% brew install gs
```

> **Note**   Installing Ghostscript will allow ImageMagick to work with PostScript files.

Now when you list the fonts, you should something like the following:

```
% magick -list font
```

```
Path: /usr/local/Cellar/imagemagick/7.0.9-14/etc/ImageMagick-7/
type-ghostscript.xml
  Font: AvantGarde-Book
    family: AvantGarde
    style: Normal
    stretch: Normal
    weight: 400
    glyphs: /usr/local/share/ghostscript/fonts/a010013l.pfb
  Font: AvantGarde-BookOblique
    family: AvantGarde
    style: Oblique
    stretch: Normal
    weight: 400
    glyphs: /usr/local/share/ghostscript/fonts/a010033l.pfb
```

Text

Now that we have a few fonts available for ImageMagick, we can draw text onto our images. For this, we will be using -gravity and -draw.

```
% magick -size 200x100 canvas:white -gravity center -draw 'text 0,0
"Welcome"' text.jpg
```

Let's look at gravity. We can query ImageMagick to see its valid options.

```
% magick -list gravity
None
Center
East
Forget
NorthEast
North
NorthWest
SouthEast
South
SouthWest
West
```

gravity controls where the text is placed on the image. We can see this in action.

```
% magick -size 200x200 canvas:white \
-bordercolor "rgb(0,0,0)" -border 1 \
-gravity none -draw 'text 0,0 "none"' \
-gravity center -draw 'text 0,0 "center"' \
-gravity east -draw 'text 0,0 "east"' \
-gravity forget -draw 'text 0,0 "forget"' \
-gravity northeast -draw 'text 0,0 "northeast"' \
-gravity north -draw 'text 0,0 "north"' \
-gravity northwest -draw 'text 0,0 "northwest"' \
-gravity southeast -draw 'text 0,0 "southeast"' \
-gravity south -draw 'text 0,0 "south"' \
-gravity southwest -draw 'text 0,0 "southwest"' \
-gravity west -draw 'text 0,0 "west"' \
gravity.jpg
```

You should end up with an image like Figure 4-3.

Figure 4-3. *Text shown in the nine different origins*

We can safely ignore the gravity options of none and forgot, as they do not appear on the image. The font size can be changed with -pointsize.

```
% magick -size 200x200 canvas:white \
-bordercolor "rgb(0,0,0)" -border 1 \
-pointsize 28 \
-gravity none -draw 'text 0,0 "none"' \
-gravity center -draw 'text 0,0 "center"' \
-gravity east -draw 'text 0,0 "east"' \
-gravity forget -draw 'text 0,0 "forget"' \
-gravity northeast -draw 'text 0,0 "northeast"' \
-gravity north -draw 'text 0,0 "north"' \
-gravity northwest -draw 'text 0,0 "northwest"' \
-gravity southeast -draw 'text 0,0 "southeast"' \
-gravity south -draw 'text 0,0 "south"' \
-gravity southwest -draw 'text 0,0 "southwest"' \
-gravity west -draw 'text 0,0 "west"' \
gravity.jpg
```

Earlier we installed a few fonts with Ghostscript. We can use -font to choose the specific font we want to use.

```
% magick -size 200x50 canvas:white \
-bordercolor "rgb(0,0,0)" -border 1 \
-font "AvantGarde-Book" \
-gravity none -draw 'text 0,0 "none"' \
-gravity center -draw 'text 0,0 "center"' \
-gravity east -draw 'text 0,0 "east"' \
-gravity forget -draw 'text 0,0 "forget"' \
-gravity northeast -draw 'text 0,0 "northeast"' \
-gravity north -draw 'text 0,0 "north"' \
-gravity northwest -draw 'text 0,0 "northwest"' \
-gravity southeast -draw 'text 0,0 "southeast"' \
-gravity south -draw 'text 0,0 "south"' \
-gravity southwest -draw 'text 0,0 "southwest"' \
-gravity west -draw 'text 0,0 "west"' \
gravity.jpg
```

northwest	north	northeast
west	center	east
southwest	south	southeast

With the -draw option, there is the 0,0 that we haven't discussed. This is the *origin* for the draw command. gravity changes the start position, and the origin is offset from there.

If all the 0,0 values were changed to 20,20, then all the text would move in toward the center by 20 pixels, as shown in Figure 4-4.

```
% magick -size 250x200 canvas:white \
-bordercolor "rgb(20,20,0)" -border 1 \
-gravity none -draw 'text 20,20 "none"' \
-gravity center -draw 'text 20,20 "center"' \
-gravity east -draw 'text 20,20 "east"' \
-gravity forget -draw 'text 20,20 "forget"' \
-gravity northeast -draw 'text 20,20 "northeast"' \
-gravity north -draw 'text 20,20 "north"' \
-gravity northwest -draw 'text 20,20 "northwest"' \
-gravity southeast -draw 'text 20,20 "southeast"' \
-gravity south -draw 'text 20,20 "south"' \
-gravity southwest -draw 'text 20,20 "southwest"' \
-gravity west -draw 'text 20,20 "west"' \
gravity.jpg
```

Figure 4-4. *Text shown with an offset*

Interestingly, we can now see the `forget` and none text, in the top-left corner.

Text Color and More

The text would be really boring if we could only have black as an option. When we use the `-draw` command, we can pass in other options, one of which is to change the text color.

```
-draw 'fill #ff0000 text 0,0 "center"'
```

Another option is to rotate the text around the origin point.

```
-draw 'rotate 45 text 0,0 "center"'
```

If we put those two options together, we can create text that looks a bit different.

```
% magick -size 200x200 canvas:white \
-pointsize 84 \
-gravity center -draw 'rotate 45 fill #ff0000 text 0,0 "center"' \
text-color.jpg
```

If we use two draw commands, we can create a shadow effect with the text.

```
% magick -size 200x200 canvas:white \
-pointsize 84 \
-gravity center -draw 'rotate 45 fill #000000 text 5,5 "center"' \
-gravity center -draw 'rotate 45 fill #ff0000 text 0,0 "center"' \
text-color.jpg
```

Another option is to change the stroke of the text. You can change the color with stroke and the size with stroke-width.

```
% magick -size 200x200 canvas:white \
-pointsize 84 \
-gravity center -draw 'rotate 45 fill #000000 text 5,5 "center"' \
-gravity center -draw 'rotate 45 fill #fff stroke #000 stroke-
width 1 text 0,0 "center"' \
text-color.jpg
```

You can also draw primitive shapes, such as points, rectangles, circles, arcs, eclipses, and lines. When drawing shapes, you will need to visualize a grid over the image, starting from the top-left corner.

Drawing a shape is similar to the way we wrote text on the image earlier. However, we need to provide two coordinates for the line—the start position and the end position.

```
-draw 'fill #000 line x1,y1 x2,y2'
```

Let's use this and draw two lines across the image.

```
% magick -size 200x200 canvas:white \
-draw 'fill blue line 10,150 180,20' \
-draw 'fill black line 30,50 110,180' \
line.jpg
```

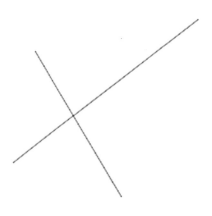

Grid

We can take this even further. It might be helpful to have a grid to help us visualize the positions for the other primitives.

```
% magick -size 198x198 canvas:white \
-bordercolor "rgb(0,0,0)" -border 1 \
-draw 'fill black line 20,0 20,200' \
-draw 'fill black line 40,0 40,200' \
-draw 'fill black line 60,0 60,200' \
-draw 'fill black line 80,0 80,200' \
-draw 'fill black line 100,0 100,200' \
-draw 'fill black line 120,0 120,200' \
-draw 'fill black line 140,0 140,200' \
-draw 'fill black line 160,0 160,200' \
-draw 'fill black line 180,0 180,200' \
-draw 'fill black line 0,20 200,20' \
-draw 'fill black line 0,40 200,40' \
-draw 'fill black line 0,60 200,60' \
-draw 'fill black line 0,80 200,80' \
-draw 'fill black line 0,100 200,100' \
-draw 'fill black line 0,120 200,120' \
-draw 'fill black line 0,140 200,140' \
-draw 'fill black line 0,160 200,160' \
-draw 'fill black line 0,180 200,180' \
grid.jpg
```

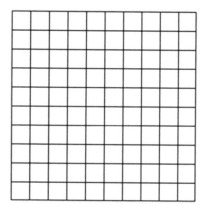

Note   The border is added to the size of the image. If you have a canvas that is 200x200 pixels in size, with a 1 -pixel border, the resulting image will be 202x202 pixels. That is why we specified the canvas as 198x198.

Combining Images

We should use the grid we've created to double-check that the primitives are drawn where we think they should be. A simple example would be to draw a red square with the four lines.

```
% magick -size 200x200 canvas:white -gravity center \
-draw 'image over 0,0 0,0 "grid.jpg"' \
-draw 'fill red line 20,20 60,20' \
-draw 'fill red line 60,20 60,60' \
-draw 'fill red line 60,60 20,60' \
-draw 'fill red line 20,60 20,20' \
combined-line.jpg
```

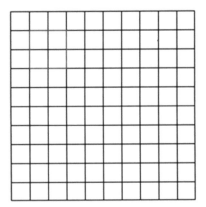

Note   I've used `fill`, but you can use `stroke` if you want to make the line thicker. You cannot use `fill` and `stroke` at the same time when drawing a line.

Here's an example of draw using stroke:

```
-draw 'stroke #000 stroke-width 2 line x1,y1 x2,y2'
```

Rectangles

It's possible to simplify this process, by using the rectangle primitive.

```
-draw 'stroke #000 stroke-width 2 line x1,y1 x2,y2'
```

Just as when you're drawing a line, rectangle takes two sets of coordinates—the top-left corner and the bottom-right corner. However, you can specify both `fill` and `stroke`, depending on whether you want to fill in the rectangle.

```
% magick -size 200x200 canvas:white -gravity center \
-draw 'image over 0,0 0,0 "grid.jpg"' \
-draw 'fill none stroke red rectangle 20,20 60,60' \
-draw 'fill red stroke red rectangle 80,80 120,120' \
combined-rectangle.jpg
```

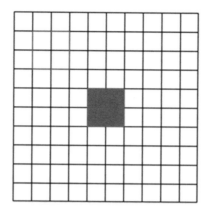

Rectangles are great, but rounded rectangles are better. The parameters are the same as the rectangle, but with additional x,y coordinates to control the roundedness of the rectangle.

```
% magick -size 200x200 canvas:white -gravity center \
-draw 'image over 0,0 0,0 "grid.jpg"' \
-draw 'fill white stroke red roundrectangle 40,40 160,160 5,5' \
combined-round-rectangle.jpg
```

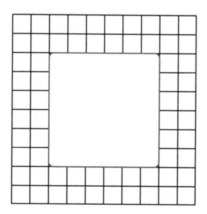

Arc

The arc is an interesting shape. You can use it to draw a circle or a semicircle. When you draw an arc, you specify three sets of parameters—the top-left corner, the bottom-right corner, and the start and stop degrees. You will specify a rectangle that the arc will be drawn in.

```
-draw 'stroke #000 stroke-width 2 arc x1,y1 x2,y2 d1,d2'
```

The degree 0 starts at the 3 o'clock position. If you want to draw a circle, you would specify the degrees as 0,360. Here are examples of arcs with different start and stop degrees.

```
% magick -size 200x200 canvas:white -gravity center \
-draw 'image over 0,0 0,0 "grid.jpg"' \
-draw 'stroke black fill red arc 0,0 100,100 0,360' \
-draw 'stroke black fill blue arc 100,100 200,200 180,0' \
-draw 'stroke black fill green arc 0,100 100,200 0,180' \
-draw 'stroke black fill yellow arc 100,0 200,100 0,270' \
combined-arc-selection.jpg
```

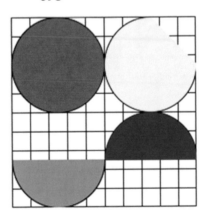

Note   Notice that the background fill is only in the area between the start and end points.

Here is an example showing you how you might use the different types of arc.

```
% magick -size 200x200 canvas:skyblue -gravity center \
-draw 'fill yellow arc 170,10 190,30 0,360' \
-draw 'fill #ff0000 arc 40,120 160,240 180,0' \
-draw 'fill #ffa500 arc 50,130 150,230 180,0' \
-draw 'fill #ffff00 arc 60,140 140,220 180,0' \
-draw 'fill #008000 arc 70,150 130,210 180,0' \
-draw 'fill #0000ff arc 80,160 120,200 180,0' \
-draw 'fill #4b0082 arc 90,170 110,190 180,0' \
-draw 'fill green rectangle 0,180 200,200' \
combined-arc.jpg
```

Note   When specifying x1,y1 x2,y2, you need to treat the arc as a whole circle. This is why some coordinates of the rainbow's arcs are greater than 200, even though it doesn't actually overhang the picture.

Circles

Drawing circles is similar to drawing rectangles, but the difference is you specify the center point and then specify where the edge is.

```
% magick -size 200x200 canvas:white -gravity center \
-draw 'image over 0,0 0,0 "grid.jpg"' \
-draw 'stroke black fill red circle 50,50 20,20' \
-draw 'stroke black fill blue circle 160,160 140,140' \
-draw 'stroke black fill green circle 50,150 50,100' \
-draw 'stroke black fill yellow circle 150,50 200,10' \
combined-circle-selection.jpg
```

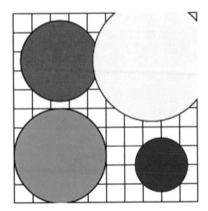

Ellipses

Ellipses are drawn in a similar way to the circle and the arc. Like the circle, you specify the center point, but this time, the second parameters are the size of the primitive. The third parameter is exactly the same as the arc; you specify the start and stop degrees.

We still cannot create a pie segment using the ellipse, but we can fake it by using a semicircle.

```
% magick -size 200x200 canvas:white -gravity center \
-gravity center -pointsize 18 -draw 'fill #000000 text 0,-70
"Pie that has been eaten"' \
-draw 'stroke black fill grey ellipse 80,120 60,60 0,360' \
-draw 'stroke black fill yellow ellipse 80,120 60,60 45,225' \
-draw 'stroke black fill yellow ellipse 80,120 60,60 180,0' \
combined-pie.jpg
```

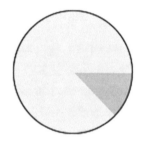

Polygon

The last primitive I want to talk about is the polygon. This is like a line that will allow you to draw arbitrary shapes that are filled in.

```
% magick -size 200x200 canvas:white -gravity center \
-draw 'stroke black fill red polygon 20,20 120,20 120,120 20,120' \
-draw 'stroke black fill red polygon 190,190 100,190 190,100' \
polygon.jpg
```

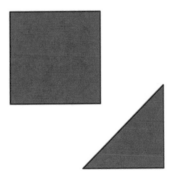

In this next example, I've used the polygon to draw the bowtie and used different primitives to create the whole face.

```
% magick -size 200x200 canvas:white -gravity center \
-draw 'image over 0,0 0,0 "grid.jpg"' \
-draw 'stroke black fill red polygon 40,120 160,180 160,120 40,180' \
-draw 'stroke black fill red circle 100,150 110,160' \
-draw 'stroke black fill lightgrey ellipse 100,70 50,60 0,360' \
-draw 'stroke black fill none ellipse 100,70 30,40 0,180' \
-draw 'stroke black fill grey ellipse 100,70 10,10 0,360' \
-draw 'stroke black fill white ellipse 80,40 10,10 0,360' \
-draw 'stroke black fill black ellipse 80,45 5,5 0,360' \
-draw 'stroke black fill white ellipse 120,40 10,10 0,360' \
-draw 'stroke black fill black ellipse 120,45 5,5 0,360' \
face.jpg
```

What could you design with ImageMagick? There is so much to ImageMagick that it would take a whole book to cover. For more information, I recommend visiting their website at https://imagemagick.org for more examples.

ffmpeg

ffmpeg is a video and audio converter. You can use ffmpeg to combine video and audio files, as well as extract the audio. Let's install it.

```
% brew install ffmpeg
```

```
==> Installing ffmpeg
==> Downloading https://homebrew.bintray.com/bottles/
ffmpeg-4.2.1_2.catalina.bottle.tar.gz
==> Downloading from https://akamai.bintray.com/11/11b16a8f9657
e0826774d41133052b088f778a50f6f8037f641923cbb6b90335?__gda__=ex
p=1577561224~hmac=e130dd97313fa7
######################################################### 100.0%
==> Pouring ffmpeg-4.2.1_2.catalina.bottle.tar.gz
🍺  /usr/local/Cellar/ffmpeg/4.2.1_2: 287 files, 56.6MB
```

Converting a video to a different format can be as simple as this.

```
% ffmpeg -i input.mp4 output.avi
```

However, what we really need are some video files to test this out. Another trick that ffmpeg has is that it can also record from macOS input devices. You can see which devices ffmpeg can capture from by using -list_devices:

```
% ffmpeg -hide_banner -f avfoundation -list_devices true -i ""
[AVFoundation input device @ 0x7f927bd26740] AVFoundation video
devices:
[AVFoundation input device @ 0x7f927bd26740] [0] FaceTime HD
Camera (Built-in)
[AVFoundation input device @ 0x7f927bd26740] [1] Capture screen 0
[AVFoundation input device @ 0x7f927bd26740] AVFoundation audio
devices:
[AVFoundation input device @ 0x7f927bd26740] [0] MacBook Pro
Microphone
: Input/output error
```

Note   -hide_banner hides the copyright notice and compiler options. -f is the format and -i is the input, which isn't needed to list devices, but still needs to be specified.

You should have at least these items in your list. There might be more, depending on whether you have any webcams, microphones, or extra screens attached.

Security

The first time you try to access a privileged service from any application, you will be prompted to allow it. In this case, the application will be Terminal, rather than the command you are trying to run. See Figure 4-5.

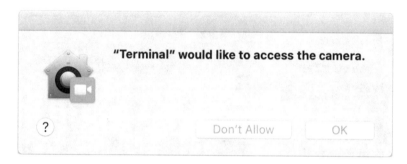

Figure 4-5. *Prompt to allow Terminal to access your camera*

You will also see a similar prompt for the microphone, as shown in Figure 4-6.

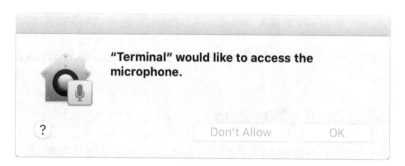

Figure 4-6. *Prompt to allow Terminal to access your microphone*

If for some reason, you accidentally clicked Don't Allow or the prompt didn't appear, you can give Terminal permission in the Security & Privacy tab in System Preferences. Make sure Terminal has a tick next to it, as shown in Figure 4-7.

Figure 4-7. *Go to Security & Privacy in the System Preferences to allow access*

Capturing from a Webcam

When you capture from some devices, they can output in different resolutions. You will need to tell ffmpeg what resolution and frame rate you want. By entering this command, we are selecting the webcam (-i "0") and ffmpeg will list all the different resolutions and frame rates for it.

```
% ffmpeg -hide_banner -f avfoundation -i "0"
[avfoundation @ 0x7fc37b008a00] Selected framerate (29.970030)
is not supported by the device.
```

```
[avfoundation @ 0x7fc37b008a00] Supported modes:
[avfoundation @ 0x7fc37b008a00]    640x480@[30.000030 30.000030]fps
[avfoundation @ 0x7fc37b008a00]    640x480@[29.000049 29.000049]fps
[avfoundation @ 0x7f9cb5009c00]   1280x720@[30.000030 30.000030]fps
[avfoundation @ 0x7f9cb5009c00]   1280x720@[29.000049 29.000049]fps
```

When you have decided which settings you will use, you can proceed.

Note   If you can't decide, keep this in mind—the bigger the numbers, the better the quality, but the bigger the file size.

The last option I'm providing to ffmpeg is the output file, out.mov.

```
% ffmpeg -hide_banner -f avfoundation -video_size "1280x720"
-framerate "30.000030" -i "0" out.mov
[avfoundation @ 0x7fd9b6009c00] Selected pixel format (yuv420p)
is not supported by the input device.
[avfoundation @ 0x7fd9b6009c00] Supported pixel formats:
[avfoundation @ 0x7fd9b6009c00]    uyvy422
[avfoundation @ 0x7fd9b6009c00]    yuyv422
[avfoundation @ 0x7fd9b6009c00]    nv12
[avfoundation @ 0x7fd9b6009c00]    0rgb
[avfoundation @ 0x7fd9b6009c00]    bgr0
[avfoundation @ 0x7fd9b6009c00] Overriding selected pixel
format to use uyvy422 instead.
Input #0, avfoundation, from '0':
  Duration: N/A, start: 8518.378600, bitrate: N/A
    Stream #0:0: Video: rawvideo (UYVY / 0x59565955), uyvy422,
    1280x720, 30 tbr, 1000k tbn, 1000k tbc
Stream mapping:
  Stream #0:0 -> #0:0 (rawvideo (native) -> h264 (libx264))
Press [q] to stop, [?] for help
```

Ffmpeg will now be recording until you press the 'q' key.
  If ffmpeg seems to hang, double check that it has security
  permissions.

Let's open the file and see what we have; see Figure 4-8.

% **open out.mov**

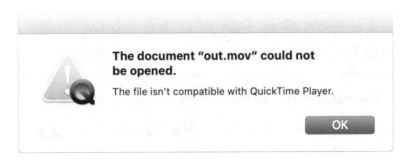

Figure 4-8. *Oh no, the video file doesn't work with QuickTime*

Note   It is possible to play this file with an alternative video player, such as VLC, but you'd have problems if you wanted it to run in programs like iMovle.

The problem comes down to the pixel format. Did you notice this in the previous output?

```
[avfoundation @ 0x7fd9b6009c00] Selected pixel format (yuv420p)
is not supported by the input device.
[avfoundation @ 0x7fd9b6009c00] Supported pixel formats:
[avfoundation @ 0x7fd9b6009c00]   uyvy422
[avfoundation @ 0x7fd9b6009c00]   yuyv422
[avfoundation @ 0x7fd9b6009c00]   nv12
[avfoundation @ 0x7fd9b6009c00]   0rgb
```

[avfoundation @ 0x7fd9b6009c00]   bgr0
[avfoundation @ 0x7fd9b6009c00] Overriding selected pixel
format to use uyvy422 instead.

The pixel format allows QuickTime to play the video. The pixel format uyvy422 didn't work. Having tried them all, I can say that yuyv422 also doesn't work. The 0rgb and bgr0 formats ended up having problems as well. So much so, that I had to use kill on ffmpeg. That leaves us with the nv12 pixel format.

As it happens, it works perfectly.

You specify the pixel format using -pixel_format, as follows:

```
% ffmpeg -hide_banner -f avfoundation -video_size "1280x720"
-framerate "30.000030" -pixel_format nv12 -i "0" out.mov
```

Display Capture

You can also capture everything that is displayed on your screen. The command we will use is very similar to capturing on the webcam. We don't need to provide the video size or the frame rate, as the computer knows these already. Otherwise, you wouldn't have a picture on your display.

Your display is able to be read much quicker than a webcam, and that poses a problem. We need to tell ffmpeg to ignore the extra frames coming from the display, and only take what is needed to be written. This is done by using -vsync vfr.

```
% ffmpeg -hide_banner -f avfoundation -pixel_format nv12 -i "1"
-vsync vfr display.mov
```

You will get a lot of output from this command and ffmpeg will keep running until you tell it to stop. You can stop ffmpeg by pressing Control+C. Ffmpeg will output some statistics about the video captured and then exit.

```
frame= 233 fps= 30 q=29.0 size= 512kB time=00:00:05.86 bitrate=
715.0kbits/s speed=0.755x
```

Finally, ffmpeg will output the following:

```
Exiting normally, received signal 2.
```

You will have a file in your current directory called display.mov, which you should have no trouble previewing with QuickLook.

Audio

So far, all our videos have not included audio. Let's capture some audio from the internal microphone. If you have a higher quality microphone, you can use that instead.

Grabbing audio is actually much easier than grabbing the video. The difference is, when we use -i, we need to specify the audio device, and not the video device. The -i option is <video>:<audio>. We previously didn't have to specify the colon, because it assumed the default of none.

```
% ffmpeg -f avfoundation -i ":0" audio.mp3
```

Combining Audio and Video

At capture time, combining audio and video is simple by specifying -i 1:0.

```
% ffmpeg -hide_banner -f avfoundation -pixel_format nv12 -i 1:0
-vsync vfr display-audio.mov
```

However, you should have a few files from previous attempts that you can combine. This can be achieved by specifying more than one -i option.

```
% ffmpeg -i display.mov -i audio.mp3 combined.mov
```

Stripping Audio or Video

Stripping the video from a file can be useful if you are producing a video, but you also want the audio in a podcast. If you want ffmpeg to drop the video of a file, you can use the -vn option.

```
% ffmpeg -i combined.mov -yn combined-video.mov
```

If you want ffmpeg to drop the audio of a file, you can use the -an option.

```
% ffmpeg -i combined.mov -an combined-audio.mp3
```

Converting Between Formats

So far, we've only used MP3 and MOV file formats. However, there are loads of different formats available.

```
% ffmpeg -hide_banner -formats
```

File formats:

```
 D. = Demuxing supported
 .E = Muxing supported
 --
 D 3dostr 3DO STR
```

This list is far too long to display here. Let's limit the formats to the ones we're interested in.

```
% ffmpeg -hide_banner -formats | grep -E " (mp4|mp3|mov|aiff)"
 DE aiff             Audio IFF
  E mov              QuickTime / MOV
 D  mov,mp4,m4a,3gp,3g2,mj2 QuickTime / MOV
 DE mp3              MP3 (MPEG audio layer 3)
  E mp4              MP4 (MPEG-4 Part 14)
```

Note   You can think of "muxing" as encoding and "demuxing" as decoding.

Previously, we used the say command to save computer -generated speech to an AIFF file.

```
% say "I like talking" -o ~/talking.aiff
```

We can use ffmpeg to convert talking.aiff into an MP3 file.

```
% ffmpeg -i ~/talking.aiff talking.mp3
```

ffmpeg will use the file extension you specify for the output file and that extension will be used to determine the output file format. This can also be used to convert video files. For example, you can convert a .mov file into the MP4 file format.

```
% ffmpeg -i combined.mov combined.mp4
```

Combining Multiple Videos

Using ffmpeg, we can combine our webcam and our display capture into a single video. This is useful for creating a talking head video, where you can see whatever video is being presented and the instructor's video is in the bottom corner, as shown in Figure 4-9.

Figure 4-9. *Example of a talking head video*

I'm going to use the backslash to split this command across multiple lines, in the hopes that it will be easier to read. This command reuses the options from the webcam and the display capture sections, which you can see on Lines 2 and 3. Line 4 specifies how the video files should be combined.

```
% ffmpeg \
-f avfoundation -pixel_format nv12 -vsync vfr -i "1" \
-f avfoundation -video_size "640x480" -framerate "30.000030"
-pixel_format nv12 -i "0:0" \
-filter_complex "[0:v][1:v] overlay=50:50" \
talkinghead.mp4
```

<talking head picture>

When I run that command, I get a talking head video, but there are issues. The video for both the webcam and display are very jumpy. And there was this message:

**Thread message queue blocking; consider raising the thread_
queue_size option (current value: 8)**

You should also see, while the video is recording, an fps indicator. This is how many frames per second ffmpeg is able to process. If this is less than the output frame rate, you will experience jumpy video.

```
fps=9.8
```

This is three times slower than the output video rate of 30 fps and explains the poor quality video. The reason for this is because we are asking ffmpeg to do a lot of processing, but it only has so many resources (threads) that are available to process the incoming data.

We can do what the warning message suggested and increase the value of thread_queue_size. This is set on the incoming stream, so we need to specify it twice, once for each input.

```
% ffmpeg -f avfoundation -thread_queue_size 256 -pixel_format
nv12 -vsync vfr -i "1" \
-f avfoundation -thread_queue_size 128 -video_size "640x480"
-framerate "30.000030" -pixel_format nv12 -i "0:0" \
-filter_complex "[0:v][1:v] overlay=50:50" \
talkinghead.mp4
```

You may be wondering where I got the values 256 and 128 from. They came from trial and error and watching the fps value each time. The display capture is working with more information, and so got a bigger number.

The filter_complex option tells ffmpeg how to combine the two videos. The values 50:50 specify the start position for the overlay video from the top-left corner (specified as left:top).

If you want to use the bottom-right corner, you will need to do some basic math, using your display resolution. Let's use my display as an example.

```
Stream #0:0: Video: rawvideo (NV12 / 0x3231564E), nv12,
2880x1800, 1000k tbr, 1000k tbn, 1000k tbc
```

The display resolution is 2880x1800 and we are capturing from the webcam at 640x480. We will also want the same 50-pixel padding from the edge of the screen.

```
Top value = screen height - webcam height - padding
1270 = 1800 - 480 - 50

Left value = screen width - webcam width - padding
2190 = 2880-640-50
```

When we take those values and plug them into the previous command as overlay=2190:1270, we get the following:

```
% ffmpeg -f avfoundation -thread_queue_size 256 -pixel_format
nv12 -vsync vfr -i "1" \
-f avfoundation -thread_queue_size 128 -video_size "640x480"
-framerate "30.000030" -pixel_format nv12 -i "0:0" \
-filter_complex "[0:v][1:v] overlay=2190:1270" \
talkinghead.mp4
```

Subtitles

Another converter that is built into ffmpeg is subtitle converting. If you produce a video with audio and upload it to a video sharing service, sometimes they will provide subtitles for your video. However, those subtitles might not be compatible with programs that you use to edit them.

You can use ffmpeg to convert between the subtitle formats. It will allow you to edit the subtitles in an application of your choosing.

```
% ffmpeg -i sub.srt subs.vtt
```

I personally use this when I'm working on subtitles in Camtasia, and I need to upload them to Udemy.

Advanced Brew Concepts

We talked about the basics of using Brew in Chapter 1. Now we can look at two more advanced ideas, Brew casks and Brew services.

Brew Casks

Casks can be used to install paid and open source applications alike.

```
% brew cask
Homebrew Cask provides a friendly CLI workflow for the administration
of macOS applications distributed as binaries.

See also "man brew-cask"
```

By default, you won't have any casks installed.

```
% brew cask list
```

An application that I use a lot for vector work is Inkscape. Normally I download it directly from the website, but it would be handy if I used a cask to install it. Then at a later date, Brew can be used to update all installed casks.

Searching Casks

```
% brew search inkscape
==> Casks
inkscape ✔

If you meant "inkscape" specifically:
It was migrated from homebrew/core to homebrew/cask.
You can access it again by running:
  brew tap homebrew/cask
And then you can install it by running:
  brew cask install inkscape
```

Brew has found Inkscape. If Brew lists Inkscape as homebrew/cask/inkscape then homebrew/cask is untapped. This isn't a problem, because the moment you try to install Inkscape, Brew will tap homebrew/cask for you.

% **brew cask install inkscape**

```
==> Downloading https://media.inkscape.org/dl/resources/file/
Inkscape-1.0beta2.dmg
######################################################## 100.0%
==> Verifying SHA-256 checksum for Cask 'inkscape'.
==> Installing Cask inkscape
==> Moving App 'Inkscape.app' to '/Applications/Inkscape.app'.
==> Linking Binary 'inkscape.wrapper.sh' to '/usr/local/bin/
inkscape'.
🍺  inkscape was successfully installed!
```

Applications in casks are not limited to open source programs. For example, you can install apps from Google.

% **brew search google**

```
==> Formulae
aws-google-auth                google-go              google-sql-tool
google-authenticator-libpam    google-java-format     googler
google-benchmark               google-sparsehash

==> Casks
google-ads-editor              google-notifier
google-backup-and-sync         google-photos-backup-and-sync
google-chat                    google-trends
google-chrome                  google-web-designer
google-cloud-sdk
```

If searching isn't inspiring enough, you can search online at https://formulae.brew.sh/cask/.

Updating Casks

If you want to see which cask is not running the latest version, you can use the outdated command.

```
% brew cask outdated
```

If nothing is returned, then everything is up to date. Normally, I just prefer to keep everything up to date, so I run the upgrade command periodically.

```
% brew cask upgrade
Updating Homebrew...
==> Auto-updated Homebrew!
Updated 1 tap (homebrew/core).
==> Updated Formulae
numpy@1.16

==> No Casks to upgrade
```

In the future, if you didn't use cask for applications and you moved to another machine, you would need to download all the apps again. With cask, you can get a list of all the installed casks, which can be used to install them on the other machine.

```
% brew cask list
inkscape
```

If you combine this with the sed command, you could make it even easier for yourself.

```
% brew cask list | sed -E -e 's/^/brew cask install /'
brew cask install inkscape
```

Brew Services

Brew has the ability to manage background tasks. This is something that we will need to use in Chapter 7. This will probably be the first time you have used Brew services. If so, Brew will have to install Brew services first.

```
% brew services
==> Tapping homebrew/services
Cloning into '/usr/local/Homebrew/Library/Taps/homebrew/
homebrew-services'...
remote: Enumerating objects: 24, done.
remote: Counting objects: 100% (24/24), done.
remote: Compressing objects: 100% (18/18), done.
remote: Total 24 (delta 0), reused 16 (delta 0), pack-reused 0
Unpacking objects: 100% (24/24), 11.43 KiB | 688.00 KiB/s, done.
Tapped 1 command (62 files, 66.8KB).
Usage: brew services subcommand:

Manage background services with macOS' launchctl(1) daemon manager
```

When Brew has finished installing services, you will be able to get the full help by using --help.

```
% brew services --help
```

If you already had Brew services installed, it will just display a list of available services.

Listing Services

Brew services has a few subcommands, or verbs. The first verb for services is list, which is the default if none is specified.

```
% brew services list
Name    Status  User Plist
```

As we install the commands that support services, they will appear in this list, as stopped. The list shows you which services are running, and which have been stopped.

At the moment we don't have any services to show, so let's install a DNS resolver. This command will be installed as a dependency later, so there is no harm in installing it now.

```
% brew install unbound
==> Installing unbound
==> Pouring unbound-1.10.1.catalina.bottle.tar.gz
==> Caveats
To have launchd start unbound now and restart at startup:
  sudo brew services start unbound
==> Summary
🍺  /usr/local/Cellar/unbound/1.10.1: 57 files, 5MB
```

Now when we list the services, we see the unbound service appear.

```
% brew services list
Name        Status      User      Plist
unbound     stopped
```

Descriptions of these columns are listed in Table 4-2.

Table 4-2. *Brew Services Columns*

Heading	Description
Name	Service name
Status	Service state, e.g., started, stopped
User	Whoever the service is running as; has the same permissions as that user
Plist	Contains the path to a file that defines how to start this service; you shouldn't need to edit this

> **Note**   The User and Plist columns won't have anything in them until the service has been started.

The trouble with Brew services is that if the service crashes, then Brew will still show that it is running.

Starting Services

To start a service as your user, you simply use the start command and the service name:

```
% brew services start unbound
Warning: unbound must be run as root to start at system startup!
==> Successfully started `unbound` (label: homebrew.mxcl.unbound)
```

> **Note**   unbound is designed to be run as root, but it won't cause any harm running it as your user.

Now when you look at the service list again, you can see that the User and Plist columns have been populated.

```
% brew services list
Name      Status  User        Plist
unbound started danielplatt /Users/danielplatt/Library/
LaunchAgents/homebrew.mxcl.unbound.plist
```

Stopping Services

If you no longer want a service to run, you can stop it.

```
% brew services stop unbound
Stopping `unbound`... (might take a while)
```

This is useful if you are upgrading to a new major version of any applications, where you can have both versions installed at once.

Restarting Services

Occasionally, you will need to restart a service because you've changed its configuration. We will go through this later in the chapter.

```
% brew services restart unbound
Stopping `unbound`... (might take a while)
==> Successfully stopped `unbound` (label: homebrew.mxcl.unbound)
==> Successfully started `unbound` (label: homebrew.mxcl.unbound)
```

The services verb restart is just a shortcut for stop and start.

Sudo

Sometimes you will need to run a command as root, to give it a lot more permissions than your user currently has. An example of this is a web server. n the Internet, the standard port for a web browser serving HTTP content is port 80. With UNIX, and thus macOS, a port number that is less than 1024 is considered privileged. The way around this is to start the web server as root.

To run Brew services as root, you need to prefix sudo to the command.

```
% sudo brew services start <service>
```

If you start a service with sudo and then to stop it, you must also use sudo. If you don't use sudo to stop the service, you won't have permission to stop it. We talked more about sudo in Chapter 2.

Utilities

This section covers various utilities that you might find handy to use on the macOS Terminal.

The archey Utility

Another command I like is archey.

% **brew install archey**

archey shows a very simple splash screen, with a retro Apple logo. It tells you information about your computer and who you are logged in as, the hostname, your uptime, and various other information. See Figure 4-10.

Again, this might not be useful for you, but it could be useful at work, or for a user with a laptop. If you want to know your external IP address, this command is helpful.

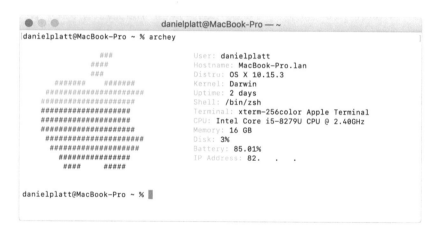

Figure 4-10. *archey tells you information about your computer*

I like to put archey in my .zshrc file so that it's displayed every time I open Terminal.

Linux Utilities for macOS

A lot of the commands that come with macOS are from BSD. These same commands also have a Linux equivalent. Typically, the Linux command equivalents will support a lot more arguments, and those arguments tend to be more readable.

For example, `tail` on the macOS takes -n to specify the number of lines to output. The Linux equivalent takes -n, but also includes `--lines`. You can install these extra commands as part of `coreutils`.

```
% brew install coreutils
==> Caveats
Commands also provided by macOS have been installed with the
prefix "g".
If you need to use these commands with their normal names, you
can add a "gnubin" directory to your PATH from your bashrc like:
  PATH="/usr/local/opt/coreutils/libexec/gnubin:$PATH"
```

These commands are installed in `/usr/local/opt/coreutils/libexec/gnubin`.

```
% ls /usr/local/opt/coreutils/libexec/gnubin
[          dirname mkdir    rmdir      timeout
b2sum      du      mkfifo   runcon     touch
base32     echo    mknod    seq        tr
base64     env     mktemp   sha1sum    true
basename   expand  mv       sha224sum  truncate
basenc     expr    nice     sha256sum  tsort
cat        factor  nl       sha384sum  tty
chcon      false   nohup    sha512sum  uname
chgrp      fmt     nproc    shred      unexpand
chmod      fold    numfmt   shuf       uniq
```

274

chown	groups	od	sleep	unlink
chroot	head	paste	sort	uptime
cksum	hostid	pathchk	split	users
comm	id	pinky	stat	vdir
cp	install	pr	stdbuf	wc
csplit	join	printenv	stty	who
cut	kill	printf	sum	whoami
date	link	ptx	sync	yes
dd	ln	pwd	tac	
df	logname	readlink	tail	
dir	ls	realpath	tee	
dircolors	md5sum	rm	test	

It might seem redundant to install the Linux versions of the same commands; however, there is a good reason to do so. At first glance, this collection of utilities might seem redundant. Let's consider the head command.

% **head --help**
```
head: illegal option -- -
usage: head [-n lines | -c bytes] [file ...]
```

As far as I can tell, there is no way to get BSD head to output the usage cleanly. Now we can try the same thing with the Linux version.

% **/usr/local/opt/coreutils/libexec/gnubin/head --help**
```
Print the first 10 lines of each FILE to standard output.
With more than one FILE, precede each with a header giving the
file name.
With no FILE, or when FILE is -, read standard input.
```

Mandatory arguments to long options are mandatory for short options too.

-c, --bytes=[-]NUM	print the first NUM bytes of each file; with the leading '-', print all but the last NUM bytes of each file
-n, --lines=[-]NUM	print the first NUM lines instead of the first 10; with the leading '-', print all but the last NUM lines of each file
-q, --quiet, --silent	never print headers giving file names
-v, --verbose	always print headers giving file names
-z, --zero-terminated	line delimiter is NUL, not newline
--help	display this help and exit
--version	output version information and exit

```
NUM may have a multiplier suffix:
b 512, kB 1000, K 1024, MB 1000*1000, M 1024*1024,
GB 1000*1000*1000, G 1024*1024*1024, and so on for T, P, E, Z, Y.
Binary prefixes can be used, too: KiB=K, MiB=M, and so on.
GNU coreutils online help: <https://www.gnu.org/software/
coreutils/>
Full documentation <https://www.gnu.org/software/coreutils/
head>
or available locally via: info '(coreutils) head invocation'
```

We get a much richer experience. We have better usage information. The options are more descriptive. Instead of using -n, we can use --lines, which, when you read it, will help you instantly understand the value.

Ultimately, it will come down to preference. I do a lot of work on Linux-based servers, so it makes sense for me to install the Linux tools.

Assuming that you want to use the Linux versions, I'll presume that you won't want to continually refer to them by the full path. There was a message about this when we installed them.

```
Commands also provided by macOS have been installed with the
prefix "g".
If you need to use these commands with their normal names, you
can add a "gnubin" directory to your PATH from your bashrc like:
  PATH="/usr/local/opt/coreutils/libexec/gnubin:$PATH"
```

You can either refer to the commands with a g in front of them, such as ghead, or you can override the path. If you're happy with the g prefix, you need take no further action. If you want to override the existing commands, you will need to edit your .zshrc file and paste the new path in.

If you ever want to go back to the BSD commands, you can remove this line (or comment it out by prefixing the line with the # symbol).

The ddrescue Command

Have you ever had a disk that your computer struggled to read or read very slowly? Maybe you kept getting errors when you tried to access files on the disk, as shown Figure 4-11.

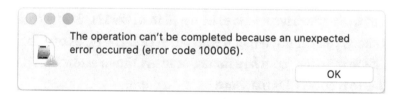

Figure 4-11. *File copy error in the Finder when the disk goes away*

If so, your disk might be on its way out and this next command might be able to help you recover data before it's too late.

```
% ddrescue
```

The purpose of ddrescue is to read the contents of a disk without trying to understand it. It will treat the drive as a single file. Although this might not sound useful on the face of it, you can combine this with another command, hdiutil, to mount it again.

Warning   If you value your data and would be willing to spend a few hundreds or thousands to get it back, then seek a professional data recovery firm.

If you cannot afford to pay someone to recover your drive and you would be forced to throw it away, then this command might help you.

Because you are going to write the contents of your drive as a file, you will need a drive that has more free space than the total size of the drive that needs to be recovered. This is because you won't know what is free until you try to mount the image.

Types of Errors

For this to work, the drive needs to be listed in diskutil list. If the drive doesn't show, you cannot target it with ddrescue. The types of error that will work are the drive, software issues, or intermittent errors. It is possible to use this to recover CDs that have holes in them.

Warning   Be aware that access to the disk might cause more damage to itself and the computer. In the case of the CD with a hole, it might damage the CD drive or the CD might break apart.

If the errors were caused by the hardware failing, mounting the disk from an image will allow the computer to fix some errors.

```
% sudo ddrescue --retry-passes=1
GNU ddrescue 1.24
Press Ctrl-C to interrupt
Initial status (read from mapfile)
rescued: 36241 kB, tried: 983040 B, bad-sector: 0 B, bad areas: 0

Current status
       ipos:  608239 kB, non-trimmed: 571964 kB, current rate:        0 B/s
       opos:  608239 kB, non-scraped:        0 B, average rate:       0 B/s
  non-tried:       0 B, bad-sector:       512 B,    error rate:       0 B/s
    rescued:   36274 kB,   bad areas:          1,     run time: 13h 13m 14s
pct rescued:    0.00%, read errors:       8714, remaining time:          n/a
                         time since last successful read:             0s
Trimming failed blocks... (forward)
```

When you recover any drive, you will need to have enough free disk space on your target drive to store the entire image. This won't be an issue with a CD, but it might be if you attempt this on a 1TB drive.

I used this technique to recover a TB hard drive that would read very slowly and would intermittently stop working. It took many weeks, but I recovered 100% of the drive.

The asciinema Command

You might sometimes need to record your Terminal session. The asciinema command is used for recording and playing back Terminal sessions. It's even possible to use asciinema to upload your sessions to a website for everyone to enjoy.

```
% brew install asciinema
```

Let's look at the help.

```
% asciinema --help
usage: asciinema [-h] [--version] {rec,play,cat,upload,auth}
...
Record and share your Terminal sessions, the right way.
positional arguments:
  {rec,play,cat,upload,auth}
    rec              Record terminal session
    play             Replay terminal session
    cat              Print full output of terminal session
    upload           Upload locally saved terminal session to
                     asciinema.org
    auth             Manage recordings on asciinema.org account
```

There are also some basic examples, but we'll go through them now instead. Now we will discuss each asciinema command in turn.

rec

The simplest way to use asciinema rec is to enter it without any additional arguments; it will save the recording locally. When you are finished, you then can upload it or save it locally.

```
% asciinema rec
asciinema: recording asciicast to /var/folders/5z/
tnwhfkg57hdfys5fxckr07_h0000gn/T/tmpbrrhs1gt-ascii.cast
asciinema: press <ctrl-d> or type "exit" when you're done
danielplatt@MacBook-Pro ~ % echo "This is my recording"
"This is my recording"
% exit
asciinema: recording finished
```

asciinema: press <enter> to upload to asciinema.org, <ctrl-c>
to save locally
asciinema: asciicast saved to /var/folders/5z/
tnwhfkg57hdfys5fxckr07_h0000gn/T/tmpbrrhs1gt-ascii.cast

I recommend moving the file to somewhere safe. If you choose to upload it, you will be given a link to view it, but also to claim it and all future recordings on your computer.

Alternatively, you can specify the file to save to as part of the command-line arguments.

% **asciinema rec ~/recording.cast**
asciinema: recording asciicast to /Users/danielplatt/recording.cast
asciinema: press <ctrl-d> or type "exit" when you're done
danielplatt@MacBook-Pro ~ %
asciinema: recording finished
asciinema: asciicast saved to /Users/danielplatt/recording.cast

One option I recommend is -i, which limits the idle time. For example, if you started recording and got distracted, only to return to it later, asciinema will have recorded all that time in the playback. Usually this is not required. The -i option will limit the idle time to the specified number of seconds.

% **asciinema rec -i 2**

This command will limit the idle time to two seconds.

play

The play command is great for rewatching items that you recorded.

% **asciinema play ~/recording.cast**

The play command can also play casts that are hosted on `asciinema.org`.

```
% asciinema play https://asciinema.org/a/17648
bash-3.2$ # I am in a new shell instance which is being
recorded now
bash-3.2$ sha1sum
```

If you recorded a cast with the rec verb, but forgot to limit idle time, then you are in luck. You can also limit the amount of idle time with the play verb.

```
% asciinema play -i 2 https://asciinema.org/a/17648
```

The other thing you can do with the playback is change the speed. This is cool, especially if you are a slow typer. The option is -s SPEED. The value of SPEED is a number that represents how fast the playback is. Normally, playback will have a SPEED value of 1.

If you wanted the playback to be 10 times faster, you'd use this:

```
% asciinema play -i 2 -s 10 https://asciinema.org/a/17648
```

If you wanted the playback to be 10 times slower, you'd use this:

```
% asciinema play -i 2 -s 0.1 https://asciinema.org/a/17648
```

cat

The cat verb will show you the output of your cast. It works on files and URLs.

```
% asciinema play https://asciinema.org/a/17648
bash-3.2$ # I am in a new shell instance which is being
recorded now
bash-3.2$ sha1sum /etc/f* | tail -n 10 | lolcat -F 0.3
da39a3ee5e6b4b0d3255bfef95601890afd80709  /etc/find.codes
88dd3ea7ffcbb910fbd1d921811817d935310b34  /etc/fstab.hd
442a5bc4174a8f4d6ef8d5ae5da9251ebb6ab455  /etc/ftpd.conf
```

```
442a5bc4174a8f4d6ef8d5ae5da9251ebb6ab455  /etc/ftpd.conf.default
d3e5fb0c582645e60f8a13802be0c909a3f9e4d7  /etc/ftpusers
bash-3.2$ # To finish recording just exit the shell
bash-3.2$ exit
```

upload

The upload verb will upload a local cast to asciinema.org. This can be useful if you want to share your Terminal session with others. You can choose to keep your upload private and only people with the URL will be able to access the video.

It is possible to embed your uploaded session into your own website. Let's look at how it works.

% **asciinema upload recording.cast**

View the recording at:

```
https://asciinema.org/a/nrUALQkjcUXI8jj9RHunbZ99q
```

This is just like uploading with the rec verb, but now your recording has been uploaded. It will look like Figure 4-12.

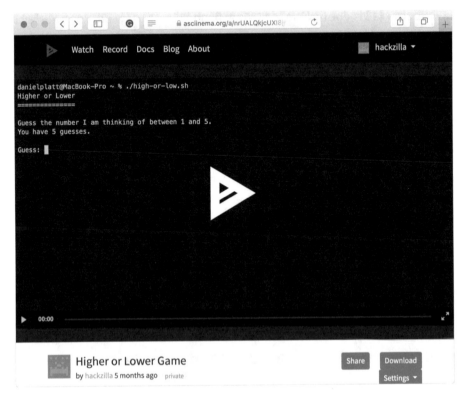

Figure 4-12. *Uploaded asciinema cast*

When you upload to asciinema, you will be prompted to link your account, if you haven't already done so.

Using the auth verb will redisplay the message about linking your computer with an asciinema account.

% **asciinema auth**

Open the following URL in a web browser to link your install ID with your asciinema.org user account:

```
https://asciinema.org/connect/3d23e2
ff-0000-0000-0000-00000000000
```

When you visit your URL, you will either need to create an account or sign in. With an account, your cast can persist longer than seven days and you can make them public.

A friend recently asked me if Terminal could record everything that happened in the session, automatically. That way, they had a historical record of everything they typed and what happened. Naturally, I thought about asciinema to capture Terminal usage. I figured we could store the logs in an out-of-the-way place and decided on ~/Library/Logs, which we needed to create.

```
% mkdir -p ~/Library/Logs/Terminal
```

Knowing that we could change the speed of the playback and skip any really long idles, I opted for a simple version of the command and did not use the -i argument.

The big difference is that we would need to give the asciinema command a filename based on the date and time to avoid using the file being stored in the temporary directory or overriding an existing file. Normally, this will be enough to stop any duplicate file issues, as you are unlikely to open tabs faster than once per second.

However, I found a scenario where I kept getting duplicate files, even based on the current date time. This was because on boot up, macOS can relaunch Terminal with all the tabs open at the same time. This causes them all to be open in the same second. Using $RANDOM is a good workaround for that.

Another change I've had to make is replacing the tilde symbol (~) with the $HOME variable. Otherwise, I was getting a Python error.

```
% asciinema rec "$HOME/Library/Logs/Terminal/terminal_`/bin/
date \"+%Y-%m-%d %H:%M:%S\"` $RANDOM.cast"
```

This works perfectly in Terminal. If you only wanted to record a single session, you simply type the command in. If you wanted to record a few sessions, you could make it easier by creating an alias.

```
% alias ars='asciinema rec "$HOME/Library/Logs/Terminal/
terminal_`/bin/date \"+%Y-%m-%d %H:%M:%S\"` $RANDOM.cast"'
```

What if you wanted to record every Terminal session automatically, without having to remember to enable it? You're probably thinking we can add the asciinema command to the end of the .zshrc file. You would be right, that could be a good place for it, if it were any other command.

However, there is an issue with adding asciinema to the end of the .zshrc file. When you run asciinema, it will start a new Zsh shell, which in turn starts a new shell and will cause asciinema to run again. You will end up with an infinite loop, as the computer keeps opening new copies of asciinema.

```
Last login: Sat Jan 11 21:23:48 on ttys010

asciinema: press <ctrl-d> or type "exit" when you're done
asciinema: recording asciicast to /Users/danielplatt/Library/
Logs/Terminal/terminal_2020-01-11 22:19:21 29769.cast
asciinema: press <ctrl-d> or type "exit" when you're done
asciinema: recording asciicast to /Users/danielplatt/Library/
Logs/Terminal/terminal_2020-01-11 22:19:21 1797.cast
asciinema: press <ctrl-d> or type "exit" when you're done
asciinema: recording asciicast to /Users/danielplatt/Library/
Logs/Terminal/terminal_2020-01-11 22:19:21 21265.cast
asciinema: press <ctrl-d> or type "exit" when you're done
asciinema: recording asciicast to /Users/danielplatt/Library/
Logs/Terminal/terminal_2020-01-11 22:19:22 5748.cast
asciinema: press <ctrl-d> or type "exit" when you're done
^C
```

We could get asciinema to use a different shell to get around this issue, or we could take advantage of a feature of Terminal.

In Terminal's preferences (⌘,) is the ability to change the command Terminal uses to open the shell. Normally this is /bin/zsh, but you can change this to a command of your choosing. Let's add the command into the Shells Open With field, as shown in Figure 4-13.

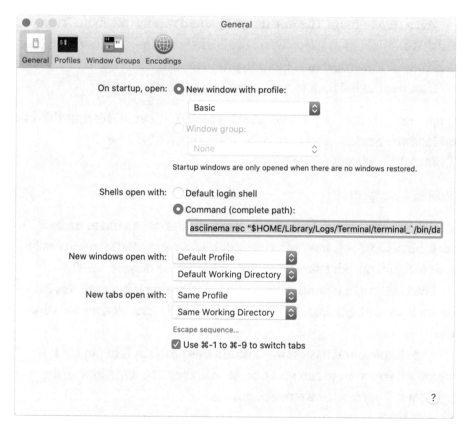

Figure 4-13. *Asciinema preferences, showing the asciinema command*

Now, when we open a new Terminal window, we are greeted with this message.

```
[Command not found: asciinema]
[Could not create a new process and open a pseudo-tty.]
```

What went wrong? The first thing I ignored was the bit about "complete path." We should have used /usr/local/bin/asciinema, rather than just asciinema. However, that is just one problem with it.

If we use the full path to asciinema, we get this message.

```
usage: asciinema [-h] [--version] {rec,play,cat,upload,auth} ...
asciinema: error: unrecognized arguments: \"+%Y-%m-%d
%H:%M:%S\"` $RANDOM.cast"

[Process completed]
```

You probably could figure out a way to fix the command to make it work, but what if you wanted to use a different command? Do you really want to figure out why the command isn't working on your own?

I can tell you that another reason it isn't working is because this isn't the shell prompt. All the niceties of the shell, with variables, won't work here.

The simplest and easiest way around this problem is to put the full command you want to run into a script and then call that script as the login shell. That is what we're going to do.

% nano ~/my-shell.sh

```
#!/bin/zsh

mkdir -p ~/Library/Logs/Terminal
/usr/local/bin/asciinema rec "$HOME/Library/Logs/Terminal/
terminal_`/bin/date \"+%Y-%m-%d %H:%M:%S\"` $RANDOM.cast"
```

% chmod +x ~/my-shell.sh

We need to use the full path to the command. For me, ~/my-shell.sh is the equivalent of /Users/danielplatt/my-shell.sh. We can confirm this is so with the which command.

```
% which ~/my-shell.sh
/Users/danielplatt/my-shell.sh
```

Now all we need to do is add this command to the Terminal preferences, as shown in Figure 4-14.

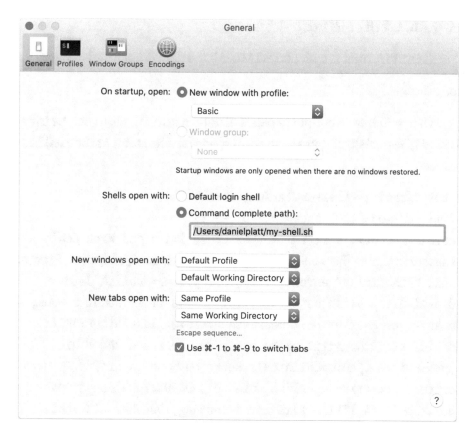

Figure 4-14. *Asciinema preferences showing my-shell.sh command*

Now, all your Terminal sessions will be recorded. Although you might not need all of them recorded, you might find that this comes in handy.

Formatting XML and JSON Files

I'm not sure how likely you are to come across these data formats. However, these commands are brilliant for formatting these files so that they are much easier to read.

The XML File Format

The XML file format is a bit like HTML. All the data is enclosed in tags.

```
<data>text</data>
```

When you have a couple of pages of data in an XML file, it can be tricky to read it, especially if there is no whitespace (spaces, tabs, or returns) in the file.

```
% cat ~/random-files-master/data/books.xml
<?xml version="1.0" encoding="UTF-8"?>
<catalog><book><id>1</id><Author>Craig Smith and Katz Cowley
</author><title>The Wonky Donkey</title><genre>Children's Fiction
Books on Animals</genre><price>4.00</price><publish_date>
2018-11-01</publish_date><description>The story about a wonky
donkey...</description></book><book><id>2</id><Author>Julia
Donaldson</author><title>The Girl, the Bear and the Magic
Shoes</title><genre>Children's Books on Fashion Crafts</genre>
<price>5.24</price><publish_date>2019-04-04</publish_date>
<description>A little girl loved running, but her old shoes
were too tight...</description></book></catalog>
```

```
% xmllint --format ~/random-files-master/data/books.xml
<?xml version="1.0" encoding="UTF-8"?>
<catalog>
  <book>
    <id>1</id>
    <Author>Craig Smith and Katz Cowley</author>
    <title>The Wonky Donkey</title>
    <genre>Children's Fiction Books on Animals</genre>
    <price>4.00</price>
    <publish_date>2018-11-01</publish_date>
    <description>The story about a wonky donkey...
    </description>
  </book>
  <book>
    <id>2</id>
    <Author>Julia Donaldson</author>
    <title>The Girl, the Bear and the Magic Shoes</title>
    <genre>Children's Books on Fashion Crafts</genre>
    <price>5.24</price>
    <publish_date>2019-04-04</publish_date>
    <description>A little girl loved running, but her old shoes
    were too tight...</description>
  </book>
</catalog>
```

That is much more readable. If you want to remove the whitespace to save space, the -nospace option will do this for you.

```
% xmllint --nospace ~/random-files-master/data/books.xml
```

The JSON File Format

The JSON format is typically used with dynamic websites, which use a lot of JavaScript. JSON is a data format, like XML, but instead of being based on tags, it is based on key: value.

% **cat ~/random-files-master/data/books.json**
```
{"book":[{"id":"1","author":"Craig Smith and Katz
Cowley","title":"The Wonky Donkey","genre":"Children's
Fiction Books on Animals","price":"4.00","publish_
date":"2018-11-01","description":"The story about a wonky
donkey..."},{"id":"2","author":"Julia Donaldson","title":"The
Girl, the Bear and the Magic Shoes","genre":"Children's Books
on Fashion Crafts","price":"5.24","publish_date":"2019-04-
04","description":"A little girl loved running, but her old
shoes were too tight..."}]}
```

The command jq (JQ) is a JSON processor, which means that it can format the JSON as well as filter it.

% **brew install jq**

Now that we have jq installed, we can format some JSON.

% **cat ~/random-files-master/data/books.json | jq**
```
{
  "book": [
    {
      "id": "1",
      "author": "Craig Smith and Katz Cowley",
      "title": "The Wonky Donkey",
      "genre": "Children's Fiction Books on Animals",
      "price": "4.00",
      "publish_date": "2018-11-01",
```

```
    "description": "The story about a wonky donkey..."
  },
  {
    "id": "2",
    "author": "Julia Donaldson",
    "title": "The Girl, the Bear and the Magic Shoes",
    "genre": "Children's Books on Fashion Crafts",
    "price": "5.24",
    "publish_date": "2019-04-04",
    "description": "A little girl loved running, but her old
    shoes were too tight..."
  }
 ]
}
```

This is what people typically think of when they think about JSON. However, to save on bandwidth, it is usually transmitted without whitespace.

```
% cat ~/random-files-master/data/books.json | jq --compact-output
{"book":[{"id":"1","author":"Craig Smith and Katz
Cowley","title":"The Wonky Donkey","genre":"Children's Fiction
Books on Animals","price":"4.00","publish_date":"2018-11-
01","description":"The story about a wonky donkey..."},{"
id":"2","author":"Julia Donaldson","title":"The Girl, the
Bear and the Magic Shoes","genre":"Children's Books on
Fashion Crafts","price":"5.24","publish_date":"2019-04-
04","description":"A little girl loved running, but her old
shoes were too tight..."}]}
```

The CSV Command

Out of all the data formats in this section, CSV is the most common. CSV stands for Comma Separated Values, and it is sometimes used interchangeably with Tab Separated Values. Most spreadsheet programs will give you options when you open a CSV file that allow you to choose the separator value.

```
% cat ~/random-files-master/data/books.csv
id,author,title,genre
1,Craig Smith and Katz Cowley,The Wonky Donkey,Children's
Fiction Books on Animals
2,Julia Donaldson,The Girl, the Bear and the Magic
Shoes,Children's Books on Fashion Crafts
```

The CSVKit package contains a selection of commands that work on CSV files. Its commands format CSV files to make them easier to read and converts CSV files to other formats.

```
% brew install csvkit
```

There is csvlook, which "pretty prints" the CSV file in a similar format to a spreadsheet, as shown in Figure 4-15.

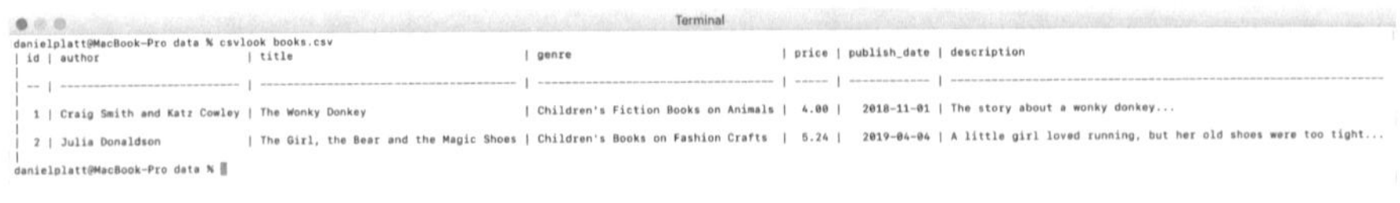

Figure 4-15. *Formatted CSV file*

csvstat gives you some useful statistics about the CSV file.

```
% csvstat ~/random-files-master/data/books.csv
  1. "id"

        Type of data:          Number
        Contains null values:  False
        Unique values:         2
        Smallest value:        1
        Largest value:         2
        Sum:                   3
        Mean:                  1.5
        Median:                1.5
        StDev:                 0.707
        Most common values:    1 (1x)
                               2 (1x)

  2. "author"

        Type of data:          Text
        Contains null values:  False
        Unique values:         2
        Longest value:         27 characters
        Most common values:    Craig Smith and Katz Cowley (1x)
                               Julia Donaldson (1x)
```

csvjson can convert a CSV file into a JSON file. The output is very close to the original JSON file, books.json.

```
% csvjson ~/random-files-master/data/books.csv | jq
[
  {
    "id": 1,
    "author": "Craig Smith and Katz Cowley",
```

```
    "title": "The Wonky Donkey",
    "genre": "Children's Fiction Books on Animals",
    "price": 4,
    "publish_date": "2018-11-01",
    "description": "The story about a wonky donkey..."
  },
  {
    "id": 2,
    "author": "Julia Donaldson",
    "title": "The Girl, the Bear and the Magic Shoes",
    "genre": "Children's Books on Fashion Crafts",
    "price": 5.24,
    "publish_date": "2019-04-04",
    "description": "A little girl loved running, but her old
    shoes were too tight..."
  }
]
```

You can also convert JSON files into CSV files. This also works with other formats, such as XLS and XLSX files.

```
% in2csv -k book books.json
```

Note   The conversion of JSON to CSV is fairly basic. We had to specify the top-level list with -k book, to select the actual list of data (the book: [ ] part of the JSON).

The watch Command

Have you ever found yourself running the same command over and over, waiting for some change to happen? I occasionally do this when I'm downloading a large file. I constantly run `ls  -h` to see how big a file is on disk. There is a command called `watch` that will do the same thing for you.

```
% brew install watch
```

The way you use it is by passing the command you want to run as an argument to `watch`. The output can be seen in Figure 4-16.

```
% watch "ls"
```

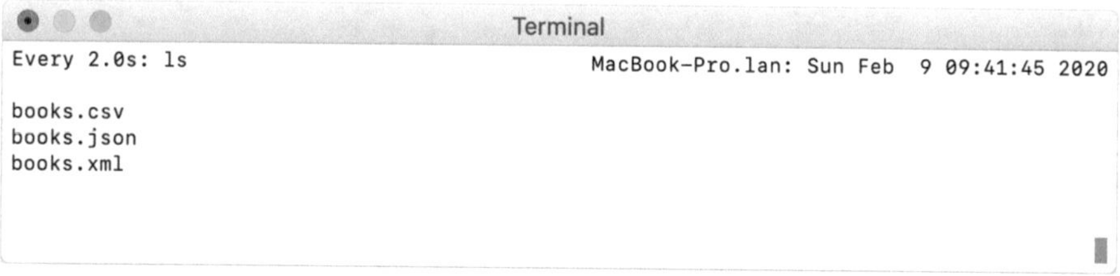

```
Every 2.0s: ls                          MacBook-Pro.lan: Sun Feb  9 09:41:45 2020

books.csv
books.json
books.xml
```

Figure 4-16. *Output of watch using the default interval*

Then `watch` will run the `ls` command every two seconds and update the screen with the new output. You can change the frequency in which the command is run with the `--interval` option. You then supply the number of seconds between runs, as shown in Figure 4-17.

```
% watch --interval 10 "ls"
```

297

Figure 4-17. *Output of watch using a 10 second interval*

I've even used watch as a quick substitute for a cron or a launchd task. It won't survive a reboot, but it is really quick to set up.

Networking

In the previous chapter, we used curl to download the random files archive.

```
% curl --location -o master.zip https://github.com/hackzilla/
random-files/archive/master.zip
```

The reason I used curl is that it is installed by default with macOS, whereas wget needed to be installed with Brew.

The wget Command

Using wget to download files is a bit easier than using curl. For this reason, I like to have both on my system.

```
% brew install wget
% wget "https://github.com/hackzilla/random-files/archive/
master.zip"
--2020-02-08 15:43:18--  https://github.com/hackzilla/
random-files/archive/master.zip
Resolving github.com (github.com)... 140.82.118.4
Connecting to github.com (github.com)|140.82.118.4|:443...
connected.
```

```
HTTP request sent, awaiting response... 302 Found
Location: https://codeload.github.com/hackzilla/random-files/
zip/master [following]
--2020-02-08 15:43:19--  https://codeload.github.com/hackzilla/
random-files/zip/master
Resolving codeload.github.com (codeload.github.com)...
140.82.113.9
Connecting to codeload.github.com (codeload.github.
com)|140.82.113.9|:443... connected.
HTTP request sent, awaiting response... 200 OK
Length: unspecified [application/zip]
Saving to: 'master.zip'

master.zip              [ <=> ]  11.46K  --.-KB/s    in 0.08s

2020-02-08 15:43:19 (139 KB/s) - 'master.zip' saved [11740]
```

wget is a great command for downloading files. It is worth noting that some symbols in an URL might trigger a functionality in Zsh. For this reason, I recommend always quoting the URL that you pass to curl or wget.

The curl Command

If you need more control, then use curl, which is installed with macOS. You can also use Brew to install a more up-to-date version. At the time of writing, the default macOS version of curl was over a year out of date.

```
% curl --version
curl 7.64.1 (x86_64-apple-darwin19.0) libcurl/7.64.1
(SecureTransport) LibreSSL/2.8.3 zlib/1.2.11 nghttp2/1.39.2
Release-Date: 2019-03-27
```

Installing `curl` with Brew is the same as any other command, but you will need to add it to your PATH.

```
% brew install curl
curl is keg-only, which means it was not symlinked into /usr/local,
because macOS already provides this software and installing
another version in
parallel can cause all kinds of trouble.

If you need to have curl first in your PATH run:
  echo 'export PATH="/usr/local/opt/curl/bin:$PATH"' >> ~/.zshrc
```

Updating `curl` is entirely up to you. I tend to leave `curl` as the default version, as if there were any security issues, Apple would upgrade it. With `curl`, we can download a series of files by using the square brackets ([ ]) to specify a series.

For example, the numbers one to ten would be written as [1-10]. If we wanted a leading zero, we could write it as [01-10]. This also works for letters, such as [a-z].

```
http://example.org/page[1-100].txt
```

We can also add a step to the range. If we wanted to only access the odd numbers, we would write [1-100:2]. If there are sets of items you want to try, you can use the braces.

For example, we could search for specific years and the number sequence.

```
http://example.org/year/{1996, 2000, 2004}/page[1-10].txt
```

How would I use this with `curl`? First, you need to make sure you use quotes around the URL, because otherwise, the shell will try to interpret it.

Note   I have set my computer to resolve `example.org` to my computer. This will be covered later in the book.

```
% curl "http://example.org/year/{1996, 2000, 2004}/page[1-10].txt"
[1/30]: http://example.org/year/1996/page1.txt --> <stdout>
--_curl_--http://example.org/year/1996/page1.txt
<html>
<head><title>404 Not Found</title></head>
<body>
<center><h1>404 Not Found</h1></center>
<hr><center>nginx/1.17.8</center>
</body>
</html>
```

You might want to output all of all the possible URLs to Terminal; however it's also possible to save them to individual files. Previously we used the -o option to save the file, but that won't work as it is.

```
% curl -o /tmp/page.txt "http://example.org/year/
{1996,2000,2004}/page[1-10].txt"
```

What will happen is for every file it will be saved to page.txt. The way around this problem is by using variables. A curl variable is the # symbol followed by a number. The number increments from 1. In this example, #1 will contain either 1996, 2000, or 2004 and #2 will be a number between 1 and 10.

```
% curl -o /tmp/page-#1-#2.txt "http://example.org/year/
{1996,2000,2004}/page[1-10].txt"
% ls /tmp/page*
page-1996-1.txt        page-2000-1.txt        page-2004-1.txt
page-1996-10.txt       page-2000-10.txt       page-2004-10.txt
page-1996-2.txt        page-2000-2.txt        page-2004-2.txt
page-1996-3.txt        page-2000-3.txt        page-2004-3.txt
```

Both commands have an extensive list of options that can be passed to them, which makes them very powerful.

Checking Internet Speed

If you are paying for an Internet connection, how do you know you are getting the speed that you are paying for? Most people will go to a website that attempts to calculate it for you. However, in my experience they are usually full of ads. There is another way. There is a speed test command you can install using Brew, called `speedtest-cli`.

```
% brew install speedtest-cli
==> Downloading https://github.com/sivel/speedtest-cli/archive/
v2.1.2.tar.gz
==> Downloading from https://codeload.github.com/sivel/
speedtest-cli/tar.gz/v2.1.2
#################################################### 100.0%
🍺  /usr/local/Cellar/speedtest-cli/2.1.2: 7 files, 84.9KB,
    built in 5 seconds
```

When you run `speedtest-cli`, it will find the closest server to you and perform a speed test.

```
% speedtest-cli
Retrieving speedtest.net configuration...
Testing from Cogent Communications (82.129.x.x)...
Retrieving speedtest.net server list...
Selecting best server based on ping...
Hosted by Iomart (Maidenhead) [37.85 km]: 11.372 ms
Testing download speed
Download: 51.29 Mbit/s
Testing upload speed
Upload: 38.91 Mbit/s
```

I have a 60MB/60MB Internet connection, and these results aren't that far away from what I actually pay for.

There are lots of reasons why these will be different. Some of these reasons will be because of your Internet supplier, and others will be things under your control. To ensure that you get the best connection to the Internet, you should be close to your Wi-Fi router or connection via Ethernet.

Logging Information

`speedtest-cli` can also save the results to a CSV file for you. This is really useful if you want to keep a historical record of your Internet connection speed. A reason for this could be that every evening around 6pm your Internet connection becomes painfully slow and you want evidence.

There are two options that you can supply to `speedtest-cli` to output to the CSV format. The first is `--csv` and the second is `--csv-header`.

```
% speedtest-cli --csv
3839,Iomart,Maidenhead,2020-03-15T09:47:26.678718Z,37.852639672
79236,9.264,56859526.677607715,51278243.8575505,,82.129.x.x
```

```
% speedtest-cli --csv-header
Server ID,Sponsor,Server Name,Timestamp,Distance,Ping,Download,
Upload,Share,IP Address
```

When you use these commands, you will want to save the data to a file. We will use `--csv-header` when we create the file, and then append to the file with the `--csv` option. We don't need the header every time we write to the file.

This command will create a CSV file with just the headers. If the file existed before, it will be overwritten.

```
% speedtest-cli --csv-header > speedtest.csv
```

Then you will call this next command as often as you need a new result.

```
% speedtest-cli --csv >> speedtest.csv
```

Note the double greater than symbol in the previous line of code. You could run this command with the `watch` command, or better yet, use built-in scheduling to automatically capture your next result. With a little bit of work, you can plot data and end up with a graph that looks similar to Figure 4-18.

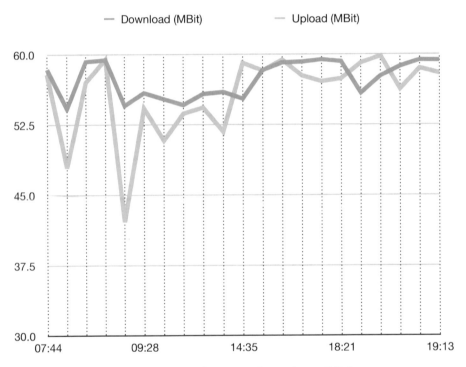

Figure 4-18. *Graph produced in Numbers from CSV*

Summary

In this chapter, you installed many commands from Brew. You started slow with the `fortune` command and added to what you could do by chaining commands together. You even learned how to use Terminal to create images and video. In the next chapter, we are going to look at how we can script in Terminal.

CHAPTER 5

Shell Scripting Basics

Some of my earlier memories of using computers involve typing a computer program into the computer. I remember hoping that I didn't make a mistake and then finally running it. In this chapter, I hope to foster a sense of accomplishment that helps you on your journey.

We have been using Zsh as our shell in all the examples so far in this book. However, there is another shell we will use for scripting, called *sh*.

Unlike Zsh, sh has been bundled with macOS for many years and is a good default for maximum compatibility with any script you write. This is especially important if you want to use what you learn in this chapter on other computers.

Your First Script

The sh command lives in /bin/sh. Now you'll write your first script. Actually, that's a lie, this will be your second script. Your first was the .zshrc file.

Create a file called "~/welcome" with these contents:

```
echo "Welcome";
```

If you need help with this step, please consult Chapter 2. This is your script and you can run it like this:

```
% bash ~/welcome
Welcome
```

Anything you can type into your Terminal can be used in a script.

© Daniel Platt 2021
D. Platt, *Tweak Your Mac Terminal*, https://doi.org/10.1007/978-1-4842-6171-2_5

Running and Debugging Scripts

Previously, we created a welcome file that we ran using Bash.

```
% cat ~/welcome
echo "Welcome";
```

While in principle this is a script, we can make it more like the commands we have used. The first thing we need to do is fix how we run the command.

```
% bash ~/welcome
```

We need to be able to run this command like this.

```
% ~/welcome
zsh: permission denied: /Users/danielplatt/welcome
```

The problem is we are trying to execute the welcome file without having the execute permission set.

```
% ls -lath ~/welcome
-rw-r--r-- 1 danielplatt staff /Users/danielplatt/welcome
```

We have the read and write permission, but the execute (x) permission is missing.

This is easy to fix with the chmod command. We can give the welcome file the execute permission.

```
% chmod ugo+x ~/welcome
% ls -lath ~/welcome
-rwxr-xr-x  1 danielplatt  staff  /Users/danielplatt/welcome
```

Now when we try to run the script again, the shell will be able to execute it.

```
% ~/welcome
Welcome
```

We can also tell the shell to look in the current directory for the script.

```
% cd ~
% ./welcome
Welcome
```

Running Scripts from the Current Directory

Before we go on, I'd like to explain why we don't just use the filename, as with other commands.

```
% welcome
zsh: command not found: welcome
```

The reason is that all the other commands are located in the PATH variable. Your current directory is not in the list of directories. Therefore, the shell will not look for the script you are trying to run in your current directory.

There is one more thing we should do to make this official. We should specify an interpreter for this script. This is straightforward; we simply add #!/bin/... as the first line in the script. The contents of ~/welcome will now look like Listing 5-1.

Listing 5-1. The Finished Welcome Script

```
#!/bin/sh
echo "Welcome"
```

We are using /bin/sh, as this has existed for a long time on macOS. This means that when you look online, you will find more support for this interpreter. This is why we are using this interpreter, rather than the Zsh interpreter that we've been discussing in this book. In fact, /bin/sh is really the Bash interpreter. You can see this if you use the version option on both.

```
% /bin/sh --version
GNU bash, version 3.2.57(1)-release (x86_64-apple-darwin19)
Copyright (C) 2007 Free Software Foundation, Inc.

% /bin/bash --version
GNU bash, version 3.2.57(1)-release (x86_64-apple-darwin19)
Copyright (C) 2007 Free Software Foundation, Inc.
```

Text Modes

The macOS Terminal can have different font styles, as shown in Table 5-1, such as bold, underlined, or blinking.

Table 5-1. *Different Text Modes in Bash*

Mode	Text Style
0	Normal, remove all style
1	Bold
2	Dim
3	Italic
4	Underline
5	Blink
7	Inverted
8	Hidden
22	Remove bold/dim
23	Remove italic
24	Remove underline
25	Remove blink
27	Remove Inverted
28	Remove hidden

Note   Mode 21 is supposed to be used to remove bold, but it doesn't work on the macOS Terminal.

By default, text that you output will not be styled.

```
% printf "Normal text"
Normal text
```

Let's experiment with the different text modes. We will create a file called textmode and enter the code in Listing 5-2.

Listing 5-2.   Filename: textmode—Script Showing the Different Text Modes

```
#!/bin/sh

printf "\e[0m"
printf "This text is \e[1mBOLD\e[22m.\n"
printf "This text is \e[2mDIM\e[22m.\n"
printf "This text is \e[3mITALIC\e[23m.\n"
printf "This text is \e[4mUNDERLINED\e[24m.\n"
printf "This text is \e[5mBLINKING\e[25m.\n"
printf "This text is \e[7mINVERTED\e[27m.\n"
printf "This text is \e[8mHIDDEN\e[28m.\n"
```

When we run the code in Listing 5-2, we get the following output.

```
% chmod +x textmode
% textmode
This text is BOLD.
This text is DIM.
This text is ITALIC.
This text is UNDERLINED.
This text is BLINKING.
```

```
This text is INVERTED.
This text is HIDDEN.
```

Note   The text will actually be blinking and the hidden text will show up when highlighted.

Clearing Text Modes

These text mode changes are persistent. If you don't end them, they will carry on until you reset the style. The Zsh shell will clear the text modes before displaying a new prompt, but this is something that the Bash shell does not do.

Listing 5-3 shows what happens if you forget to turn off the textmode, in this case, bold.

Listing 5-3. Commands Showing the Difference When Bold Is Accidentally Not Turned Off

```
% printf "This text is \e[1mBOLD.\n"
This text is BOLD.
% printf "This text is Normal.\n"
This text is Normal.
```

In a script, that outcome is slightly different and the commands in Listing 5-4 illustrate this point.

Listing 5-4. Filename: boldtext—Enabling Bold Without Ending It

```
#!/bin/sh

printf "This text is \e[1mBOLD.\n"
printf "This text is Normal.\n"
```

When we run the `boldtext` command, we can see the bold text on the second line of text, where we didn't end the bold mode.

```
% ./boldtext
This text is BOLD.
This text is Normal.
```

After this command has been run in Zsh, the text mode will be reset to normal.

Combining Text Modes

We can also combine these styles by starting multiple text modes without closing them.

```
% printf "This text is \e[1m\e[4mBOLD and UNDERLINED\e[22m\
e[24m.\n"
This text is BOLD and UNDERLINED.
```

Text Color

Did you know you can change the text color? You can set the text color and the background color and can choose from a color palette of 256 colors. To help visualize all the different colors in your palette, use the code in Listing 5-5.

Listing 5-5. Output Color Palette

```
#!/bin/sh
# Original Script - https://askubuntu.com/a/681719
for((i=0; i<256; i++)); do
```

```
    printf "\e[48;5;${i}m%03d" $i;
    printf '\e[0m';
    [ ! $((($i + 1) % 8)) -eq 0 ] && printf ' ' || printf '\n'
done
```

Now add the code to a file called color.

```
% nano ~/color
% chmod +x ~/color
```

When you run this script, you will get output that looks like Figure 5-1, which is the ANSI color code for each color. However, it is likely that Figure 5-1 is shown in grayscale in the book. If this is the case, you will need to run this command yourself.

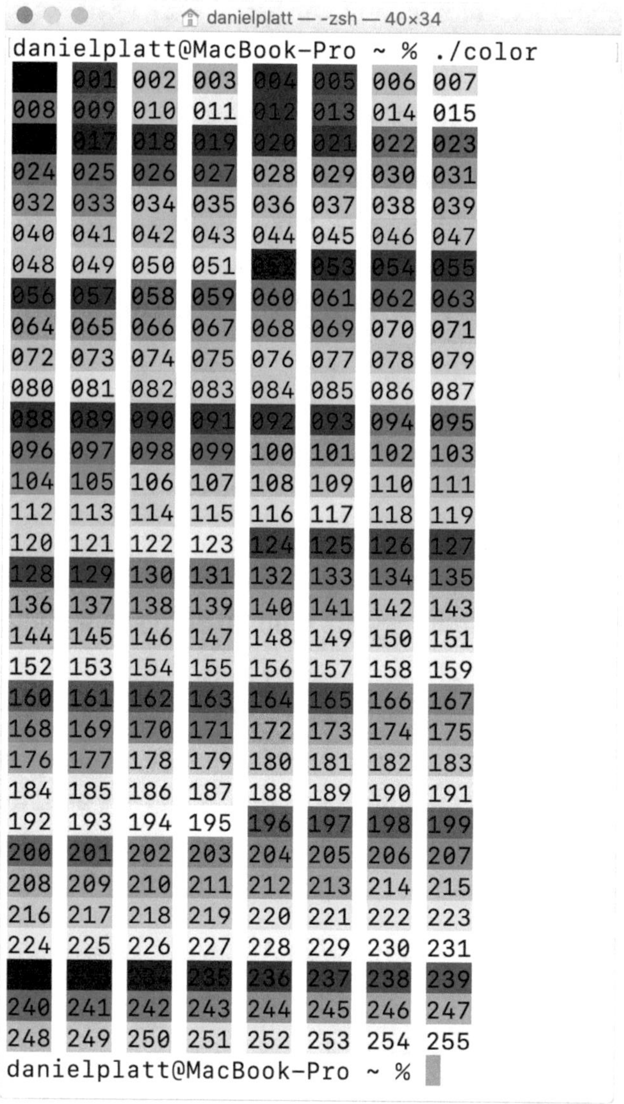

Figure 5-1. *Output of the color command*

Changing the text color is similar to how we changed the text mode in the previous section.

```
printf '\e[<fg_bg>;5;<ANSI_color_code>m'
```

fg_bg needs to be replaced with either 38 (foreground) or 48 (background). Then you have \e[0m, which is used to reset the colors back to their defaults.

For example, let's say we wanted blue text on a red background.

```
printf '\e[38;5;12m'
printf '\e[48;5;9m'
printf 'blue text on a red background\n'
printf '\e[0m'
```

Note   This works only if they are entered at the same time, rather than typed out one by one.

Remember, Zsh resets the colors and styles after every command. All the commands could be combined into one, but I have used four to help with readability. If you want to run them as one command, all the text needs to be combined into a single printf command.

```
printf '\e[38;5;12m\e[48;5;9mblue \e[1mtext\e[22m on a red background\n\e[0m'
```

If you don't include the mode reset, the colors will carry on until you change them again. You can also combine the text mode and color.

```
printf '\e[38;5;12m'
printf '\e[48;5;9m'
printf 'blue \e[1mtext\e[22m on a red background\n'
printf '\e[0m'
```

Variables

In Chapter 2, we covered creating environment variables. Variables in scripts work the same way as shell variables, with the main difference being that they will disappear when the script finishes running. A variable can be used inside a string, which can be output or used to create a new variable.

```
echo "My home directory is ${HOME}."
```

The braces around the variable name are optional, but they help define the bounds of the variable name. Without the braces, you wouldn't be able to have a string directly follow the variable.

We can use this to combine existing variables to create a new variable.

```
STRING1="Hello"
STRING2="World"
STRING3="${STRING1} ${STRING2}"
echo $STRING3
```

Special Variables

There are a few special variables that we didn't cover. When we've executed other commands, we have sometimes given them options or arguments.

```
% say "hello"
```

These special variables help us grab the text that started the program. The first variable is $# and it will tell us how many arguments we've passed in. Let's create a quick script to demonstrate, as shown in Listing 5-6. I will use args as the filename.

Listing 5-6. Output Command Arguments

```
#!/bin/sh
echo "You used $# arguments."
```

Don't forget to make it executable, like we discussed in Chapter 2.

```
% chmod +x args
```

Now we can run the program without arguments.

```
% ./args
You used 0 arguments.
```

We can run the command again and make up some arguments.

```
% ./args "hello" "world"
You used 2 arguments.
```

Using Arguments

It's one thing to know that there are arguments, but another to use them. There are two main ways to access the arguments to the script with Bash—using $* and $@ or using $0, $1, $2, and so on.

$*

The $* argument will treat all the arguments as a single string, with a single space between them. Let's change the args echo script to $*, as shown in Listing 5-7.

Listing 5-7. Arg Script Using $*

```
#!/bin/sh
echo $*
```

```
% ./args "hello" "world"
hello world
```

$@

The $@ variable works the same as $* when used with echo. However, you can use $@ as an array in a loop. Let's change the script args to a loop, as shown in Listing 5-8.

Listing 5-8. Outputting Arguments with a Loop

```
#!/bin/sh
for arg in $@
do
  echo "$arg"
done
```

Now, every argument passed to args will be displayed on a newline.

```
% ./args "hello" "world"
hello
world
```

$0, $1, $2, and So On

These variables represent the position of the argument on the shell when you ran the command. If you know the position of the argument, you can access it by using the offset.

```
$0 is the program name.
```

Every argument will be given to a new variable with an incremental number. Let's change the script in Listing 5-9.

Listing 5-9. Outputting the Arguments Based on Offset

```
echo $0
echo $1
echo $2
```

```
% ./args "hello" "world"
./args
hello
world
```

The If Statement

Outputting variables is one thing, but what if we want to perform different tasks depending on some condition? We need to use a structure known as the if statement.

```
if [[ <condition> ]] ; then
    <commands if condition is true>
elif [ <condition ]] ; then
  <commands if this condition is true>
else
    <commands if condition is false>
fi
```

The possibilities are endless with if statements. This information is only the beginning, but it will be enough to get you started.

There are lots of different tests you can run using the if statement. Table 5-2 shows a selection of conditions you are most likely to need.

Table 5-2. *Different if Conditions That Can Be Used*

Condition (Test)	Description
-e path	Does path point to a file?
-d path	Does path point to a directory?
string1 == string2	Does string1 equal string2?
string1 != string2	Are string1 and string2 different?
string1 < string2	Does string1 appear before string2 alphabetically?
string1 > string2	Does string2 appear before string1 alphabetically?
variable1 -eq variable2	Does variable1 equal variable2?
variable1 -ne variable2	Does variable1 not equal variable2?
variable1 -lt variable2	Is variable1 less than variable2?
variable1 -le variable2	Is variable1 less than or equal to variable2?
variable1 -gt variable2	Is variable1 greater than variable2?
variable1 -ge variable2	Is variable1 greater than or equal to variable2?

To run a test, we just surround the expression with double square brackets, as shown in Listing 5-10.

Listing 5-10. Example of Conditional Checking if 10 Is Greater Than 5

```
if [[ 10 -gt 5 ]] ; then
    echo "10 is greater than 5";
else
    echo "5 is greater than 10";
fi
```

319

Did you notice that the test in Listing 5-10 was impossible to evaluate as false? Just by changing the expression in the test, we can see if a file exists on the filesystem. This code is shown in Listing 5-11.

Listing 5-11. Testing if ~/testfile Exists

```
if [[ -e ~/testfile ]] ; then
    echo "testfile exists";
else
    echo "testfile doesn't exist";
fi
```

Try running the code before and after you create the file.

```
% touch ~/testfile
```

You can find much more about this topic in the Bash manual, by searching for "Evaluation."

Arithmetic

There might be times when you want to work with numbers. By default, Bash will treat all input as strings, which would make doing arithmetic tricky.

```
% echo 1+3
1+3
```

We need to tell Bash it is dealing with numbers. There is an easy way to do this, by using *arithmetic expansion*. To use arithmetic expansion, you need to surround your expression with a dollar sign and double parentheses, as follows:

```
$((expression))
```

Inside the arithmetic expansion, we can use all the standard arithmetic operators, as shown in Table 5-3.

Table 5-3. *Listing of the Different Arithmetic Operators*

Operation	Example	Result
Addition	echo $((1+3))	4
Subtraction	echo $((1-3))	-2
Multiplication	echo $((1*3))	
Division	echo $((7/3))	2
Modulo	echo $((7 % 3))	1

When you use division, you need to be aware that it only returns whole numbers. If there is a reminder, you can get it by using the modulo symbol.

Loops

Earlier in the section entitled "Text Color," there was a script that displayed the ANSI color codes. You may not have noticed, but it used a loop to generate that table. This code is shown again in Listing 5-12.

Listing 5-12. The Script That Prints the Color Palette Available to Terminal

```
# Original Script - https://askubuntu.com/a/681719
for((i=0; i<256; i++)); do
      printf "\e[48;5;${i}m%03d" $i;
      printf '\e[0m';
      [ ! $((($i + 1) % 8)) -eq 0 ] && printf ' ' || printf '\n'
done
```

Let's break this script down. This is the basis of the for loop.

```
for((<initial value>; <end condition>; <increment>)); do
       <commands>
done
```

The loop will keep going until it meets the end condition. There are four components in a for loop.

1. *The initial value*

   ```
   i=0
   ```

   This part is concerned with setting the variable, i, to a known value.

   Without this, i would be undefined, or possibly set to something unexpected if it is being reused.

2. *The end condition*

   ```
   i<256
   ```

   The end condition is needed to understand when the loop should exit.

3. *Increment*

   ```
   i++
   ```

   This is the equivalent to i=i+1 and is used to change the value of i between each iteration of the loop.

4. *Commands*

   The commands are anything that needs to execute during every iteration of the loop. In our case, the specific commands are in Listing 5-13.

Line 1 prints the color number and changes the background color to match. Line 2 clears the color. Line 3 outputs a newline or a space.

Listing 5-13. Commands of the for Loop in Listing 5-9

```
printf "\e[48;5;${i}m%03d" $i;
printf '\e[0m';
[ ! $((($i + 1) % 8)) -eq 0 ] && printf ' ' || printf '\n'
```

Since line 3 in Listing 5-13 is doing many different things, we should look at it more closely. In Table 5-4, we are going to step through how the line is interpreted. This should give you a good understanding of how it works.

Table 5-4. *Breakdown of Line 3 in Listing 5-12*

Step	Expression	Description	Result
A	($i + 1)	Add 1 to $i	1 to 256
B	$((a % 8))	Remainder when divided by 8	1, 2, 3, 4, 5, 6, 7, 0
C	b -eq 0	Is it equal to 0?	1 (true) or 0 (false)
D	[! c]	Negate output of c	0 (false) or 1 (true)
E	d && printf ' '	Only print a space if d is true	
F	e || printf '\n'	Only print a newline if d is false	

Note   Steps C and D could have been combined by using **[b -ne 0]**.

Break and Continue

A special note about the keywords continue and break. Let's look at a simple loop that outputs the line numbers 0 to 9, as shown in Listing 5-14.

Listing 5-14. Example of a Loop Printing the Value of i

```
for((i=0; i<10; i++)); do
    printf "Line: %d\n" $i;
done
```

The continue statement in a loop will cause the current iteration to end, and it will move to the next iteration. The break statement will end the loop before the end condition.

I'm going to modify Listing 5-14, in order to add break and continue statements. Consider the loop in Listing 5-15.

Listing 5-15. A Loop Using continue and break

```
for((i=0; i<10; i++)); do
    if [[ i -lt 4 ]] ; then
        continue;
    fi

    printf "Line: %d\n" $i;

    if [[ i -gt 6 ]] ; then
        break;
    fi
done
```

This loop will output the following:

```
Line: 4
Line: 5
Line: 6
Line: 7
```

The `continue` will keep being called until i is at least 5, and the loop will end when i is greater than 6, but not before outputting line 7.

Exit Code

Have you ever wondered if the system knows if a script ran successfully or not? Maybe you would like to know the status of a command that you ran? There is shell variable that holds the last command's exit status.

```
% echo $?
0
```

Let's try that again, but with a command that fails.

```
% ./missing-command
zsh: no such file or directory: ./missing-command
% echo $?
127
```

Exit codes are useful for programmatically handling errors and each command will define its own list of error codes that it will emit. It is worth noting that the exit code will be a value between 0 and 255.

There is an easy way to understand them. If the exit code is 0, then the command ended successfully. If the exit code is greater than 0, then the command ended with an error.

If you want to know what the exit codes are for a particular command, their man page normally lists them.

```
% man curl
```

There are nearly a hundred exit codes for curl.

Exiting

When you write your own script, there might be times when you want your script to end early. It might be a success, or maybe the user didn't provide all the arguments required to run the command successfully.

You can use the exit keyword to end the currently executing process, and you can see the effect of doing so in your Terminal window.

```
% exit
[Process completed]
```

Using exit within a script will cause it to exit in the same way as your shell. The full usage of exit is exit <error code>. If you don't supply an exit code, it will default to the exit status of the last run command. Therefore, it is recommended to always supply an exit code when using exit.

What error code should you use? Well, that entirely depends on why you want to exit. However, for simplicity, I would stick with 0 if your script is exiting without error, or 1 if there was an error.

Reading Input

Much has been said about displaying output from a script by using echo and printf, but we haven't covered anything about getting input into a script. What if, in the middle of a script, we have a question?

We've seen it before, when searching the manual and we get prompted to display a particular manual entry. How can we do this ourselves?

```
read <variable>
```

read takes all the input from the user until a newline and stores it in a variable. In this example, we type what goes in, which is stored in $input. Then the same text will be outputted.

```
% read input; echo $input
what goes in
what goes in
```

We can use echo to help create a prompt that allows the user to see what they are entering.

```
% echo -n "Input: "; read input; echo $input
Input: must come out
must come out
```

Note   If you use the -n option with echo, then echo will not output a newline.

Projects

It's one thing being told how to use Bash. It's another thing to try some projects that illustrate these principles, which you'll do in this section.

Each project is split into three sections—"You Will Need," "Expected Output," and "Suggested Answer."

The "You Will Need" section is about helping you identify what will be useful in completing the project. The "Expected Output" section is the code that your project will need to output for the given script. The script should work for all the given arguments. The "Suggested Answer" section explains how I would have tackled the project.

Remember, there are many ways to produce the answers for these projects. Don't worry if you have an answer that doesn't exactly match this book.

Project 5-1: Print Arguments

This project tests your ability to print certain arguments, as well as to print a message if no arguments were provided. Let's create a file called args.

You Will Need

- if
- loop
- $0
- $#
- Variable arithmetic

Expected Output

When your script is run without any arguments, I want you to display a helpful message that tells the user how to use the script.

```
% ./print-args
Usage: ./print-args message
```

The script will also need to output each argument in turn with its argument number.

```
% ./print-args "hello" "world" 1 2 3
Arg 1: hello
Arg 2: world
```

```
Arg 3: 1
Arg 4: 2
Arg 5: 3
```

How would you solve this?

Suggested Answer

This script should first check the number of arguments that have been passed in with $#. If the number is less than 1, (i.e., is 0), the script will print the usage instructions and exit. Otherwise, the script will loop over the arguments in $0 and print them. See Listing 5-16.

Listing 5-16. print-args Suggested Answer

```
#!/bin/sh

if [ $# -lt 1 ]
then
  echo "Usage: $0 message"
  exit 1
fi

count=0

for arg in $@
do
  count=$((count+1))
  echo "Arg $count: $arg"
done
```

Project 5-2: Quicker Say Command

In this project, let's assume that you are frequently using the say command to save computer-generated speech with the Fiona voice to an .aiff file. The filename can be based on the current date.

Rather than having to type the same argument every time, you can create a script with the arguments hard-coded. The only thing that needs to be passed into this script is the message. Let's create a file called saytofile.

You Will Need

- if
- $0
- $#
- $@ or $*
- /bin/date
- say

Expected Output

When your script runs without any arguments, I want you to display a helpful message that tells the user how to use the script.

% ./saytofile
```
Usage: ./saytofile message
```

Your script will take all the arguments and pass them to the say command. To be quicker for the user, say needs to save the output to the filesystem using a filename that contains the current date and time.

% ./saytofile "this is my message to the world"
```
Saved to speech-2020-01-04 12:11:54.aiff
```

How would you solve this?

Suggested Answer

The script first needs to see if the usage needs to be printed. Then the script creates a variable called filename, which is speech.aiff. It then uses /bin/date to format the current date and time to ensure the filename is unique, assuming that it doesn't run more than once a second.

Then we add the say command, along with a specific voice and the filename. Finally, we use $@ to pass all the arguments to the script into the say command as the message. See Listing 5-17.

Listing 5-17. saytofile Suggested Answer

```
#!/bin/sh

if [ $# -lt 1 ]
then
  echo "Usage: $0 message"
  exit 1
fi

filename="speech-`/bin/date "+%Y-%m-%d %H:%M:%S"`.aiff"
say -v fiona -o "$filename" $@

echo "Saved to $filename"
```

Project 5-3: Higher or Lower

In this project, we will create a simple program in which you have to guess a random number that the computer picked between 1 and 10.

The script will give you hints as to whether the answer is higher or lower, but it will limit you to five guesses. Let's create a file called higher-or-lower.

You Will Need

- `if`
- `while`
- `read`
- `$RANDOM`

Expected Output

This script will not take any arguments, so you will not need to display a help message. Instead you can go straight into the game.

```
% ./higher-or-lower
Higher or Lower
================

Guess the number I am thinking of between 1 and 10.
You have 5 guesses.

Guess: 1
Higher!
Guess: 2
Higher!
Guess: 3
Higher!
Guess: 4
Higher!
Guess: 5
Higher!
Sorry, you didn't guess it correctly.
The answer was 6.
```

Suggested Answer

The first thing this script does in Listing 5-18 is generate a random number.
It then outputs the rules of the game. Then the script loops as many times
as there are guesses. During each iteration, the script asks the player for a
guess and reads the next thing they type.

   If the guess is incorrect, the script will tell the player that the answer
is higher or lower. If the guess is correct, the script will tell the player and
then exit with the success code. When the guesses are used up, the loop
will exit. Then the player will be told that they didn't win and what the
answer is. See Listing 5-18.

Listing 5-18. higher-or-lower Suggested Answer

```
#!/bin/sh

guess=0

randomNumber=$(( ($RANDOM % 10) + 1))

echo "Higher or Lower
===============

Guess the number I am thinking of between 1 and 10.
You have 5 guesses.
"

for((i=0; i<5; i++)); do
  /bin/echo -n "Guess: ";
  read guess;

  if [[ $guess -lt $randomNumber  ]]
  then
    echo "Higher!"
```

```
  elif [[ $guess -gt $randomNumber   ]]
  then
    echo "Lower!"
  elif [[ $guess -eq $randomNumber   ]]
  then
    echo "You guessed correctly!"
    exit 0;
  fi

done

echo "Sorry, you didn't guess it correctly.
The answer was $randomNumber.
";
```

Project 5-4: Higher or Lower with Changeable Limits

In this project, we will take the simple program where you have to guess the random number the computer has picked between 1 and 10 and improve on it. This time we will take optional arguments to adjust the upper range of the guessing. As we increase the difficulty, it makes sense to make the number of guesses adjustable as well.

The other issue with the previous script was it treated any input as a number, but it was evaluated as 0. In this project, you should instead output a message to say when the input wasn't understood to be a number. Extra credit if you add a help option to the script.

Let's duplicate the higher-or-lower script and call it higher-or-lower2.

You Will Need

- `if`

- `while`

- `read`

- `$RANDOM`

Expected Output

The script will have built-in defaults, which means when you run the script without any arguments, it can start the game. This means you need another way to show the usage information. We've seen other commands use `--help` and this feels like a good solution.

```
% ./higher-or-lower2 --help
Higher or Lower Game
./higher-or-lower2 [upper limit=10] [guesses=5]
```

```
% ./higher-or-lower2 50 2
Higher or Lower
===============

Guess the number I am thinking of between 1 and 50.
You have 2 guesses.

Guess: a
I didn't understand that.

Guess: 2
Higher!

Sorry, you didn't guess it correctly.
The answer was 4.
```

I would like you to make the number of guesses optional. This means you can start the game by only specifying the upper limit, without specifying the number of guesses.

Suggested Answer

The first thing the script needs to do is check to see if `--help` has been provided as an argument. If it has, it will print the usage information and exit.

Next, I am defining `upperLimit` and `totalGuesses` so that they are always defined regardless of whether they have been provided. We can now check to see if the guesses and an upper limit have been provided. If they have been provided, we set them to the variables `upperLimit` and `totalGuesses`, respectively.

The last part of the setup is to check `upperLimit` and `totalGuesses` to see if they are less than 1. We could easily set the check to be equal to 0, but I wanted to ignore any variable that was set to a negative value. Now that the setup has been performed, the rules can be displayed.

We can now iterate for as many guesses as the player gets and read the player's current guess (see Listing 5-19). Anything that the player types in that isn't a number will be treated as 0. This is why we check to see if the player's guess is lower than the answer. We are checking to see if it is not equal to 0. We have a check for a guess that's higher than the answer, as well as when the answer matches the player's guess. The last check determines if the player's guess matches 0, and if it does, it outputs a message to say that it didn't understand.

Listing 5-19. higher-or-lower2 Suggested Answer

```sh
#!/bin/sh

if [[ $# -eq 1 && $1 == '--help' ]]
then
```

```
  echo "Usage: $0 [upper limit=10] [guesses=5]";
  exit 0
fi

upperLimit=0
totalGuesses=0

if [[ $# -gt 0 ]]
then
  upperLimit=$1

  if [[ $# -gt 1 ]]
  then
    totalGuesses=$2
  fi
fi

if [[ $upperLimit -lt 1 ]]; then
  upperLimit=5
fi

if [[ $totalGuesses -lt 1 ]]; then
  totalGuesses=5
fi

guess=0
randomNumber=$(( ($RANDOM % upperLimit) + 1))

echo "Higher or Lower
===============

Guess the number I am thinking of between 1 and $upperLimit.
You have $totalGuesses guesses.
"
```

```
for((i=0; i<$totalGuesses; i++)); do
  /bin/echo -n "Guess: ";
  read guess;

  if [[ $guess -lt $randomNumber && $guess -ne 0 ]]
  then
    echo "Higher!"
  elif [[ $guess -gt $randomNumber  ]]
  then
    echo "Lower!"
  elif [[ $guess -eq $randomNumber  ]]
  then
    echo "You guessed correctly!"
    exit 0;
  elif [[ $guess -eq 0 ]]
  then
    echo "I didn't understand that."
  fi

  echo ""
done

echo "Sorry, you didn't guess it correctly.
The answer was $randomNumber.
";
```

Finally, if the loop exits, that means the player failed to guess the correct answer. It will then display the correct answer.

Summary

When you're scripting, you can do just about anything. It's worth starting small and adding extra functionality over time. In this chapter, we took a more relaxed approach and looked at sh, which is bundled with macOS and is a good default for maximum compatibility with any script you write.

In the next chapter, we take a closer look at another scripting language—PHP.

CHAPTER 6

PHP

PHP is a popular web scripting language. According to w3techs.com, in December 2019, 78.9% of server-side websites with a known language used PHP. It happens that PHP was installed on your computer as part of Catalina.

For some, it might be a stretch to talk about PHP in a book about Terminal. However, if you've never used Terminal before, chances are you won't know about PHP. I will show you some of the basic concepts of PHP, like variables and control statements, and finally finish with some projects. Let's dive in.

Determining Your PHP Version

Before you start learning about coding in PHP, it is a good idea to determine what version you have installed. As of Catalina, macOS ships with PHP 7.3. With Catalina 10.15.6, PHP has had a few security releases, but is still following the 7.3 branch.

```
% php -v
PHP 7.3.11 (cli) (built: Jul  5 2020 03:23:39) ( NTS )
Copyright (c) 1997-2018 The PHP Group
Zend Engine v3.3.9, Copyright (c) 1998-2018 Zend Technologies
```

Each new branch of PHP introduces new features and removes out-of-date ones. Eventually a branch of PHP will cease to receive updates.

© Daniel Platt 2021
D. Platt, *Tweak Your Mac Terminal*, https://doi.org/10.1007/978-1-4842-6171-2_6

Basic Usage

This file shows different aspects of a PHP file. By default, PHP will output the contents of the file to the screen, until it encounters `<?php` to enable the PHP parser. As part of the previous chapter, we downloaded a ZIP file that contained many different files.

PHP Configuration

The `info.php` file is a PHP file that is designed to show you all the different settings available within PHP.

```
% cat ~/random-files-master/info.php
<?php

// PHP File to show information about PHP and your system

phpinfo();
```

By changing these values, you can control how PHP operates. For example, the `memory_limit` setting will cause PHP to terminate if it uses more memory than is specified. By default, the memory limit is set to 128MB, which is fine for simple scripts. However, if you have a script that builds a report, you might need more memory.

PHP Configuration on Cli

`phpinfo()` is a function in PHP that outputs all the settings. It's very handy for diagnosing problems, but also for making sure PHP doesn't have any startup errors. Now that we've seen the contents, let's run it. You can get PHP to parse this file by passing it in as an argument.

```
% php ~/random-files-master/info.php
```

```
phpinfo()
PHP Version => 7.3.11

System => Darwin MacBook-Pro.lan 19.6.0 Darwin Kernel Version
19.6.0: Sun Jul  5 00:43:10 PDT 2020; root:xnu-6153.141.1~9/
RELEASE_X86_64 x86_64
Build Date => Jul  5 2020 03:22:53
```

There is a lot of information in the phpinfo file, and when you are looking for a specific configuration variable, it makes sense to use grep to filter for what you are looking for.

PHP Configuration File

There is a PHP configuration file that controls all of these settings and it is named php.ini. Depending on how PHP has been set up, this file can be anywhere on your filesystem. Thankfully there is a line in the phpinfo that tells you where to look for this file.

```
Configuration File (php.ini) Path => /etc
```

If the file does not exist, then PHP is using default values for settings that are baked into it when it was originally compiled. In the past, these default settings needed to be modified before you could use PHP on a web server. The memory limit used to be only 8MB, which caused problems for all but the smallest of scripts.

It is also possible to change most of the settings in the php.ini file, inside of your PHP scripts, with the PHP function ini_set(). Note that changing the settings in this way is only temporary.

PHP Configuration in a Browser

Some installations of PHP use a different `php.ini` file for the browser version of PHP. Currently, Brew uses the same `php.ini` file for the command line and the browser. It is worth doubling-checking this, because if you try to change settings in the wrong version, you will invariably become frustrated.

PHP Web Server

PHP has a built-in web server. It should only be used for testing and never be used in production. Let's start PHP's built-in web server.

```
% cd ~/random-files-master
% php -S 127.0.0.1:8000
PHP 7.3.11 Development Server started at Thu Jul 23 23:59:35
2020
Listening on http://127.0.0.1:8000
Document root is /Users/danielplatt/random-files-master
Press Ctrl-C to quit.
```

You can see from this output which folder PHP is looking in for files, by looking at the line that starts `Document root`. This should be set to your current directory.

```
Document root is /Users/danielplatt/random-files-master
```

If you visit `http://127.0.0.1:8000/` from your web browser, you'll see that PHP doesn't have a file to give you, as shown in Figure 6-1.

Figure 6-1. *Opening* `http://127.0.0.1:8000` *in Safari*

Note   If you want PHP to serve a file for `http://127.0.0.1:8000/`, you can create a default file called `index.php`. Try the `info.php` file that you created earlier, by going to `http://127.0.0.1:8000/info.php`, as shown in Figure 6-2.

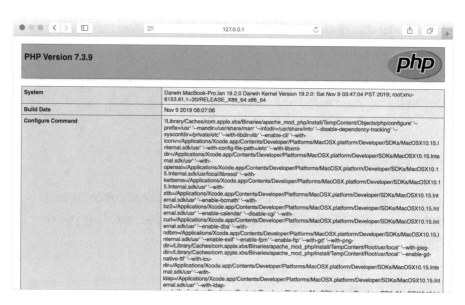

Figure 6-2. *PHP info when viewed in a web browser*

You should find this format easier to read than the same information on the command line. Look back at your Terminal, where you started the PHP web server. Every request to the PHP server has been logged for you to see.

```
Listening on http://127.0.0.1:8000
Document root is /Users/danielplatt/random-files-master
Press Ctrl-C to quit.
php -S 127.0.0.1:8000
[Sun Jan 19 13:29:51 2020] 127.0.0.1:50302 [404]: / - No such
file or directory
[Sun Jan 19 13:29:51 2020] 127.0.0.1:50303 [404]: /favicon.
ico - No such file or directory
[Sun Jan 19 13:29:55 2020] 127.0.0.1:50304 [404]: / - No such
file or directory
[Sun Jan 19 13:29:56 2020] 127.0.0.1:50307 [404]: /favicon.
ico - No such file or directory
[Sun Jan 19 13:29:58 2020] 127.0.0.1:50310 [200]: /info.php
[Sun Jan 19 13:29:58 2020] 127.0.0.1:50311 [404]: /favicon.
ico - No such file or directory
```

Being able to see the requests to the web server greatly helps when trying to create your own applications with PHP.

PHP Basics

In this section, we are going to look at some of the core concepts and structures in PHP. These will be enough to get started building your own scripts.

Language

PHP has a lot of the same core concepts that we've seen with shell scripting, but you will quickly find out that the structure or syntax is quite different.

We are going to go through a lot of the common concepts to help you get started, but we will only be scratching the surface of what you will be able to do.

Comments

When you start writing a script, you will not know how everything is going to work. It's beneficial to write pseudocode to help you figure out what will go where and how it will flow. You use comment markers to tell PHP to ignore whatever has been commented out.

Comments are typically used to describe a piece of code, without someone having to read the code fully. It may also be that the code block is quite complex and would require some time to fully understand it. A comment can be a single line of text that describes the function or the reason for doing the next few lines of code. A bad comment is one that isn't updated when the code is and therefore becomes misleading. Comments come in two different forms—single-line and multiple-line comments.

Single-Line Comments

Single-line comments use either the hash (#) symbol or two backslashes (//), as shown in Listing 6-1.

Listing 6-1. Example of Single-Line Comments

```
<?php
// This is a comment
# And this is another comment.
```

The single-line comments can occur anywhere on a line, and even after a piece of code:

```php
<?php
echo "Hello"; # Output greeting
```

Multi-Line Comments

Multi-line comments, like single-line comments, have a start symbol, but they also have an end symbol. They begin with a forward slash and an asterisk (/*) and end with an asterisk and a forward slash (*/). Everything between the /* and */ is ignored by PHP:

```php
<?php
/*
  This is a multi-line comment.
  PHP ignores everything on these lines.
  Since they are surrounded by the comment symbols.
*/
```

Constants

By default, all variables are changeable. However, a *constant* is a special variable that cannot be changed. Constants are named using all capital letters. A constant is defined by using the define function:

```php
define("MY_CONSTANT", 123);
```

Then you can access this constant using MY_CONSTANT or using constant('MY_CONSTANT'):

```php
echo MY_CONSTANT;
echo constant('MY_CONSTANT');
```

What Can You Store in a Constant?

You can store any simple (scalar) value, such as a string, int, float, and Boolean. You can also use the array.

Can You Change Constants?

Constants can never be changed once they have been created.

```
define("MY_CONSTANT", 123);
MY_CONSTANT = 1;
```

If you ran that code, you would get an error.

```
Parse error: syntax error, unexpected '='
```

Why Use Constants?

Constants are used typically for settings in PHP programs. They are really good at this, because you cannot accidentally change their value.

Predefined Constants

There are a few predefined constants available in PHP. We will see a couple of these in action when exploring ints and floats. Another predefined constant that you should know about is PHP_EOL. This constant contains a string for a newline for your current system and can be used in place of \n.

```
echo "Example" . PHP_EOL;
```

There are a lot more constants available on the PHP website, at `https://www.php.net/manual/en/reserved.constants.php`.

Variables

Variables in PHP are similar to shell variables. The difference is that PHP variables can store different types of values. When referencing a variable, you use the dollar ($) symbol in front of the name, regardless of whether you are reading or setting the value. The different types of variables that we cover are:

- Strings
- Integers
- Floats
- Arrays
- Objects
- Nulls

Let's explore them in more detail.

String Variables

A string is just a series of characters, enclosed in quotes.

```
$a = '1 string';
```

It doesn't matter if the string contains letters, numbers, or symbols. You can use the single quote (') or the double quote (") symbols to define a string. Whichever symbol you use, you must start and end a string with the same type, and include it within the string without first escaping it with backslash.

```
$a = 'PHP ';
```

Combining strings, called *concatenating*, is easy to do using the dot (.) symbol.

```
echo "hello" . " " . "world";
hello world
```

There is also a shorthand method for combining strings. Consider adding an extra string to $a.

```
$a = 'hello';
$a = $a . ' world';
```

We can condense that into one operation with `.=` symbol.

```
$a = 'hello';
$a .= ' world';
```

One thing to note is that the double quote version of a string allows you to use more than the single quoted string. With the double quoted string, you can actually reference variables, like we did in shell programming.

Integer Variables

With the integer type (usually called an int), you can store any number, positive or negative.

```
$a = -5;
```

There is a limit to the size of the number that you can store in an int.

In PHP, there are a few constants that define PHP limits. For integers, there are PHP_INT_MIN and PHP_INT_MAX, which define the bounds (see Listing 6-2).

Listing 6-2. Display Lower and Upper Bounds for an Int

```
echo "The smallest int is " . PHP_INT_MIN . PHP_EOL;
echo "The largest int is " . PHP_INT_MAX . PHP_EOL;
```

```
% php int.php
The smallest int is -9223372036854775808
The largest int is 9223372036854775807
```

You can do basic math on these variables.

```
$a = (10 + 4) / 2;
echo $a; // The output will be 7
```

The result will be an int, unless the answer isn't a whole number. Then the result will be a float.

Binary Representation of an Integer

It is worth noting that PHP internally stores your integer as a binary. Binary is your computer's native way to process and store numbers. For example, an 8-bit number can store a number between 0 and 255, which is 256 different numbers. Table 6-1 shows you the different numbers that each size can store.

Table 6-1. *Number of States a Binary Number Can Store*

8-Bit	7-Bit	6-Bit	5-Bit	4-Bit	3-Bit	2-Bit	1-Bit
256	128	64	32	16	8	4	2

The maximum number of states a bits can store is calculated as 2 to the power of the number of bits (n) or 2^n. In mathematical terms, it is written as 2 ^ n. Therefore, the largest number that can be stored is (2 ^ n) - 1, because the numbers start counting at zero.

Apple has standardized its whole computer lineup on 64-bit processors. Let's look at a 64-bit number.

```
(2 ^ 64) -1
= 18446744073709551615
```

We can see this in action with the Calculator app in macOS Catalina. When you open the calculator, you need to change the view to Programmer, as shown in Figure 6-3.

Figure 6-3. *The view menu in Calculator*

Enter the value of 18446744073709551615 or press the one's complement (1's) when the calculator displays 0 and the calculator should look like Figure 6-4.

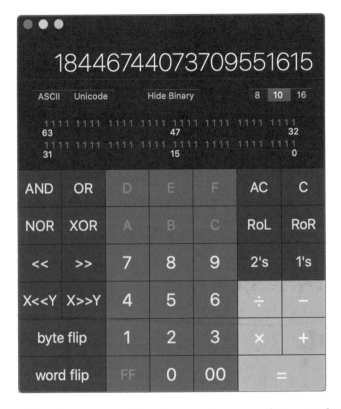

Figure 6-4. *The largest number that can be stored in a 64-bit number*

This is larger than the maximum number that PHP can store, which in my case is 9223372036854775807. There is a very good reason for this and it has to do with the smallest number that PHP can store.

When we talked about the largest 64-bit number, we knew that the smallest number was 0. We also know that the smallest number PHP can store is -9223372036854775808. The most significant bit stores whether an integer is positive or negative. We can see this in Figure 6-5, where the number is now the same as PHP's largest number.

Figure 6-5. *Largest number using 63 bits*

Calculating a Value in Binary

The simplest way to determine binary numbers is to lay out the numbers that each binary bit represents. When there is a 1, you add that to the total number, and you skip it when there is a 0. For example, the number 200 is shown in Table 6-2.

Table 6-2. *Binary Representation of the Number 200*

128	64	32	16	8	4	2	1
1	1	0	0	1	0	0	0

We see this in PHP by using `printf` to print the binary representation of the value we supply, as shown in Listing 6-3.

Listing 6-3. Displaying an Integer in Binary

```php
<?php

$value = 200;
printf("%d in binary is %b\n", $value, $value);
// 200 in binary is 11001000
```

Floating-Point Numbers

Floating-point numbers (usually called floats, but sometimes they are called a doubles) are similar to ints, but they also have a decimal fraction to them.

```php
$a = 0.1;
```

Floats have two constants—PHP_FLOAT_MIN and PHP_FLOAT_MAX—that define the bounds (see Listing 6-4).

Listing 6-4. Displaying Lower and Upper Bounds of a Float

```php
echo "The smallest positive float is " . PHP_FLOAT_MIN . PHP_EOL;
echo "The largest float is " . PHP_FLOAT_MAX . PHP_EOL;
```

```
% php float.php
The smallest positive float is 2.2250738585072E-308
The largest float is 1.7976931348623E+308
```

The PHP_FLOAT_MAX value can be converted from e-notation by multiplying by 10 to the power of the number.

```
1.7976931348623 * 10^308
```

Effectively, the decimal place will move 308 digits to the right. Suffice it to say, you can store some pretty large numbers in a float. As with integers, you can do basic math with floating-point numbers.

However, the result will always be a float. This happens, even if you think the answer should be an integer.

```
var_dump(0.5 + 0.5);
float(1)
```

Binary Representation of a Float

You would be forgiven in thinking that computers are perfect at storing floating-point numbers. However, this isn't always possible. Earlier we saw how computers stored binary numbers of integers.

Floats are split into the integer part of the number and the decimal fraction, but this is internally stored, so you don't need to worry about that. The split is determined by the precision and is currently set to 14 digits in PHP. The precision value is controlled by your php.ini file.

```
% php --info | grep precision
precision => 14 => 14
```

A 64-bit float uses 48 bits to store the integer and 16 bits to store the float. When PHP stores the decimal fraction of the number, the binary represents a fraction of 1, as shown in Table 6-3.

Table 6-3. *Storing a Decimal in Binary*

Bits	1-Bit	2-Bit	3-Bit	4-Bit	5-Bit	6-Bit	7 -it	8-Bit
Fraction	1/2	¼	1/8	1/16	1/32	1/64	1/128	1/256
Value	0.5	0.25	0.125	0.0625	0.03125	0.015625	0.0078125	0.00390625

It's easy for PHP to store decimal numbers like 0.25 and 0.5, as they are 01000000 and 10000000, respectively. A number like 0.03125 is still straightforward and requires five bits to successfully store it as 00100000. However, numbers like 0.1 and 0.2 are much more difficult to store.

In Listing 6-5, the set of instructions calculate the binary representation of a positive float. It works by multiplying the fraction by 2 and seeing if that result is greater than 2. If it is, that is a binary 1. It also subtracts 1 from the number. Otherwise it is a binary 0. It will keep looping to 8 bits.

Listing 6-5. Calculating the Binary Representation of a Float

```php
<?php
$num = 0.1;
$int = intval($num);
$fraction = $num - $int;

$binary = '';
$position = 1;

for ($i = 0; $i<8; $i++) {
  $fraction *= 2;

  if ($fraction >= 1) {
    $fraction -= 1;
    $binary .= '1';
  } else {
    $binary .= '0';
  }
}

printf("%f in binary is %08b.%s\n", $num, $int, $binary);
```

When we run Listing 6-5, we get the binary 00011001 from the output:

```
0.100000 in binary is 00000000.00011001
```

However, 00011001 works out to be 0.097656125, which isn't 0.1. Let's try the same Listing 6-5, but change the number of bits from 8 to 16. This time, the binary is 0001100110011001, which works out to be 0.0999908447265625:

```
0.100000 in binary is 00000000.0001100110011001
```

No matter how many bits we use, some decimal numbers cannot be stored correctly. This is something to be mindful of when you're comparing floating-point numbers.

Shorthand Operators for Integers and Floats

PHP allows you to use shorthand for arithmetic operations.

```
$b = 10;
```

Normally, if you wanted to change $b, you would have to include $b in the calculation.

```
$b = $b / 5;
```

Table 6-4 shows the mathematical operations that you can use.

Table 6-4. *Mathematical Operators*

Symbol	Operation
+	Addition
-	Subtraction
*	Multiplication
/	Division
%	Modulo
**	Raise to the power of

However, you can shorten is and remove the additional $b variable.

```php
$b /= 5;
```

Table 6-5 lists the shorthand operations.

Table 6-5. *Shorthand Mathematical Operators*

Symbol	Shorthand	Operation
+	+=	Addition
-	-=	Subtraction
*	*=	Multiplication
/	/=	Division
%	%=	Modulo

Array Variables

An array is a collection of elements. Each element represents a variable that can be of any type, including another array. There are two different types of array—*numeric arrays* and *associative arrays*. They both have their place and the difference between them is related to how you access the elements stored in the array.

Numeric Arrays

Numeric arrays are indexed using an integer. Unless specified, they will start at zero. The following two examples will produce the same array:

Example 1:

```php
$a = [1, 2.0, 3, "string"];
```

Example 2:

```php
$a = [
  0 => 1,
```

```
   1 => 2.0,
   2 => 3,
   3 => "string",
];
```

We can see what this looks like with var_dump:

```
var_dump($a);

array(4) {
  [0]=>
  int(1)
  [1]=>
  float(2)
  [2]=>
  int(3)
  [3]=>
  string(6) "string"
}
```

The best way to think about an array is like a row of boxes with a robot arm for a picker, as shown in Figure 6-6.

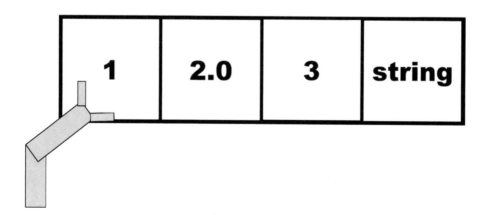

Figure 6-6. *Representation of an array using boxes*

How would you read the number 1 value from the array, in Figure 6-6? You have to tell the robot (PHP) how many boxes to move across to get the value you want. You start at the first box, so we don't have to move. So, we have to tell PHP to move 0 boxes across. In PHP, you do that using square brackets:

```
echo $a[0];
1
```

To get a different number, you just have to assign a new value, as shown in Listing 6-6.

Listing 6-6. An Element to a Numeric Array

```
$a[0] = 'New value'
echo $a[0];
New value
```

Adding a new value to the array is just as straightforward. We use the square brackets again, but without a value. This will cause PHP to append a value into the array:

```
$a[] = 'Additional value'
```

Let's use var_dump to see how our array now looks:

```
array(4) {
  [0]=>
  string(9) "New value"
  [1]=>
  float(2)
  [2]=>
  int(3)
  [3]=>
  string(6) "string"
```

```
   [4]=>
   string(16) "Additional value"
}
```

Removing elements from the array is as easy as unsetting them:

```
unset($a[4]);
```

Associative Arrays

Associative arrays are like numeric arrays, but the value you use to access them is different. The index is based on a string, rather than a number.

```
$a = [
  'key1' => 'carrot',
  'key2' => 'potato',
];
```

Adding and removing elements is the same as with numeric arrays:

```
$a['key'] = 'cherry';
unset($a['key']);
```

Booleans

A Boolean value is a simple true or false.

```
$a = false;
```

Not to be confused with 'false', which is the word false in a string. These values are used a lot in conditional statements and are the result of *comparison operators.* I will discuss this more in the section covering if statements.

Object Variables

Objects are an important part of PHP.

```php
$a = new stdClass();
```

There is a lot you can put into a class, but for the moment, know that you can store variables and code in them.

Null Variables

Null means no value and it is used to define a variable without a value.

```php
$a = null;
```

Type-Checking Variables

A variable isn't locked into a specific type; it can be changed by writing a value of a different type. How do you know what value is in a variable? There is a function called gettype(), which will return the type of a variable as a string.

```php
echo gettype($a);
```

The possible values that will be echoed are:

```
"string"
"integer"
"float"
"array"
"object"
"NULL"
"resource"
```

"resource closed"

"unknown type"

There are also built-in functions that can check that a variable is a particular type. A full list is shown in Table 6-6.

Table 6-6. *List of Built-In Type Checking Functions*

Variable Type	Built-in Function
string	is_string()
integer	is_int() or is_integer()
Float	is_float()
array	is_array()
boolean	is_bool()
object	is_object()
null	is_null()

You can use the functions with an if statement to handle different types of variables, as shown in Listing 6-7.

Listing 6-7. Checking if $a is a String

```
if (is_string($a)) {
    echo "\$a is a string";
} elseif (is_bool($a)) {
    echo "\$a is a boolean";
}
```

We will discuss the if statement in more detail later on in this chapter.

Superglobals

PHP has a few variables that are called *superglobals*. As superglobal is a variable that can be accessed anywhere in your project. Some superglobals are:

- $_SERVER
- $_GET
- $_POST
- $_REQUEST
- $_SESSION

These variables are associative arrays and, for the most part, should be treated as read-only, with the exception of $_SESSION.

$_SERVER

You've seen this variable before, when we were looking at phpinfo() in the Basic Usage section.

Note   These variables will change depending on whether you are accessing them within a Terminal PHP script or as a web request.

When accessed through a web browser, you will see the following variables about the server and the client:

$_SERVER['SERVER_NAME']	dev.example.org
$_SERVER['SERVER_PORT']	80
$_SERVER['SERVER_ADDR']	127.0.0.1
$_SERVER['REMOTE_PORT']	52394
$_SERVER['REMOTE_ADDR']	127.0.0.1
$_SERVER['SERVER_SOFTWARE']	nginx/1.17.8

Whereas, on Terminal, you have details about that environment.

```
$_SERVER['TERM_PROGRAM'] => Apple_Terminal
$_SERVER['SHELL'] => /bin/zsh
$_SERVER['TERM'] => xterm-256color
$_SERVER['TMPDIR'] => /var/folders/5z/tnwhfkg57hdfys5fxckr07_
h0000gn/T/
```

Out of all these superglobals, this is the only one that is populated on Terminal.

Command-Line Arguments

You might remember, back in the beginning of the chapter, we showed an example using phpinfo().

```
% php ~/random-files-master/info.php
```

```
phpinfo()
PHP Version => 7.3.9

System => Darwin MacBook-Pro.lan 19.2.0 Darwin Kernel Version
19.2.0: Sat Nov  9 03:47:04 PST 2019; root:xnu-6153.61.1~20/
RELEASE_X86_64 x86_64
```

If you look at the end of the output, you will see something similar to this.

```
$_SERVER['argv'] => Array
(
    [0] => /Users/danielplatt/random-files-master/info.php
)

$_SERVER['argc'] => 1
```

Note   These only show up when run from Terminal. You won't see argv or argc in the browser version of phpinfo.

These variables define how the command was started.

$_GET

This variable is made up of parameters from the URL used to access the PHP script. Given the following URL, http://127.0.0.1/info.php?a=1&b=2, you can expect the $_GET variable to look like this.

```
array(2) {
  ["a"]=>
  string(1) "1"
  ["b"]=>
  string(1) "2"
}
```

We can see this in action with the PHP web server:

```
% sudo /usr/bin/php -S 127.0.0.1:80
Password:
PHP 7.3.11 Development Server started at Thu Jul 30 10:23:18 2020
Listening on http://127.0.0.1:80
Document root is /Users/danielplatt/random-files-master
Press Ctrl-C to quit.
```

PHP Variables

Variable	
$_REQUEST['a']	1
$_REQUEST['b']	2
$_GET['a']	1
$_GET['b']	2

Everything from the question mark until the end of the URL or hash symbol is considered the query string. The bit before the equals sign is the key and after is the value. The ampersand is the separator.

You can even pass an array into the query string by using the square brackets. PHP will interpret them and append the next instance in the array. Given the URL `http://127.0.0.1/info.php?arr[]=1&arr[]=2`, the variable will show up as follows:

PHP Variables

Variable	

$_REQUEST['arr']	Array
	(
	    [0] => 1
	    [1] => 2
	)

$_GET['arr']	Array
	(
	    [0] => 1
	    [1] => 2
	)

$_POST

The $_POST variable is similar. However, the data can be sent differently from the browser. One way of sending this data is using a HTML form, with the post method.

$_REQUEST

The request variable is a combination of $_GET and $_POST. Where possible, use $_GET or $_POST directly.

Note   The order is defined in `phpinfo`, by the `request_order` directive.

$_SESSION

The session variable has the ability to persist between page reloads, given the right circumstances. It will be unique for every different user/browser that visits your page. Listing 6-8 is a very simple page counter to show the user/browser page loads.

Listing 6-8. Simple Page Counter for Each User/Browser

```php
<?php

session_start();
$i = 0;

if (isset($_SESSION['i'])) {
  $i = $_SESSION['i'];
}

$_SESSION['i'] = $i+1;
var_dump($_SESSION);
```

Every time you load the page, $_SESSION['i'] will increment by 1. However, if you were using Safari, and then you used Chrome, the count would reset back to 1.

Other Superglobals

There are other superglobals that help you do other things. You can find more information from the manual on php.net, at https://www.php.net/manual/en/language.variables.superglobals.php.

Functions

A function is a label you give to a block of PHP code, which you can call from anywhere. We've already used one function, called `var_dump`. The label is made up of the function name, `var_dump`, and the arguments within the brackets. This function outputs the type of value in the variable and the value.

```
var_dump(1.0);
float(1)
```

We can also create our own functions. Let's try to re-create the `var_dump` function. To start a function, we need to use the `function` keyword, then provide the label and arguments. After this, we need to surround the code with curly braces { }.

```
function var_dump($variable) {
  # code
}
```

We just need the code now. You have seen all the required components.

```
function var_dump($variable) {
  echo gettype($var) . "(" . $var . ")" . PHP_EOL;
}
```

If we try to run this in PHP, we will get an error.

```
Fatal error: Cannot redeclare var_dump()
```

This error is because we are trying to create a function with the same name as an existing function. We need to give the function a unique name.

```
function my_var_dump($variable) {
  echo gettype($var) . "(" . $var . ")" . PHP_EOL;
}
```

Listing 6-9 shows how this function compares to the PHP version. I will put the output in a comment after the function.

Listing 6-9. Full Example my_var_dump

```php
<?php
function my_var_dump($variable) {
  echo gettype($variable) . "(" . $variable . ")" . PHP_EOL;
}

var_dump("string");
# string(6) "string"
my_var_dump("string");
# string(string)

var_dump(1.0);
# float(1)
my_var_dump(1.0);
# double(1)

var_dump(42);
# int(42)
my_var_dump(42);
# integer(42)
```

As you can see, the output is similar, but not exactly the same. What happens if you want to do something in a function and then return the result?

```php
$answer = addTwo(4);
# $answer = 6
```

You have seen all the components required to create a function that returns a value, except one. The last component you need is the ability to return a value from within a function, which is the return statement.

Let's create that function now.

```php
function addTwo($int) {
  return $int + 2;
}
```

The thing to note about the return statement is that no instructions that happen after the return will be run.

```php
function addTwo($int) {
  return $int + 2;
  echo "This will never been seen";
}
```

If Statements

So far, you've seen PHP programs that start at the top and run through, line after line, until they finish, with no opportunity to skip any lines. An if statement is used to change the flow of the program, in order to execute different code depending on an expression. It's like coming to a fork in the road.

You can go left or right, but you need something to help you decide which way to go. Maybe it's a sign telling you which way to go, or maybe it's a flip of a coin. PHP is similar. The *something* that I spoke of is a Boolean expression, something that works out to be true or false.

```php
if (<expression>) {
  # if expression is true
  echo 'Go Left' . PHP_EOL;
} else {
  # if expression is false
  echo 'Go Right' . PHP_EOL;
}
```

You may be aware that the else in the if statement is optional.

```
if (<expression>) {
  # if expression is true
  echo 'Go Left' . PHP_EOL;
}
```

It is also possible to include more than one expression check. You can include additional if checks with the elseif keyword, as shown in Listing 6-10.

Listing 6-10. Example Using elseif

```
$a = rand (0, 1000 );

if ($a > 500) {
  echo "\$a is greater than 500.";
} elseif ($a > 250) {
  echo "\$a is greater than 250.";
} elseif ($a > 99) {
  echo "\$a is greater or equal to 100.";
} else {
  echo "\$a is less than to 100.";
}
```

It is possible to have as many or as few elseif checks as you want. However, you need to make sure that they are performed in the correct order. Imagine if the check for $a > 99 was first.

Boolean Expression

A Boolean expression is a logical statement that works out to a simple Boolean answer. The expression could be a simple, true or false. Some built-in functions return Boolean values. An example of a function that returns a Boolean is file_exists('/a/file/path'). It's based on a file existing or not.

```
if (file_exists('~/random-files-master')) {
  echo 'file or folder exists' . PHP_EOL;
} else {
  echo 'file or folder does not exist' . PHP_EOL;
}
```

We will cover a few more functions, but there are far too many to list them all here. You can find a complete list at `https://www.php.net/manual/en/funcref.php`.

Comparison Operators

Comparison operators are used to compare two values and produce a Boolean. The values could be literally strings or variables. It doesn't matter. If you wanted to see if a variable equaled a string, you could use the following:

```
if ($var1 === 'people') {
  echo 'Var1 is a string and equals.' . PHP_EOL;
}
```

Table 6-7 lists most of the comparison operators available in PHP.

Table 6-7. *Comparison Operators in PHP*

Type	Symbol	Notes
Equals	==	
Not Equal	!=	
Identical	===	Checks variable type
Not Identical	!==	Checks variable type
Greater than	>	
Greater than or equal	>=	
Less than	<	
Less than or equal	<=	

When you compare two values, PHP will convert both sides of the expression to the same type before performing the comparison.

Note It is best to use === and !== to check the comparison type, before checking if they are equal.

Does the Variable Exist?

Occasionally, you might not know if a variable has been set. This comes up a lot with superglobals. What happens if we try to use a superglobal that doesn't exist? The easiest way to find out is to try it. The following code is trying to access an associate by an element that doesn't exist.

```php
<?php
echo $_GET['a'];
```

When this runs, we get an undefined index, as shown here:

```
% php /tmp/test.php
PHP Notice: Undefined index: a in /private/tmp/test.php on line 2
```

How do you check that a particular query parameter has been set? You can wrap the variable in a function called isset(), to test if a variable exists, and isset will return either true or false. You can see this in Listing 6-11.

Listing 6-11. Using isset with an if Statement

```php
<?php

if (isset($_GET['a'])) {
  echo "The variable $_GET['a'] exists.";
} else {
  echo "The variable $_GET['a'] does not exist.";
}
```

Loops

In the real world, a loop is something that goes around something else. Like looping a rope around a post. In PHP, some loops have an end and others do not, but they always loop around a piece of code. The purpose of a loop in PHP is to keep running that code until they reach an end condition.

The end condition is a Boolean expression, just like with the if statements. There are a few different types of loops in PHP. We will discuss the four different types of loops next.

The for Loop

The for loop uses a variable for counting that you define as part of the loop. The loop has three parts to it. It declares the start value for the variable ($i), then the Boolean expression ($i<4) allows the for loop to run. While the expression is evaluated as true, the loop will keep running.

Third is the increment ($i++), which moves your variable closer to the end condition. Here's an example of a for loop that produces the output 0 - 3, followed by a newline:

```php
for ($i=0; $i<4; $i++) {
  echo $i . PHP_EOL;
}
```

Note   The variable can be called anything you like.

The increment can also reduce the variable; you could make the for loop count down to 1 from 4, with $i--.

```php
for ($i=4; $i>0; $i--) {
  echo $i . PHP_EOL;
}
```

Or you could change the step from 1 to 2.

```php
for ($i=0; $i<10; $i+=2) {
  echo $i . PHP_EOL;
}
```

Another way the for loop can be used is to step through a numeric array.

```php
$arr = ['a', 'b', 'c'];
$count = count($arr);

for ($i=0; $i<$count; $i++) {
  echo $arr[$i] . PHP_EOL;
}
```

This will print every element in the array. However, this will work only with numeric arrays that are in sequence.

The while Loop

The while loop typically works the same way as a for loop and can be easily used like one.

```php
$i = 0;

while ($i<4) {
  echo $i . PHP_EOL;
  $i++;
}
```

However, the real power of the while loop is that it keeps doing an action until it results in the action you require. For example, you can use a while loop to read the contents of a file until the end of the file is reached, as shown in Listing 6-12.

Listing 6-12. PHP Script to Read and Echo the Contents of a File

```php
$filePointer = fopen('random-files-master/spook.txt', 'r');

if (!$filePointer) {
  die('Could not open file' . PHP_EOL);
}

while ($line = fgets($filePointer)) {
  echo $line;
}

fclose($filePointer);
```

In a while loop, it is possible that the expression is never evaluated as true, and the loop will never have been run. In effect, the loop will be skipped over.

The do while Loop

The do while loop is very similar to the while loop. However, the difference is that the expression is evaluated at the end of the loop. This means that the loop will always happen at least once.

```php
$i = 0;

do {
  echo $i . PHP_EOL;
  $i++;
} while ($i < 4);
```

The foreach Loop

With the for loop, we can use the variable to loop through an array.

```php
$arr = ['a', 'b', 'c'];
$count = count($arr);

for ($i=0; $i<$count; $i++) {
  echo $arr[$i] . PHP_EOL;
}
```

The downside with this is you have to count the elements first. You also need to provide a numeric array. If any of the numbers are missing from the sequence, you will have errors. There are ways around this, using a method called array_keys(); however, you can also use the foreach loop.

```php
foreach ($arr as $value) {
  echo $value . PHP_EOL;
}
```

The foreach loop doesn't care which type of array is iterated. It doesn't care if there are numbers missing from the sequence. If you want to know what position a value is in the array, you can tweak the foreach syntax to give you that variable as well.

```php
foreach ($arr as $index => $value) {
  echo $value . PHP_EOL;
}
```

Exiting a Loop Early

If you want to break out of a loop before the end condition, you can use the break keyword.

```php
$count = 0;

while (true) {
  echo $count . PHP_EOL;
  $count++;

  if (rand(0, 10) === 0) {
    break;
  }
}
```

This example will keep printing numbers in ascending order until rand() returns 0. Another keyword to alter the loops is continue, which will skip to the next iteration of the loop. The example here will only output odd numbers. It skips the even numbers by using the modulo symbol (%) and continue, when $i is even.

```php
for ($i=0; $i<10; $i++) {
  if ($i % 2 === 0) {
    continue;
  }

  echo $i . PHP_EOL;
}
```

Both break and continue will alter any of these loops.

Improved my_var_dump

In our attempt to make a function that worked like var_dump, we didn't test it with an array. If we had, we would have noticed that it didn't work as expected. Assume this is the output variable we want to dump.

```php
$arr = [
    1,
    2,
```

```
    '',
    [],
];
```

var_dump would show the third element as an empty array.

```
var_dump($arr);
/*
array(4) {
  [0]=>int(1)
  [1]=>int(2)
  [2]=>string(0) ""
  [3]=>array(0) {}
}
*/
```

However, our my_var_dump function lists the third element as Array.

```
my_var_dump($arr);
# array(Array)
```

If you try to use an array as a string, PHP will treat it as a string ("Array"). We need to add more code to handle an array.

```
function my_var_dump($variable) {
  echo gettype($variable) . "(" . $variable . ")" . PHP_EOL;
}
```

If we use an if statement, we can check if the variable is an array with is_array(). We can then iterate over the array and call my_var_dump for the elements inside.

```
function my_var_dump($variable) {
  if (is_array($variable)) {
    echo "array(" . count($variable) . ") {" . PHP_EOL;
```

```php
    foreach ($variable as $key => $value) {
      echo "   [{$key}] => ";
      my_var_dump($value);
    }
    echo "}" . PHP_EOL;
  } else {
    echo gettype($variable) . "(" . $variable . ")" . PHP_EOL;
  }
}

array(4) {
  [0] => integer(1)
  [1] => integer(2)
  [2] => string()
  [3] => array(0) {
}
}
```

Although this still isn't perfect, it is good enough to show you many different concepts of programming in PHP, including recursion.

Dependencies

On macOS, Bash has a dependency manager that we installed. It's Brew. The dependency manager is great at helping you keep all the installed commands up to date.

When building websites in PHP, developers will need to add other people's code to their projects. These pieces of code are called libraries, components, plugins, or bundles. PHP has a dependency manager for it called *Composer*. Composer refers to these as dependencies as *packages*.

This is useful for anyone who needs to track their dependencies in their projects. This is especially important when more than one person can make changes to a project. Each new release of a package could have any combination of new features and bug fixes. Let's install Composer.

```
% brew install composer
```

Anything that you have installed will eventually go out of date. With software, it can happen quickly due to new features or fixes for recently discovered bugs. You define your project's dependencies in a file called composer.json.

Composer can also create this file for you with composer init in your project directory. These examples assume that your project directory is ~/php-project.

Note   The composer init command will ask you a series of questions. Each question will have square brackets, [ ], at the end which will be the defaults, when you press the Return key without typing anything.

Let's now run through a basic composer init example but skip all dependencies, which we will add later. You can see this example in Listing 6-13.

Listing 6-13. Example Output from composer init

```
% mkdir ~/php-project && cd ~/php-project
% composer init

Welcome to the Composer config generator
```

This command will guide you through creating your composer.json config.

Package name (<vendor>/<name>) [danielplatt/php-project]:
Description []: **my project**
Author [Daniel Platt <github@ofdan.co.uk>, n to skip]:
Minimum Stability []: **stable**
Package Type (e.g. library, project, metapackage, composer-plugin) []: **project**
License []:
Define your dependencies.

Would you like to define your dependencies (require) interactively [yes]? **no**
Would you like to define your dev dependencies (require-dev) interactively [yes]? **no**

```
{
    "name": "danielplatt/php-project",
    "authors": [
        {
            "name": "Daniel Platt",
            "email": "github@ofdan.co.uk"
        }
    ],
    "require": {}
}
```

Do you confirm generation [yes]?

The information that was entered matters only if you are sharing the project with anyone or are publishing it online.

Searching for Packages

In my PHP projects, I use a group of packages called Symfony. They are well maintained and used by many members of the PHP community. To find packages to install, you can use `composer search <term>`. I'm going to search for Symfony packages.

```
% composer search symfony
symfony/process Symfony Process Component
symfony/polyfill-mbstring Symfony polyfill for the Mbstring extension
symfony/http-foundation Symfony HttpFoundation Component
symfony/finder Symfony Finder Component
symfony/event-dispatcher Symfony EventDispatcher Component
```

You might prefer searching for packages using the companion website `https://packagist.org/`, which also provides the `readme` package and the usage statistics, as shown in Figure 6-7.

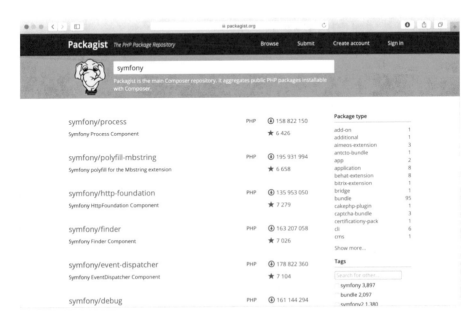

Figure 6-7. *Searching for symfony on packagist.org*

Updating Packages

Composer can update your dependencies whenever you run the update command and then saves them to a file called `composer.lock`.

```
% composer update
Loading composer repositories with package information
Updating dependencies (including require-dev)
Nothing to install or update
Generating autoload files
```

> **Note**   The only time the `composer.lock` file is updated is when you run `composer update` or `composer require`. We will cover `composer require` in the next section.

Installing Packages

Composer install will only install the specific dependencies from the `composer.lock` file. If this file doesn't exist, Composer will treat it as if you ran `composer update`.

The idea is, you can give the `composer.json` file to anyone and it will install the latest versions of all the dependencies. If you want the other person to install exactly the same dependencies as you have, you will need to provide them with the `composer.json` and `composer.lock` files.

Then they will be able to run Composer install from the project directory, which includes these Composer files. They can then run `composer install` to install all the required packages and their specific versions.

```
% composer install
Loading composer repositories with package information
Updating dependencies (including require-dev)
Nothing to install or update
Generating autoload files
```

Adding Packages

When I used `composer init`, I specifically skipped defining the dependencies. Normally, you would know what dependencies you wanted to add and would add them at that time.

However, you can use `composer require` to add them now and Composer will guide you through the process. It will add the dependencies to the `require` section of the `composer.json` file.

```
% composer require
Search for a package:
```

You then need to enter the name of the package your project requires.

I will use `symfony/finder`, which is a package that helps you find files on your filesystem.

```
% composer require
Search for a package:
Enter the version constraint to require (or leave blank to use
the latest version):
Using version ^5.1 for symfony/finder
```

Version Constraint

The version constraint is a way to express which version of a package you want to be installed. There are a few different ways to express the version constraint, depending on what you are trying to achieve.

It's worth noting that most version numbers are made of three parts, which define the differences between the different versions of a package.

```
Major . Minor . Revision
```

This is called *semantic versioning*. If package maintainers follow this definition, we should be free to install the latest revision of a package without it breaking anything. We should also be able to install any newer minor versions without issue, but occasionally some issues happen. The Symfony components have a backward-compatibility promise, which means the minor updates will not break applications. When a package moves its version to a major release, you know that they have made a break.

Exact Constraint

At the time of this writing, the current version of `symfony/finder` is 5.1.3. If you entered 5.1.3, or any other version number, you are using the exact constraint. With an exact constraint, Composer will never be able to upgrade that package to a newer release.

Wildcard Constraint

The wildcard constraint uses the asterisk symbol to tell Composer that we do mind what value that part of the constraint is. We can use the asterisk to replace the revision part, `5.1.*`, or the minor part, `5.*`, of the version constraint. It's entirely acceptable to replace the whole constraint with the wildcard symbol, if you always want to install the latest version of a package. It is worth noting that it is entirely possible to match an older version of a package with the wildcard constraint by mistake.

Caret Constraint

The caret constraint is similar to the wildcard constraint, but it solves the problem of accidentally allowing an older version of the package to be installable.

An example of the caret constraint is ^5.1.3. This will allow Composer to install any version that is 5.1.3 or greater, but not allow the next major release. That means ^5.1.3 will allow version up to, but not including, 6.0.0. With the caret constraint, you do not need to specify the revision part of the version. If it is omitted, it will be treated as 0. For example, ^5.1 will be treated as ^5.1.0.

Development Dependencies

The --dev argument allows you to add dependencies that your project needs for development, but that are not needed when the website goes live.

```
% composer require --dev
```

The process is exactly the same as before, but the dependencies are added to a require-dev section of the composer.json file.

After Dependencies Have Been Specified

When you have finished adding packages, just press Enter on the Searching for Package Prompt to end this process. Composer will write the composer.json and composer.lock files.

The other thing Composer will do is download the dependencies and store them in a directory called vendor, as shown here.

```
Search for a package:
./composer.json has been updated
Loading composer repositories with package information
Updating dependencies (including require-dev)
Package operations: 1 install, 0 updates, 0 removals
  - Installing symfony/finder (v5.1.3): Downloading (100%)
Writing lock file
Generating autoload files
```

> **Note**   Once you have a composer.json file, you should no longer use composer init, as it will overwrite your existing composer. json and composer.lock files.

Using Packages in PHP

Now that you have Composer set up for your project and have installed a dependency, you need a way to be able to use them. Using the dependencies inside a PHP file is as simple as requiring the autoload.php script that Composer sets up:

```php
<?php
require "vendor/autoload.php";
```

Web Browser Projects

Now it's a matter of understanding how the packages work and reading the package's readme file to take full advantage of them.

Project 6-1: Person API

We're going to create an API that returns data about a person. Normally, we would be getting this data from a database, but because we don't have a database, we are going to make it all up. We are going to fake it.

You Will Need

- Arrays
- The Faker library
- json_encode
- PHP web server

Faker is a PHP library that generates fake data for you. The data that it generates is helpful when you're building a database, because it allows you to populate it with semi-realistic data. Faker will generate fake phone numbers, addresses, and much more, but also allow you to specify different regions. Let's get the initial setup.

```
% mkdir ~/person-api
% cd ~/person-api
% composer require fzaninotto/faker
```

The script in Listing 6-14 can help you get started.

Listing 6-14. index.php Starting Script

```php
<?php

require "vendor/autoload.php";

$faker = Faker\Factory::create();

$gender = 'male';

if ($faker->boolean) {
  $gender = 'female';
}

$person = [
  'title' => $faker->title($gender),
];

echo json_encode($person);
```

When you are ready to test your code, you will need to fire up your web server. Hint: For more information on how to use Faker, look at the project documentation at https://github.com/fzaninotto/Faker.

Expected Output

I am using curl to see the output from the script, as we can format the response nicely, and this will work in Safari.

Note   127.0.0.1 is an IP address that you can use on your own computer but its content is not visible on another computer.

```
% curl -s http://127.0.0.1/ | jq
{
  "title": "Prof.",
  "firstName": "Jonas",
  "lastName": "Hauck",
  "address": "46290 Liza Rest\nEast Virginiaside, NE 83960-4858",
  "country": "United States Minor Outlying Islands"
  "jobTitle": "Speech-Language Pathologist",
  "emailAddress": "uadams@example.org",
  "phoneNumber": "+1 (383) 614-3188"
}
```

When you are ready to test your script, you will need to start the PHP web server from within your project.

```
% sudo php -S 127.0.0.1:80
PHP 7.3.11 Development Server started at Thu Jul 30 09:49:
47 2020
Listening on http://127.0.0.1:80
Document root is /Users/danielplatt/person-api
Press Ctrl-C to quit.
```

Suggested Answer

Notice in Listing 6-15 that the array keys I chose mostly match up with Faker.

Listing 6-15. index.php Suggested Answer

```php
<?php

require "vendor/autoload.php";

$faker = Faker\Factory::create();

$gender = 'male';

if ($faker->boolean) {
  $gender = 'female';
}

$person = [
  'title' => $faker->title($gender),
  'firstName' => $faker->firstName($gender),
  'lastName' => $faker->lastName,
  'address' => $faker->address,
  'country' => $faker->country,
  'jobTitle' => $faker->jobTitle,
  'emailAddress' => $faker->email,
  'phoneNumber' => $faker->phoneNumber,
];

echo json_encode($person);
```

Project 6-2: People API

We're going to extend our API that returned data about a person and return multiple people based on a query parameter.

You Will Need

- Person API

- A loop

- Array appending

- $_GET

Let's get the initial setup, which is shown in Listing 6-16.

```
% cp -r ~/person-api ~/people-api
```

Listing 6-16. index.php Starting Script

```php
<?php

require "vendor/autoload.php";

$faker = Faker\Factory::create();

$people = [];

echo json_encode($people);
```

When you are ready to test your script, you will need to start the PHP web server from within your project.

```
% sudo php -S 127.0.0.1:80
PHP 7.3.11 Development Server started at Thu Jul 30 09:49:47 2020
Listening on http://127.0.0.1:80
Document root is /Users/danielplatt/people-api
Press Ctrl-C to quit.
```

Expected Output

Here's the expected output:

```
% curl -s http://127.0.0.1/?count=2 | jq
[
  {
    "title": "Mrs.",
    "firstName": "Rhoda",
    "lastName": "Predovic",
    "address": "44811 Norma Trail Apt. 823\nTressashire, MD
    91023-6551",
    "country": "Guyana",
    "jobTitle": "Stock Broker",
    "emailAddress": "kelsi32@example.net",
    "phoneNumber": "276.932.3867 x43340"
  },
  {
    "title": "Ms.",
    "firstName": "Deborah",
    "lastName": "Durgan",
    "address": "476 Genoveva Hill\nBergnaumfurt, NV 73979-1649",
    "country": "Mali",
    "jobTitle": "Fence Erector",
    "emailAddress": "marshall.thompson@example.com",
    "phoneNumber": "385.294.9630 x5924"
  },
}
```

Once we return a list of people, we can also convert the JSON output into the CSV format.

```
% curl -s http://127.0.0.1/ | jq | in2csv --format csv
```

Suggested Answer

In my answer in Listing 6-17, I made the count parameter optional, by
checking it has been set and putting that value in $count and otherwise
defaulting $count to 10. I forced $_GET['count'] to be an int, to make
sure the script works as expected if someone entered something other
than a number. Then I use a loop to decrement the $count variable until it
reaches zero.

Listing 6-17. index.php Suggested Answer

```php
<?php

require "vendor/autoload.php";

$people = [];
$faker = Faker\Factory::create();

$count = 10;

if (isset($_GET['count']) && $_GET['count'] > 0) {
  $count = (int) $_GET['count'];
}

while ($count > 0) {
  $gender = 'male';

  if ($faker->boolean) {
    $gender = 'female';
  }

  $person = [
    'title' => $faker->title($gender),
    'firstName' => $faker->firstName($gender),
    'lastName' => $faker->lastName,
```

```
    'address' => $faker->address,
    'country' => $faker->country,
    'jobTitle' => $faker->jobTitle,
    'emailAddress' => $faker->safeEmail,
    'phoneNumber' => $faker->phoneNumber,
  ];

  $people[] = $person;
  $count--;
}
echo json_encode($people);
```

Command-Line Projects

The following two projects involve using the command line to perform various functions.

Project 6-3: Arguments

In this project, I want you to print out the arguments and a message if no arguments have been provided. This is the same project you did for shell programming.

You Will Need

- if
- $_SERVER['argv']
- $_SERVER['argc']
- A foreach loop

Expected Output

When no arguments have been provided, you need to output the usage instructions.

```
% php print-args.php
Usage: print-args.php message...
```

When arguments have been provided, I want to you iterate over them and print them out, along with their position.

```
% php print-args.php "hello" "world" 1 2 3
Arg 1: hello
Arg 2: world
Arg 3: 1
Arg 4: 2
Arg 5: 3
```

How would you solve this?

Suggested Answer

The first thing you need to do is check if $_SERVER['argc'] is less than 2 to print out the usage instructions (see Listing 6-18). The reason this is less than 2, rather than less than 1, is because the script name is counted as an argument. Once you know that there are arguments, you can use a foreach loop to iterate over them. Make sure you skip position zero, as that is the script filename.

Listing 6-18. print-args.php Suggested Answer

```php
<?php

if ($_SERVER['argc'] < 2) {
  echo "Usage: " . $_SERVER['argv'][0] . " message...\n";
  die;
}
```

```
foreach ($_SERVER['argv'] as $position => $message) {
  if ($position === 0) {
    continue;
  }
  echo "Arg $position: $message\n";
}
```

Project 6-4: Higher or Lower

In this project, we will create a simple program where you have to guess the random number the computer has picked between 1 and 10. The script will give you hints as to whether the answer is higher or lower, but limit you to five guesses. Let's create a file called `higher-or-lower.php`.

You Will Need

- `if`
- `while`
- `readline($prompt)`
- `rand($min, $max)`

We haven't used the `readline` function before, but it is straightforward. The `$prompt` that you pass to it is just a string that will be printed to the screen. Then `readline` will wait for the user to type something in and press the Return key to return whatever can be captured into a variable.

```
$guess = readline("Guess: ");
```

Expected Output

I'm expecting your script to start by outputting how many guesses are left. The script should then output whether each guess is lower than, higher than, or matches the answer. Finally, when all the guesses are used up, the script should end by outputting the answer.

```
% ./higher-or-lower.php
Higher or Lower
===============

Guess the number I am thinking of between 1 and 10.
You have 5 guesses.

Guess: 1
Higher!
Guess: 2
Higher!
Guess: 3
Higher!
Guess: 4
Higher!
Guess: 5
Higher!
Sorry, you didn't guess it correctly.
The answer was 6.
```

Suggested Answer

Listing 6-19 starts by generating a random number for the answer. There is a for loop with the number of guesses built into it. For every iteration, or guess, the loop will check to see if the answer is higher or lower than the random number. If the answer is guessed correctly, the script will exit. If the loop eventually exits, the script will print the answer and finish.

Listing 6-19. higher-or-lower.php Suggested Answer

```php
<?php

$guess = 0;
$randomNumber = rand(1, 10);

echo "Higher or Lower
===============

Guess the number I am thinking of between 1 and 10.
You have 5 guesses.
";

for ($i=0; $i<5; $i++) {
  $guess = (int) readline("Guess: ");

  if ($guess < $randomNumber) {
    echo "Higher!" . PHP_EOL;
  } elseif ($guess > $randomNumber) {
    echo "Lower!" . PHP_EOL;
  } elseif ($guess === $randomNumber) {
    echo "You guess correctly!" . PHP_EOL;
    exit;
  }
}

echo "Sorry, you didn't guess it correctly.
The answer was $randomNumber.
";
```

If you want to take this project further, try to make the limits changeable, just like you did in in the shell scripting project in Chapter 5 (Project 5-4: Higher or Lower with Changeable Limits).

Summary

In this chapter we looked at PHP, another scripting language that is available within Terminal. It's a popular general-purpose scripting language that is perfect for web development. To help illustrate its value, we reviewed a couple of web-based command-line projects. In the next chapter, we will explore how to keep track of changes in text files and scripts with version control.

CHAPTER 7

Version Control

Have you ever worked on a large document on your computer? When I was at university, I frequently had to write long documents. This was back when computers still had a 3 ½-inch floppy drive, which should give you some idea how long ago we're talking. I was forever worried that the computer would corrupt my document.

To get around this, I would duplicate the document before making changes. When I'd finished writing the document, I'd usually have 10 or 20 different versions of the file, with names like "Document Copy 11" or "Latest New Document."

This was the student version control of the time. Version control is very similar to my story. It keeps track of the changes in documents and allows you to go back and retrieve a previous version of a file. Version control can also store the contents of a whole directory of files. In this chapter, we'll look at version control today.

Version Control at a Glance

Each new version that is stored in a repository is called a *commit*. A commit will contain the file differences, as well as who committed them, when they happened, a description of the changes, and a reference to the parent commit, as shown in Figure 7-1.

© Daniel Platt 2021
D. Platt, *Tweak Your Mac Terminal*, https://doi.org/10.1007/978-1-4842-6171-2_7

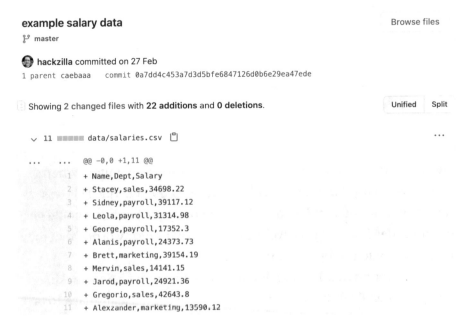

Figure 7-1. *An example of a git commit*

With all this information, git will then create an identifier for the commit, which can be referenced at a later date. This identifier is referred to as a *commit hash*. A group of files that are managed by version control are referred to as a *repository*.

You can browse the commits in a repository and revert any files to a previous commit. This is true even if you deleted the file, as long as it was previously committed. The version control system that I use on a daily basis is called *git*. There are other version control systems in use on the Internet at the moment and, according to Wikipedia, the most popular hosted version control system is Github.com, which uses git.

Version control has helped save the day for me many times. It's helped me answer questions like these:

- Who deleted that file?

- Who made this change ?

- What changes were made to this feature?

Version control also allows you to take the current project and create a *branch* of it. In this branch, you can make all the changes you wanted. Eventually, you might want to merge the changes back into the master branch. Version control can help you do that.

Getting Started

You've interacted with git already, because Brew uses git to keep track of all the updates. When Brew says it is updating, it is downloading information from a git repository.

All the applications and commands that we've been using will have originally been checked out by Brew, using the version control repository.

You might not have noticed, but when you downloaded the random-files directory from GitHub.com, you were actually downloading it from a git repository. To be fair, it was downloaded as a zip, but the files are hosted in a version control system. If you want to see the repository, you can access it from https://github.com/hackzilla/random-files.

There are a few terms that GitHub uses in the interface that are worth defining, and they are explained in Table 7-1.

Table 7-1. *GitHub Terms*

Commits	Individual code changes.
Issues	Bug reports and feature requests.
Pull requests	Commits that contain bug fixes or features. They have yet to be integrated into the master branch.
Releases	Packaged versions of the application.

407

Getting started using a website like GitHub is easy, but the point of this book is about doing things in Terminal to help you get a better understanding of how things work. It is worth knowing how to do it from Terminal as well.

Getting started is easy, as macOS includes the git client, so there is nothing to install.

Cloning Repositories

The good thing about git is it is really good at collaborating with others. Originally git was seen as a distributed version control system, which meant it was designed to collaborate with your friends and colleagues. Over time, companies created the hosted git repository model, where everyone sends and receives updates. They offer both *private* and *public* repositories, whereby private is where you want to limit access to certain people or organizations.

If you created a public repository, everyone will be able to read from it, but only select people will be able to write to it. My repository for `random-files` can be seen in Figure 7-2; it's is a public repository that is hosted on GitHub.

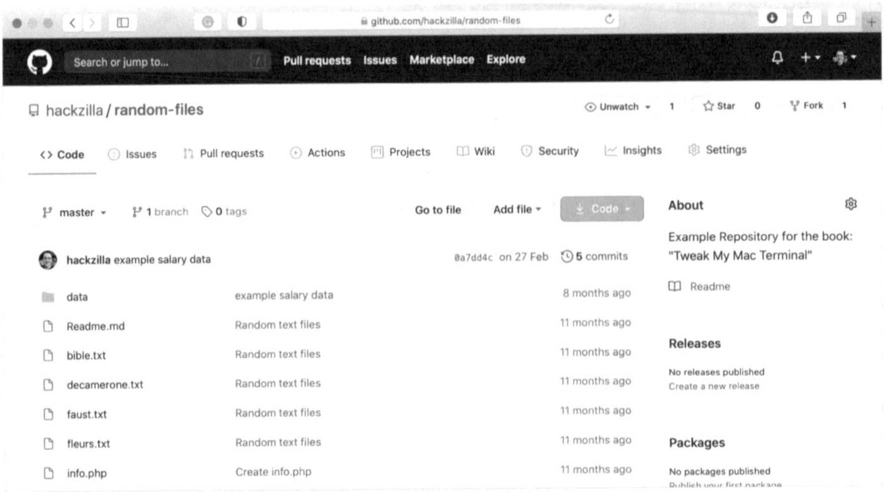

Figure 7-2. `https://github.com/hackzilla/random-files`

If you wanted to download this repo, you could use the Download ZIP option, which is effectively what you did at the beginning of Chapter 3. Or you could grab this URL from the Clone or Download option, as shown in Figure 7-3.

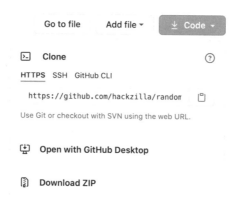

Figure 7-3. *The Clone or Download button on a GitHub repository*

With the URL from Figure 7-3, you can download the repository, which not only includes the files, but the history as well. The command I will be using is git clone.

```
% git clone https://github.com/hackzilla/random-files.git
Cloning into 'random-files'...
remote: Enumerating objects: 19, done.
remote: Counting objects: 100% (19/19), done.
remote: Compressing objects: 100% (19/19), done.
remote: Total 19 (delta 3), reused 11 (delta 0), pack-reused 0
Unpacking objects: 100% (19/19), 11.23 KiB | 1.02 MiB/s, done.
```

Git will create a folder with the same name as the repo, and you can see this in the output as Cloning into 'random-files'. This is now an exact copy of the repository. The URL you cloned will now be known as the *remote* repository.

Branches

All repositories have at least one branch, which is called *master*. The random-files repository only has this one branch, but we can create more.

Let's create a branch called my-branch.

```
% git checkout -b my-branch
Switched to a new branch 'my-branch'
```

The -b argument tells git checkout to create the new branch. You can switch freely between the branches using the git checkout command.

```
 % git checkout master
Switched to branch 'master'
Your branch is up to date with 'origin/master'.
```

When you see 'origin/master', this refers to the master branch of origin. Origin is just a label for the remote, which means that origin/master is the remote master branch.

The HEAD Branch

The HEAD is a special branch. It is a pointer to the commit that you are working with. You can think of the HEAD as your working directory in git.

Tags

Tags are labels that point to specific commits. Imagine you are working on a project where you release different versions. Without tags, you would have all your commits in the master, but no way to know which commit applied to which released version.

Tags allow you to specify which commit matches which release. They can be published for all to see. This is how the composer knows which version of the source code to download.

Updating the Repository

When you clone a repository, you are getting everything stored at that moment in time. When the owner of the repository makes additional commits, you will not automatically receive them.

The server that you get your repository from is called the *remote* in git. The git commands we run will need to be run when we are inside of the repository.

```
% cd random-files
```

Fetch

The git fetch command will check the remote server and compare the log with what it has stored locally. If there are no changes, then git fetch will exit without displaying anything.

```
% git fetch
```

Let's check a repository that I haven't updated in a while and you will see the difference.

```
% git fetch
remote: Enumerating objects: 413, done.
remote: Counting objects: 100% (413/413), done.
remote: Compressing objects: 100% (66/66), done.
remote: Total 3118 (delta 355), reused 381 (delta 346), pack-
reused 2705
Receiving objects: 100% (3118/3118), 506.30 KiB | 1.95 MiB/s,
done.
Resolving deltas: 100% (1815/1815), completed with 34 local
objects.
From github.com:hackzilla/TicketBundle
```

```
   7d19a08..2c13f7f  master      -> origin/master
* [new branch]       3.x         -> origin/3.x
* [new tag]          3.3.0       -> 3.3.0
* [new tag]          3.3.1       -> 3.3.1
```

At this point, git is now aware of new changes, but will not have made any changes to the files on your drive, or updated you to the latest commit. The HEAD will remain pointing to the same commit, the one before the fetch.

Status

After you fetch and make git aware of the latest commits, you need to see what has changed. This is where git status comes in.

git status will tell you where you are in relation to the remote repository. When we look at my out-of-date TicketBundle repository, we see it is 525 commits behind.

```
% git status
On branch master
Your branch is behind 'origin/master' by 525 commits, and can
be fast-forwarded.
  (use "git pull" to update your local branch)

nothing to commit, working tree clean
```

However, when we look at the random-files repository, we see that I am up to date and there is nothing new.

```
% git status
On branch master
Your branch is up to date with 'origin/master'.

nothing to commit, working tree clean
```

In both cases, git status told me there was "nothing to commit." This is letting you know that there are no file differences between what is stored in git and on your local filesystem. This will depend on which commit your HEAD is pointing to.

If you have made changes to the contents of the random-files repository, then git status will tell you about them. I am going to create a new file and edit the Readme.md to illustrate new and modified files.

```
% touch new-file
% nano Readme.md
% git status
On branch master
Your branch is up to date with 'origin/master'.

Changes not staged for commit:
  (use "git add <file>..." to update what will be committed)
  (use "git restore <file>..." to discard changes in working
  directory)
    modified:   Readme.md

Untracked files:
  (use "git add <file>..." to include in what will be
committed)
    new-file

no changes added to commit (use "git add" and/or "git commit -a")
```

I will discuss what to do about changes later.

Pulling

You've seen how to make git aware of changes and how to see how many commits behind you are. What you need to do now is bring the latest changes into the repository. This is where git pull comes in.

When you use git pull, you can limit it to download a single branch or everything. There are reasons for wanting to do both.

You will likely want to download everything for repositories you own, but a public repository that has many thousands of commits on many different branches will likely be more than you need.

To pull in the changes from just a remote branch, which will update and set the HEAD to the most recent commit, use the following:

```
% git pull origin master
```

Alternatively, you can pull down everything by omitting the origin master. This will do everything that pulling a specific branch will do, but will also store all the changes in the other branches.

```
% git pull
```

Your First Repository

It's time to create your first repository, or *repo* for short. First, you need to create a folder that the git repo will live in; this is also where you will store all your files that you want to be versioned.

```
% mkdir "my life's work"
% cd "my life's work"
```

Now that you have the folder and you are inside, you can use git to convert this folder into a repo.

```
% git init
Initialized empty Git repository in /Users/danielplatt/my
life's work/.git/
```

Everything that makes this folder a git repo is in that .git folder. We can see if there are any commits, by using git log.

```
% git log
fatal: your current branch 'master' does not have any commits
yet
```

First, we need some files.

```
% touch "Great Essay" "First Symphony"
```

These are just empty files, but they will help to illustrate the point. We can use git status to check on the state of our git repository. status can help us identify which changes have not yet been committed to the repo.

```
% git status
On branch master

No commits yet

Untracked files:
  (use "git add <file>..." to include in what will be
committed)
    First Symphony
    Great Essay

nothing added to commit but untracked files present (use "git
add" to track)
```

We can see that git status knows about the two files that we created and is calling them *untracked files*. An untracked file is a file that has never been saved to this git repo.

When you start a commit, you load the changes into a staging area. Once you are happy with all the changes in the staging area, you tell git to commit them.

Adding Files to a Repository

Adding files to the staging area is straightforward.

```
% git add "Great Essay"
% git add "First Symphony"
```

You could have easily added everything by using a wildcard or by specifying the current directory with a dot.

```
% git add .
```

The git add command won't produce any output, but you can see what it has done by issuing another status.

```
 % git status
On branch master
Your branch is up to date with 'origin/master'.

Changes to be committed:
  (use "git restore --staged <file>..." to unstage)
    new file: Great Essay
    new file: First Symphony
```

Removing Files from a Repository

If you accidentally added a file that you didn't want to commit, you can remove it.

```
% git rm "First Symphony"
error: the following file has changes staged in the index:
    First Symphony
(use --cached to keep the file, or -f to force removal)
```

When you tell git to remove a file, it will want to know whether you want to just remove it from the staging environment, or completely from the filesystem. Use --cached to remove it from the staging environment, and -f to remove it from the filesystem.

```
% git rm --cached "First Symphony"
rm 'First Symphony'
```

We should have the file called "Great Essay" staged for committing and "First Symphony" should still exist and be untracked.

Let's run git status and check.

```
% git status
On branch master

No commits yet

Changes to be committed:
  (use "git rm --cached <file>..." to unstage)
    new file: Great Essay

Untracked files:
  (use "git add <file>..." to include in what will be
committed)
    First Symphony
```

Committing to a Repository

We can now commit this change to the repo. The simplest way to commit into git is using git commit with the -m option to specify a message for the log.

Note   If you just run git commit, you will be taken to the default editor, with the ability to leave a much longer commit message. If you haven't changed the $EDITOR variable, the default editor will be vi.

Let's make your first commit.

```
% git commit -m "My first commit"
[master (root-commit) 0d75b45] My first commit
 Committer: Daniel <daniel@MacBook-Pro.lan>
Your name and email address were configured automatically based
on your username and hostname. Please check that they are accurate.
You can suppress this message by setting them explicitly. Run the
following command and follow the instructions in your editor to edit
your configuration file:

    % git config --global --edit
```

After doing this, you may fix the identity used for this commit with the following:

```
    % git commit --amend --reset-author
```

```
1 file changed, 0 insertions(+), 0 deletions(-)
create mode 100644 Great Essay
```

Great, you have now saved your commit, but what about this message?

Your Identity

By default, git has no idea who you are and will guess what your name and email address are, based on your user and computer name.

```
 Committer: Daniel <daniel@MacBook-Pro.lan>
```

When we run the command to edit the git config, we will be launching the default text editor, which I changed to nano in Chapter 2. Remember that what you enter will be freely available for all to see.

```
% git config --global --edit
```

The contents of this file are shown in Figure 7-4.

Figure 7-4. *Editing the .gitconfig in nano*

You need to update .gitconfig with your name and email address as it will appear in the git logs. This is something that you need to do only once, as this information is saved in your user account inside ~/.gitconfig.

Amending a Commit

If you need to change your user details, you will want to amend the previous commit. This will bring up the text editor and allow you to change the previous commit message.

```
% git commit --amend --reset-author
[master 80f762e] My first commit
 1 file changed, 0 insertions(+), 0 deletions(-)
 create mode 100644 Great Essay
```

Repository Log

You should now be able to see this change reflected when you run git log.

```
% git log
commit 80f762ec1b04b41999ea68397abdf8f24ae8a5e8 (HEAD ->
master)
Author: Daniel Platt <github@ofdan.co.uk>
Date:    Fri Jan 31 21:42:56 2020 +0000

    My first commit
(END)
```

Note   When in the git log, you can use the Up and Down arrows keys to move around. When you are done, press *q* to quit.

Publishing Your Repository

Git repositories are a great way to keep track of changes in a directory full of files. They are even better when shared with others.

You could zip up the directory and give it to other people. However, there is a better way. It involves having a company host your git repo for you, so that you and others can share the same commits.

The top three companies that provide hosting for git repos are:

- GitHub (https://github.com)

- Bitbucket (https://bitbucket.org/)

- GitLab (https://about.gitlab.com/)

They all offer free public and private repos hosting.

Note   The restriction is how many people you can share private repos with.

I use GitHub in the following examples.

Signing Up

The first thing you will need to do is create an account with GitHub. You can see the signup form in Figure 7-5.

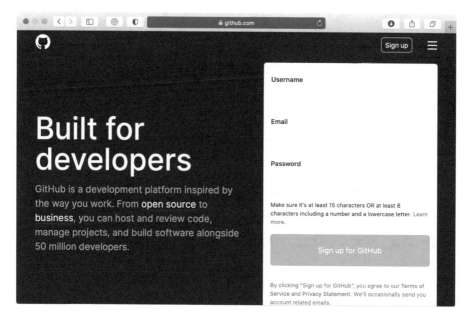

Figure 7-5. *GitHub signup form*

Once you have verified your email address, you will be able to proceed.

Creating a Repository

After you are verified, GitHub will show you a screen that allows you to create a repository. It will look like Figure 7-6 or Figure 7-7.

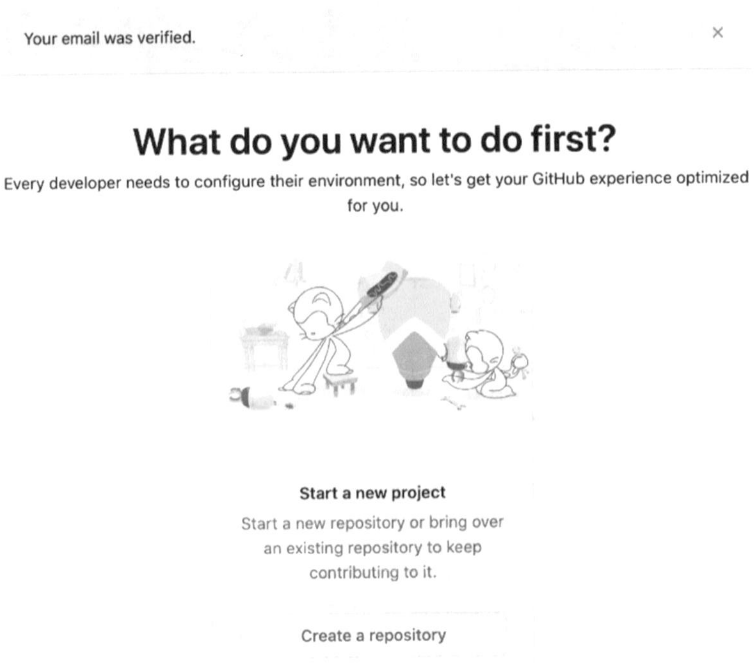

Figure 7-6. *First sign in to GitHub*

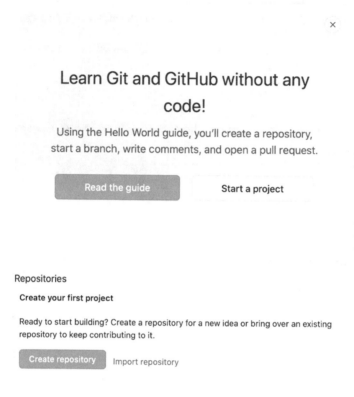

Figure 7-7. *Your account homepage*

Whichever screen you see, click Create Repository and you will be taken to a page that looks like Figure 7-8. This screen allows you to specify the name of the repository and the visibility. If you are unsure whether to make your repo public or private, choose private. When you are happy with your choices, click Create Repository.

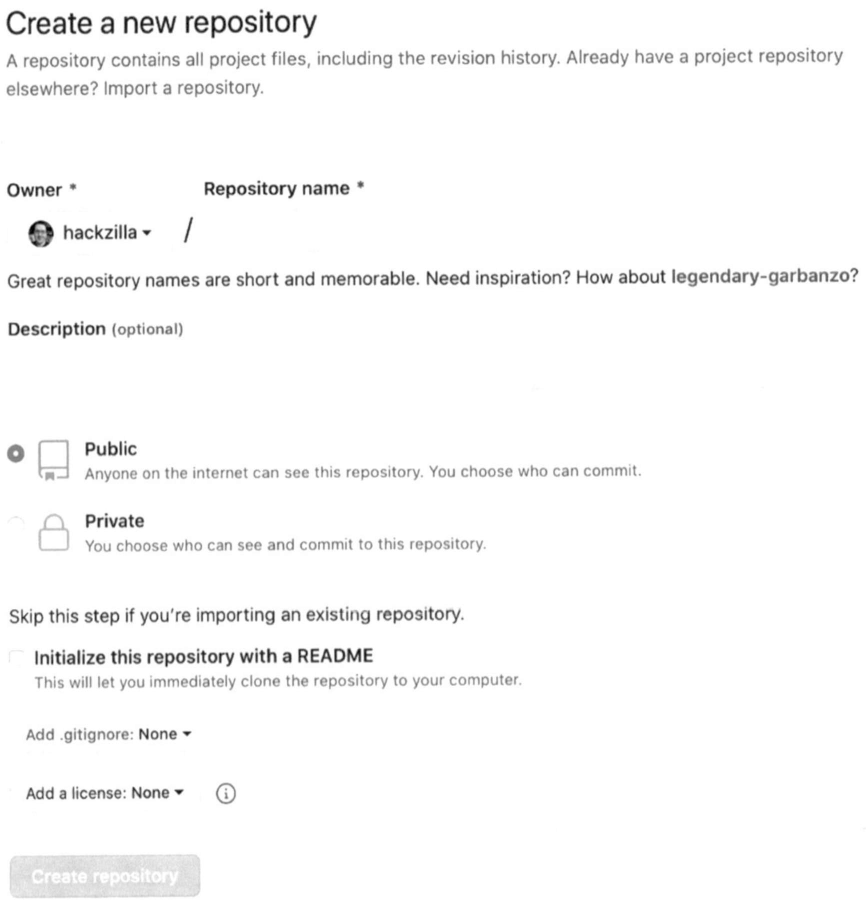

Create a new repository

A repository contains all project files, including the revision history. Already have a project repository elsewhere? Import a repository.

Owner *   Repository name *

🙂 hackzilla ▾   /

Great repository names are short and memorable. Need inspiration? How about legendary-garbanzo?

Description (optional)

⦿ 📖 **Public**
     Anyone on the internet can see this repository. You choose who can commit.

○ 🔒 **Private**
     You choose who can see and commit to this repository.

Skip this step if you're importing an existing repository.

☐ **Initialize this repository with a README**
     This will let you immediately clone the repository to your computer.

Add .gitignore: **None** ▾

Add a license: **None** ▾   ⓘ

[Create repository]

Figure 7-8. *Creating a new repository*

Authentication

Before you can use this hosted repository with your local repository, you need to be able to prove who you are.

There are two different ways to authenticate yourself and it depends on which version of the repository URL you choose. You can see the choice in Figure 7-9 where there is a selector between HTTPS and SSH. The SSH URL will start with git@ and the HTTPS URL will start with https://.

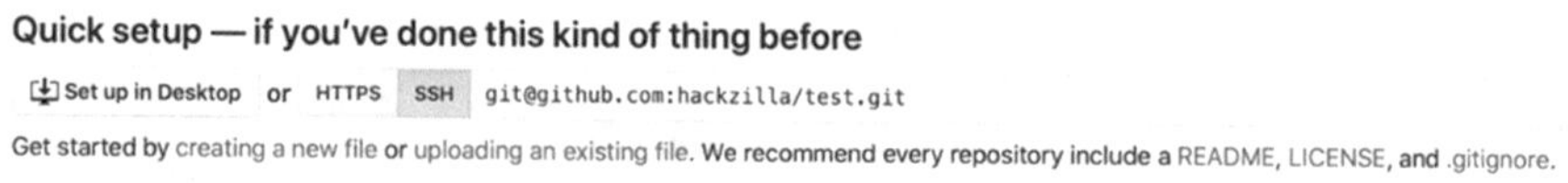

Quick setup — if you've done this kind of thing before

⬇ Set up in Desktop   or   HTTPS   SSH   git@github.com:hackzilla/test.git

Get started by creating a new file or uploading an existing file. We recommend every repository include a README, LICENSE, and .gitignore.

Figure 7-9. *New repository quick setup*

Personally, I always try to use the SSH URL when I can, but this isn't always possible, so I cover both. Whichever you choose to set up, and it is possible to set up both, you need to go into your GitHub account settings, as shown in Figure 7-10.

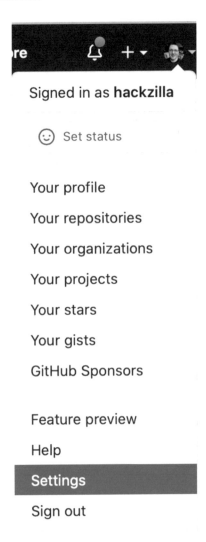

Figure 7-10. *The Settings menu for your account in GitHub*

SSH

When you are in your account settings, you will need to select SSH and GPG Keys. If you haven't used this before, you will find this section empty, as shown in Figure 7-11.

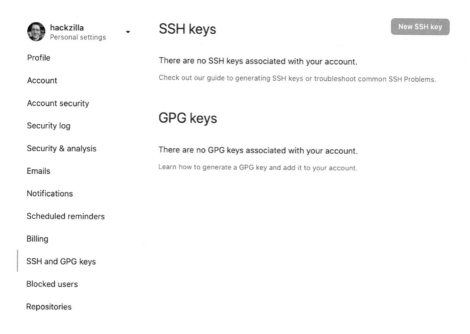

Figure 7-11. *SSH keys section in GitHub*

SSH keys

If you have never used SSH before, you will need to generate your own SSH key. It is always worth checking before you do, in case an application has done this on your behalf.

The files you are looking for are named id_rsa and id_rsa.pub. These files will live in ~/.ssh. If these files exist, you can skip the next part where we generate your SSH keys. Otherwise, you risk overwriting your existing ones.

```
% ls -lath ~/.ssh
total 8
-rw-r--r--   1 danielplatt  staff   405B 31 Jul 18:29 known_hosts
drwx------   3 danielplatt  staff    96B 31 Jul 18:29 .
drwxr-xr-x+ 16 danielplatt  staff   512B 31 Jul 18:28 ..
```

SSH keys are known as a key pair, because there is a private key and a public key. The idea is that you can encrypt a piece of information with the private key and only the public key can decrypt it. The reverse is also true—you can encrypt a piece of information with the public key and only be able to decrypt it with the private key.

You can freely give the public key to anyone and everyone, but you should never reveal your private key to anyone. This is the basis of how the remote connection, or SSH connection, works.

However, both the client and the server have their own key pairs.

Generating an SSH Key

As my account doesn't have any issue keys, I will be able to generate a pair for this account. Generating an SSH key is easy with ssh-keygen. If you want to keep your private key extra secure, you can provide ssh-keygen with a passphrase that must be provided every time you use it.

```
%  ssh-keygen
Generating public/private rsa key pair.
Enter file in which to save the key (/Users/danielplatt/.ssh/
id_rsa):
Enter passphrase (empty for no passphrase):
Enter same passphrase again:
Your identification has been saved in /Users/danielplatt/.ssh/
id_rsa.
Your public key has been saved in /Users/danielplatt/.ssh/
id_rsa.pub.
The key fingerprint is:
SHA256:JD14nC8bBjS6pX39/rgOHRwhzLPEFzjEm66a8S8ENOU danielplatt@
MacBook-Pro.lan
The key's randomart image is:
+---[RSA 3072]----+
|       o    BE.o. |
|      o = .  @... |
|     . = B  o B.  |
```

```
|    = =.+o +. . |
|   o . Sooo  o  |
|     o +.....  .|
|      o. .+ .   |
|      +oo o     |
|      o..o=o.   |
+----[SHA256]-----+
```

We now have an SSH key pair, which we can provide to GitHub to use for authentication. In SSH Keys, click New SSH Key, as was shown previously in Figure 7-11. I will paste the contents of id_rsa.pub into the key field, as shown in Figure 7-12. The title field is for your reference; if you don't provide anything, GitHub will use the label at the end of the key, in my case, it's danielplatt@MacBook-Pro.lan.

% **cat ~/.ssh/id_rsa.pub**
ssh-rsa AAAAB3NzaC1yc2EAAAADAQABAAABgQCutPTezzW/6tInOLiUapAIvKw
OvIlfh+Z+y7r5XVtruVsew5RjM= danielplatt@MacBook-Pro.lan

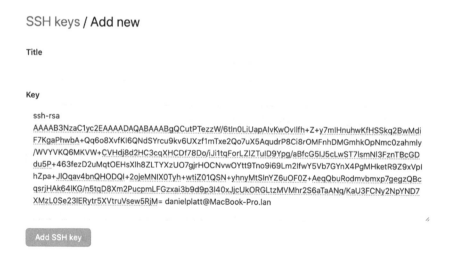

Figure 7-12. *Adding a new SSH key*

After you add the key, it will be displayed in SSH Keys, as shown in Figure 7-13. If you ever lose your private key, or someone else gets access to it, you should delete it from your GitHub account.

Figure 7-13. *My public key on GitHub*

That is all you need to do in order to authenticate with GitHub. The easiest way to test that everything is working correctly is to try to connect to GitHub using SSH.

```
% ssh git@github.com
Hi hackzilla! You've successfully authenticated, but GitHub
does not provide shell access.
Connection to github.com closed.
```

If you need to authenticate more than one computer or user, you can follow the same steps and add extra SSH keys.

HTTPS

The alternative authentication is to use HTTPS. The username and password can be the same as you use to log in to GitHub. However, I wouldn't recommend it, as git will save the details for subsequent login attempts.

```
% git clone https://github.com/hackzilla/secure.git
Cloning into 'secure'...
Username for 'https://github.com': hackzilla
Password for 'https://hackzilla@github.com':
```

You see, whatever you enter in the username and password will be stored somewhere on your computer in order for git to be able to use them the next time.

Personal Access Tokens

Alternatively to using your password, you can create a personal access token that can be used in its place. Like SSH keys, you create more than one. This is useful if you need to use your details on multiple computers or users or keep track of which tokens are still being used.

To create an access token, you need to head to your account settings, like you did in Figure 7-11, and choose Developer Settings from the menu.

When you are in the Developer Settings, select Personal Access Tokens from the menu, as shown in Figure 7-14.

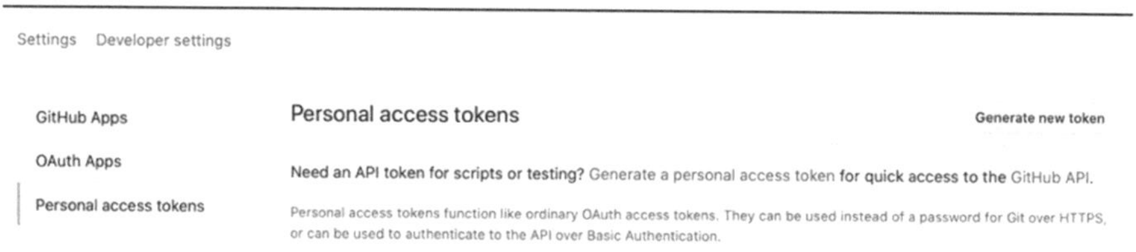

Figure 7-14. *Personal Access Tokens page in GitHub*

Now that you are in the Personal Access Tokens section, you can create a new token, as shown in Figure 7-15. There are many different permissions that you can assign to this token, but I have found that you only need to assign the repo permission for full control of private repos. It is worth giving the token a meaningful note, as this will be the only thing to remind you what this token is for. When you are done, click the Generate Token button.

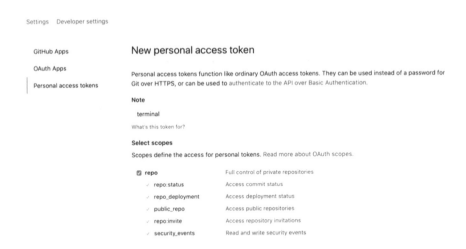

Figure 7-15. *Creating a new personal access token in GitHub*

After the page loads, you will be shown the screen in Figure 7-16. This is the only time that GitHub will show you the token, so you must copy down the token before you leave this page. If you do lose the token, you can delete and recreate it.

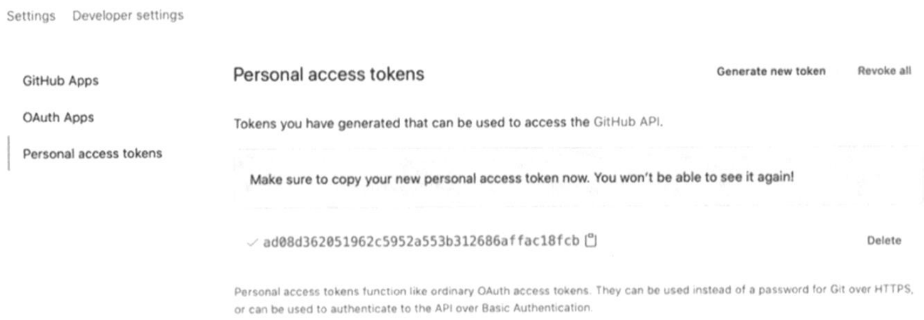

Settings   Developer settings

GitHub Apps	**Personal access tokens**
OAuth Apps	
Personal access tokens	

Generate new token   Revoke all

Tokens you have generated that can be used to access the GitHub API.

Make sure to copy your new personal access token now. You won't be able to see it again!

✓ ad08d362051962c5952a553b312686affac18fcb 🗐   Delete

Personal access tokens function like ordinary OAuth access tokens. They can be used instead of a password for Git over HTTPS, or can be used to authenticate to the API over Basic Authentication.

Figure 7-16. *The new personal access token in GitHub*

This token can be used in place of your GitHub password when authenticating with git on Terminal.

Removing Saved Details

If you find yourself accidentally deleting your token or changing your account password, GitHub will no longer authenticate correctly. You will need to remove your current login credentials.

git on macOS stores the login credentials inside keychain, as shown in Figure 7-17.

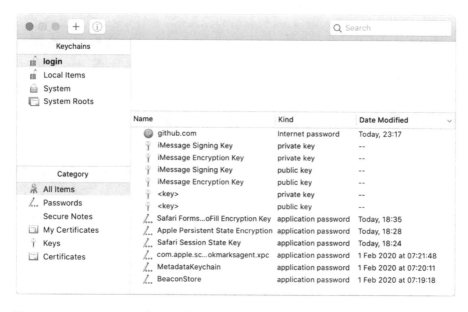

Figure 7-17. *Git credentials stored inside Keychain*

An alternative is to use git to remove these details for you. When you run this erase command, you will not be returned to the shell prompt. The command is waiting for you to tell it what to remove. You need to type in which host to remove and which protocol.

```
% git credential-osxkeychain erase
host=github.com
protocol=https
<RETURN>
```

There is no output to that command. However, the next time you try to clone a HTTPS repo, you will be prompted for login credentials.

Uploading to the Repository

When you created the repository, you were taken to a page that looks like Figure 7-18.

Figure 7-18. *A new repository in GitHub without any commits*

There are two sets of instructions. The first is to create a new repo, and the second is to upload an existing repo. As I have a repo I want to upload, I will follow the second set of instructions.

```
% git remote add origin git@github.com:hackzilla/work.git
% git push -u origin master
Enumerating objects: 3, done.
Counting objects: 100% (3/3), done.
Writing objects: 100% (3/3), 220 bytes | 220.00 KiB/s, done.
Total 3 (delta 0), reused 0 (delta 0)
```

```
To github.com:hackzilla/work.git
 * [new branch] master -> master
Branch 'master' set up to track remote branch 'master' from
'origin'.
```

The git remote command is linking GitHub and your repository and git push is telling git to upload it. The -u option tells git to track this remote branch. This tracking process tells you how many commits your branch is behind. Now that I have pushed once, I can shorten the command to just git push.

% **git push**
```
Everything up-to-date
```

When you check back on the GitHub repo, you will see your commit, as shown in Figure 7-19.

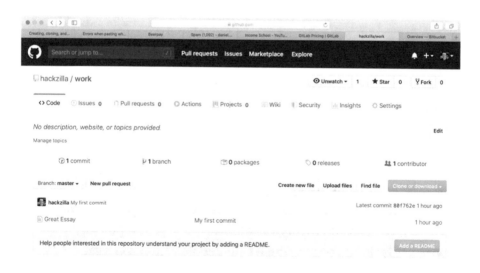

Figure 7-19. *The git repo with a single commit that I uploaded*

In this setup, you have read and write access to your repo, and everyone else only has read access, as I chose a public repository. If you want the repo to be private, you can change the preference in Settings. It's at the bottom of the options tab, as shown in Figure 7-20. GitHub will make certain you want to delete the repository by asking you to type the repo name and enter your password.

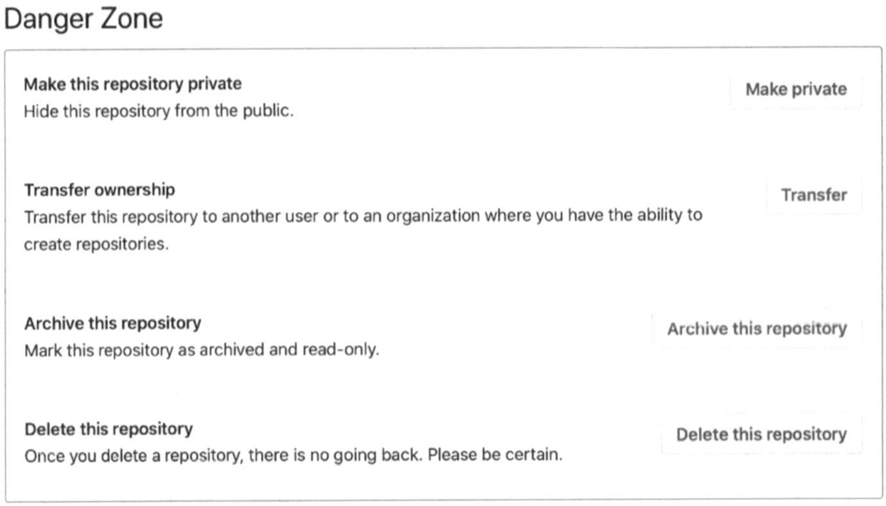

Figure 7-20. *The danger zone of a repository*

This setup is typical of an open source project. You wouldn't want just anybody changing your project without your permission, as this could lead to security and quality issues.

If you did want to give another user full control to commit to your repository, you can add them as a collaborator to your repository. However, this should only be done with people whom you trust completely. The section to add collaborators is shown in Figure 7-21.

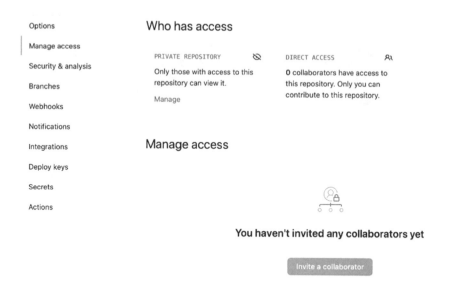

Figure 7-21. Inviting a user to collaborate on your repository

The way around allowing other people to commit to your repository is to vet their submits first. The way we do that is with pull requests, which we will cover in the "Forking the Repository" section.

Making Commits in GitHub

You can make changes directly to a repository inside of GitHub, but this will work only if you are the owner or a collaborator.

Creating/Uploading Files

I can make commits directly to the repository from within GitHub, by creating uploads or uploading files, as shown in Figure 7-22.

Figure 7-22. *The menu to upload or create a new file*

If you don't have a README.md file, GitHub will offer to create this file for you, as shown in Figure 7-23.

Figure 7-23. *GitHub offering to create a README file*

When you add a new file to GitHub, you will see the commit form, as shown in Figure 7-24.

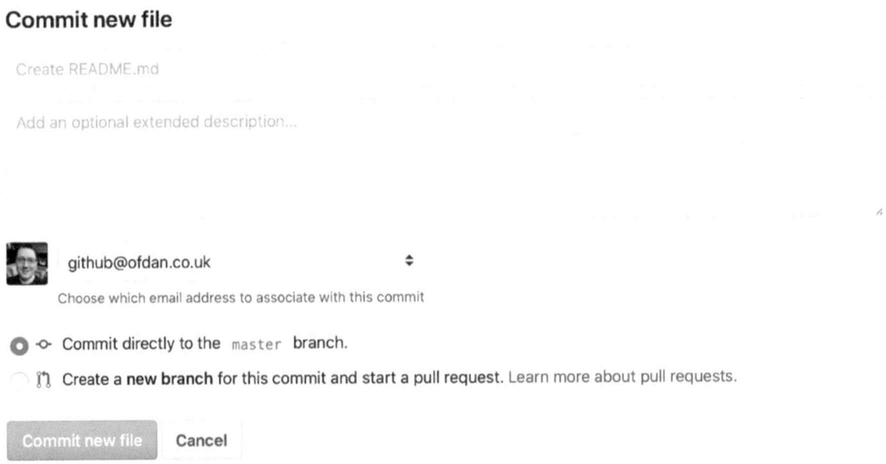

Commit new file

Create README.md

Add an optional extended description...

github@ofdan.co.uk

Choose which email address to associate with this commit

○ ⦿ Commit directly to the `master` branch.

○ ⭢ Create a **new branch** for this commit and start a pull request. Learn more about pull requests.

Commit new file   Cancel

Figure 7-24. *Creating a new commit in GitHub*

I'll stick with committing directly to the master branch for the moment and will cover pull requests later in this chapter. After I commit the new file, I see the new file, as shown in Figure 7-25.

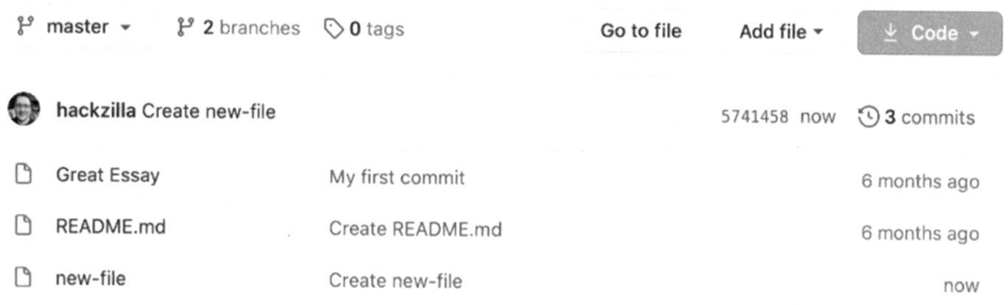

Figure 7-25. *My new commit in GitHub*

Editing Files

Editing files in git is similar to creating them. If you want to add content to new-file, you simply click on the filename, which takes you to the screen shown in Figure 7-26.

Figure 7-26. *Viewing a file in GitHub*

If you look closely at the image, you will see a pencil icon in the bottom left, as shown in Figure 7-27. When you click this edit button, you will be taken to a page that looks very similar to the Add File page.

Figure 7-27. *Close-up of the file editing and delete buttons*

Deleting Files

I can also delete files from my repository on GitHub, using the delete icon, which is shown in Figure 7-27. Delete works exactly the same as edit, whereby you need to commit the deletion.

Forking the Repository

Earlier in this chapter, in the section called "Cloning a Repository," I downloaded the random-files repository.

I would like you to do this, as it will be a good example of making a change to another person's repository.

```
% git clone https://github.com/hackzilla/random-files.git
```

I would like you to go into the random-files directory and make a commit to the repository.

```
% cd random-files
% touch my-change
% git add my-change
% git commit -m "Making a change to the repo"
```

When I do a git status, I can see that I have one commit that is ready to push.

```
% git status
On branch master
Your branch is ahead of 'origin/master' by 1 commit.
  (use "git push" to publish your local commits)

nothing to commit, working tree clean
```

However, using git push, you will find that you cannot push to my repository.

```
% git push
ERROR: Permission to hackzilla/random-files.git denied to
<another user>.
fatal: Could not read from remote repository.

Please make sure you have the correct access rights
and the repository exists.
```

This is because you are neither the owner nor a collaborator of the repo. The way around this is to *fork* the original repo, which is to take a complete copy of the original repo and push your changes to that. A repository can be copied by clicking the Fork button, as shown in Figure 7-28.

Figure 7-28. *Different buttons available for a repository*

Depending on the size of the repository, the forking could take a few minutes, but hopefully will only be a few seconds, as shown in Figure 7-29.

Forking hackzilla/random-files

It should only take a few seconds.

↻ Refresh

Figure 7-29. *Forking the random files repository*

Changing the Remote

I now have a new repo, but I still need to change the current repo to point to the forked repo. We could download it again, but that would take time and would lose any new commits. We need to change the origin of the repo to this new repo.

Grab the new URL from Clone or Download. I am going to use the ssh URL rather than the HTTPS URL.

```
git@github.com:ofdan/random-files.git
```

Manual Method

If you are comfortable editing configuration files, you can edit .git/ config directly, as shown in Figure 7-30.

```
% nano .git/config
```

Figure 7-30. *The .git/config file before making the change*

We need to change the line that says "url = ", in the Remote Origin section, as shown in Figure 7-31.

Figure 7-31. *The .git/config file after making the URL change*

It should read:

```
url = git@github.com:ofdan/random-files.git
```

Official Way

There is a more official way to make this change. That is to have git edit the config file for you.

```
% git remote remove origin
% git remote add origin git@github.com:ofdan/random-files.git
```

Now you can push your changes. At the next refresh, you'll see your new commit on GitHub.

Pull Requests

Imagine if you had made a fix to my original repo in your fork. How can you let me know about it? The best way is to create a *pull request*. The best place to make the change is in a new branch in your fork.

Wherever you made the change, when you go into GitHub, it will ask if you would like to create a pull request, as shown in Figure 7-32.

Figure 7-32. *GitHub asking if you would like to create a pull request*

When you create your pull request (PR), you are asked to confirm which branches and which repos to merge, as shown in Figure 7-33.

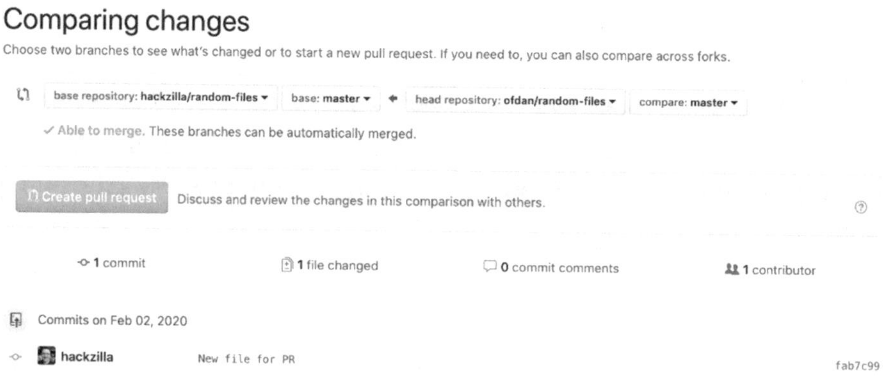

Comparing changes

Choose two branches to see what's changed or to start a new pull request. If you need to, you can also compare across forks.

base repository: **hackzilla/random-files ▼**   base: **master ▼**   ◆   head repository: **ofdan/random-files ▼**   compare: **master ▼**

✓ Able to merge. These branches can be automatically merged.

Create pull request   Discuss and review the changes in this comparison with others.   ⑦

◇ **1** commit   📄 **1** file changed   💬 **0** commit comments   👥 **1** contributor

Commits on Feb 02, 2020

◇ 🐢 hackzilla   New file for PR   fab7c99

Figure 7-33. *GitHub asking for confirmation of which branches and repos to merge*

When you are happy with your pull request, you create it. It will then show up for the owner of the other repo. The owner can then decide whether to accept your commits. This is a good way to offer your changes back to the original repo and the community.

Going Further with Git

I would love to cover everything there is in git. This chapter should be enough to help get you started. GitHub has some lovely documentation, and I recommend you read it, as it will be in more depth than I can provide here. See `https://docs.github.com/en/github/creating-cloning-and-archiving-repositories`.

I recommend you get a git application that allows you to visually see what your git repo looks like on your Mac. My recommendation is to use a GUI application, either Source Tree (free) or Git Tower (paid).

Also, check out the video called "Git For Ages 4 And Up," as it explains git in a lot more detail. You can find it at `https://www.youtube.com/watch?v=1ffBJ4sVUb4`.

Summary

In this chapter, we looked at version control and at git. You created your first repository and were able to upload it to GitHub. You also looked at how you can fork another repository and suggest commits using the pull request feature.

CHAPTER 8

Web Development

I use my Mac for web development all day long, and Terminal is one of many applications I use all the time.

In this chapter, I show you how you can use your Mac to run web apps. According to Wordpress.org, 35% of the web uses WordPress, which is a blogging platform that is written in PHP.

I will show you how to install WordPress and blog on your own computer. WordPress has a few requirements that you need to install before you can install it. You will need to install a proper web server, set up PHP, and install a database.

By installing a web app on your computer, you can perfect how your program works without any spending money on hosting before you are ready to go live. WordPress is no different. You can create content and change how it looks.

Installing a Web Server

A web server is an application that takes incoming requests and figures out what the response should be—whether that is returning a file, calling another process, or returning an error.

You've already had a taste of what a web server looks like with the built-in PHP web server. PHP's built-in web server is very limited in what it can do. There are many reasons that the PHP web server should never be used in production. It's mostly because it doesn't have a lot of the security features that full-fledged web servers have.

© Daniel Platt 2021
D. Platt, *Tweak Your Mac Terminal*, https://doi.org/10.1007/978-1-4842-6171-2_8

However, there is another reason. The PHP web server cannot handle more than one request at once. This might not seem like a big problem until you realize that popular websites can deal with hundreds or thousands of requests a second. I have managed to hit this limitation with only two web requests.

The top three web servers at the moment are Apache, Microsoft IIS, and nginx. According to netcraft.com, Apache and Microsoft seem to be losing market share, while nginx is growing. We will talk about nginx, because historically it has been the fastest web server, but more importantly, it is straightforward to set up on your Mac.

Installing nginx

Getting started with nginx is as simple as installing it.

```
% brew install nginx
==> Pouring nginx-1.17.8.catalina.bottle.tar.gz
==> Caveats
Docroot is: /usr/local/var/www

The default port has been set in /usr/local/etc/nginx/nginx.
conf to 8080 so that
nginx can run without sudo.

nginx will load all files in /usr/local/etc/nginx/servers/.
```

To have launchd start nginx now and restart at login, use this:

```
  brew services start nginx
```

Or, if you don't want/need a background service, you can just run the following:

```
  nginx
==> Summary
🍺  /usr/local/Cellar/nginx/1.17.8: 25 files, 2.1MB
```

We now have a new service called nginx.

```
% brew services list
Name     Status  User Plist
nginx    stopped
unbound  stopped
```

Starting nginx

Let's check out what has been set up by default. First, we need to start nginx.

```
% brew services start nginx
```

Then we need to open a browser to http://localhost:8080/, as shown in Figure 8-1.

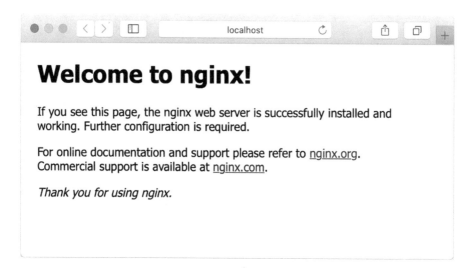

Figure 8-1. *The default nginx page*

Configuring nginx

By default, nginx has a single server set up to handle requests at localhost:8000. You can see the configuration in /usr/local/etc/nginx/nginx.conf. (Look for the section that starts with server.)

This can get complicated quickly, depending on what you want to do. So, let's keep it simple. We will leave nginx.conf as it is, because at the bottom of the file, we can see that it will pull config files from another source.

```
include servers/*;
```

This means that all we need to do is create our own file in just the right spot and it will be included when nginx.conf is processed. That location is /usr/local/etc/nginx/servers/.

For the moment, we will create a basic server config that serves the existing files from /usr/local/var/www. This means that the server will look the same as the page we just saw.

Multiple Sites That Differ by Port

The simplest option is to create a new nginx server that you access using http://localhost:8081/. We cannot listen on port 8080, as nginx is already listening on that port and no two processes can listen to the same port.

Let's create the following new server file and then enter the code from Listing 8-1 into it.

% nano /usr/local/etc/nginx/servers/localhost

Listing 8-1. /usr/local/etc/nginx/servers/localhost

```
server {
    listen 8081;
    server_name localhost;

    root /usr/local/var/www;
```

```
    location / {
        try_files $uri $uri/ =404;
    }
}
```

If you were creating multiple servers, you can create another file using a different port number. As the port we are listening on is greater than 1024, we don't need to use sudo to restart nginx.

```
% brew services restart nginx
Stopping `nginx`... (might take a while)
==> Successfully stopped `nginx` (label: homebrew.mxcl.nginx)
==> Successfully started `nginx` (label: homebrew.mxcl.nginx)
```

Now load http://localhost:8081/ in your browser to confirm that this works.

Default HTTP Port

I'm not a fan of using a non-standard port for a web server, because it can get confusing. When you type in an URL like http://www.google.com into your browser, your browser will try port 80.

We can modify this config and change the listen directive from 8081 to 80:

```
server {
    listen 80;
    server_name localhost;

    root /usr/local/var/www;

    location / {
        try_files $uri $uri/ =404;
    }
}
```

Now, we need to restart nginx. However, we can't just restart nginx as a user, and we can't use sudo. You will need to use your user to stop nginx and then use sudo to start nginx.

```
% brew services stop nginx
Stopping `nginx`... (might take a while)
==> Successfully stopped `nginx` (label: homebrew.mxcl.nginx)
```

```
% sudo brew services start nginx
Warning: Taking root:admin ownership of some nginx paths:
  /usr/local/Cellar/nginx/1.17.8/bin
  /usr/local/Cellar/nginx/1.17.8/bin/nginx
  /usr/local/opt/nginx
  /usr/local/opt/nginx/bin
This will require manual removal of these paths using `sudo rm` on
brew upgrade/reinstall/uninstall.
==> Successfully started `nginx` (label: homebrew.mxcl.nginx)
```

Note   In the future, you must use sudo for both start and stop.

You can now access this server on `http://localhost/`.

There's Another Way

Using port 80 is good, but it will allow you to create only one server. As I said earlier, no two processes can listen on the same port. However, nginx can assign multiple processes that listen on the same port. Instead of changing the port, we can change the server_name.

In the section on pretending a website is somewhere else, we created example.org. We now need a server name that we can use. I've picked dev.example.org.

First, we need to add this to our /etc/hosts file, so the browser knows where to direct our request. With this command, we can append dev.example.org to the end of /etc/hosts:

```
% echo "127.0.0.1 dev.example.org" | sudo tee -a /etc/hosts
```

Note   The tee command is used because sudo interferes with directly appending to the file.

Now we can use dev.example.org as server_name:

```
server {
    listen 80;
    server_name dev.example.org;

    root /usr/local/var/www;

    location / {
        try_files $uri $uri/ =404;
    }
}
```

Finally, we can restart nginx.

```
% sudo brew services restart nginx
```

This method is my favorite, because it gives you an unlimited number of development sites on your computer.

Using PHP

When we looked at PHP earlier, we used the built-in version 7.3. This time we will install PHP from Brew so we can control how PHP runs with Brew services.

Brew has a few different versions of PHP available to install. The older versions of PHP that Brew has are still supported. You can identify the older version by the @ symbol.

Let's search for just PHP, or PHP with the @ symbol.

```
% brew search "/^php($|@)/"
==> Formulae
php
php@7.2
php@7.3
```

If we search for just php@, the list that Brew returns will show php@7.4 instead of just php.

```
% brew search "/^php@/"
==> Formulae
php@7.2
php@7.3
php@7.4
```

Why would we want to install php, when we could install php@7.4? Well, the php command tracks the latest major version of PHP. When the next major release of PHP is released, you will be able to use Brew to upgrade to it.

```
% brew upgrade php
```

If you want to install programs to stay consistent, you only want to upgrade your version of PHP to the latest when you are ready to do so. The newer the version that is installed, the longer it will be supported.

You can install more than one version of PHP, but you shouldn't need to, unless you have a specific reason. However, only one can be active at any one time. I assume that will install PHP 7.4, as that will keep everything consistent as you follow along.

Let's install the PHP 7.4.

```
% brew install php@7.4
```

Now that we have PHP installed, we can see there is an option for it in Brew services.

```
% brew services list
Name    Status  User Plist
nginx   started root /Library/LaunchDaemons/homebrew.mxcl.
nginx.plist
php     stopped
unbound stopped
```

The configuration of PHP can be found in /usr/local/etc/php/. Inside this folder is a folder for every version of PHP installed with Brew. Although you won't need to edit these, there are lots of comments in the config files that explain what everything means.

What we do need to know is where PHP is listening for new instructions. We will need this for nginx and PHP to be able to communicate.

```
% grep "listen =" /usr/local/etc/php/7.4/php-fpm.d/www.conf
listen = 127.0.0.1:9000
```

Now we can make PHP listen for nginx commands.

```
% brew services start php
==> Successfully started `php` (label: homebrew.mxcl.php)
```

To allow nginx to run PHP files, we need to add some extra config to the nginx config.

```
location ~ .php$ {
    fastcgi_pass    127.0.0.1:9000;
    fastcgi_index   index.php;

    include fastcgi.conf;
}
```

The full configuration file is shown in Listing 8-2.

```
% nano /usr/local/etc/nginx/servers/localhost
```

Listing 8-2. */usr/local/etc/nginx/servers/localhost*

```
server {
    listen 80;
    server_name dev.example.org;

    root /usr/local/var/www;

    location / {
        try_files $uri $uri/ =404;
    }

    location ~ .php$ {
        fastcgi_pass    127.0.0.1:9000;
        fastcgi_index   index.php;

        include fastcgi.conf;
    }
}
```

In this example, it is assumed the `listen` directive we saw in the PHP config was `127.0.0.1:9000`. You will need to modify it to match. If the `listen` directive was a path to a file, you will need to prefix the path with `unix:`, such as:

```
fastcgi_pass unix:/usr/local/var/run/php/php7.4-fpm.sock;
```

This nginx configuration is enough to get you going, but isn't production safe. I recommend visiting `nginx.org`'s page on PHP to see the latest configuration (at `https://www.nginx.com/resources/wiki/start/topics/examples/phpfcgi/`).

As we've updated the nginx config, we will need to restart nginx.

```
% sudo brew services restart nginx
```

Finally, we need to test that PHP is working correctly. The quickest way to do that is to copy the info.php file from the random-files directory into the web directory for nginx.

```
% cp ~/random-files/info.php /usr/local/var/www/
```

If you open http://dev.example.org/info.php in your favorite web browser, you should now see the PHP information page, as shown in Figure 8-2.

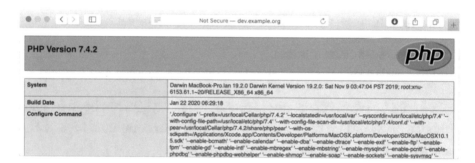

Figure 8-2. *PHP info output on the custom domain name*

Installing a Database

Next on our list of requirements is to install a database. WordPress uses a database to store all the content for the blog. The database we will install is called MySQL. Let's jump straight in and install MySQL.

```
% brew install mysql@8.0
==> mysql
We've installed your MySQL database without a root password. To
secure it run:
    mysql_secure_installation
```

MySQL is configured to only allow connections from localhost by default

To connect run:
```
mysql -uroot
```

To have `launchd` start MySQL now and restart at login, use this:

```
brew services start mysql
```

Or, if you don't want/need a background service, you can just run the following:

```
mysql.server start
```

The first thing we need to do is start the MySQL server.

```
% brew services start mysql
==> Successfully started `mysql` (label: homebrew.mxcl.mysql)
```

It would be remiss of me not to mention that MySQL has been installed without a password for the users. Just like with your computer, MySQL has its own users, with differing levels of permissions.

By default, the account with most permissions (root) exists without a password. This isn't a problem, but it is a risk you should be aware of.

If you are uncomfortable leaving the root user without a password, you can secure it with the `mysql_secure_installation` command.

If you run `mysql_secure_installation`, make sure you make a note of the new password. You will need it later.

Creating the WordPress Database

We need to do one last thing before we are done. WordPress will need somewhere in MySQL to store its data, a database. The database is where WordPress saves the content and it is what makes your site, yours.

By default, MySQL comes with some databases already. However, these databases are for running MySQL.

```
% echo "SHOW DATABASES" | mysql -uroot
Database
information_schema
mysql
performance_schema
sys
```

Note   If you set a password for MySQL, you will need to add the -p option to the command so that MySQL prompts you for the password: mysql -uroot -p.

We need to create our own database for the WordPress installation. I will call my database wordpress; however, it's better that you call your database a name that reflects how you'll use it.

We will pipe SQL directly into MySQL to create the database.

```
% echo "CREATE DATABASE wordpress" | mysql -uroot
```

When we look at the databases, we can see the newly created database.

```
% echo "SHOW DATABASES" | mysql -uroot
Database
information_schema
mysql
performance_schema
sys
wordpress
```

We need not do anything more with MySQL, because WordPress will do the rest for us.

Installing WordPress

Now that we have installed all the requirements for WordPress, we can move on to installing it. When we set up nginx, we used the default directory:

```
% cd /usr/local/var/www
```

Note   This directory can be anywhere on your computer.

Now we have to download the WordPress-compressed archive. In all my years of using WordPress, the download URL has remained the same:

```
https://wordpress.org/latest.tar.gz
```

Let's download it now:

```
% wget https://wordpress.org/latest.tar.gz
```

Now we need to decompress the file, as follows:

```
% tar -xf latest.tar.gz
```

We now have a folder called wordpress, which contains all the files.

```
% ls
50x.html index.html info.php latest.tar.gz wordpress
```

Let's move those files into the main folder, as follows:

```
% mv wordpress/* .
```

Finally, we should tidy up the files that are not part of WordPress.

```
% rm index.html info.php latest.tar.gz
% rmdir wordpress
```

To get WordPress to work correctly with nginx, we need to make some changes to the config, as follows:

```
% nano /usr/local/etc/nginx/servers/localhost
server {
    listen 80;
    server_name dev.example.org;

    index index.php;
    root /usr/local/var/www;

    location / {
        try_files $uri $uri/ =404;
    }
}
```

Finally, we need to restart nginx:

```
% sudo brew services restart nginx
```

Now, when you go to http://dev.example.org/, you will see the WordPress install, as shown in Figure 8-3.

Note   The URL you see depends on how you choose to set up your version of nginx.

Figure 8-3. *WordPress Language selection*

For the next step, we will need our database details, as shown in Figure 8-4.

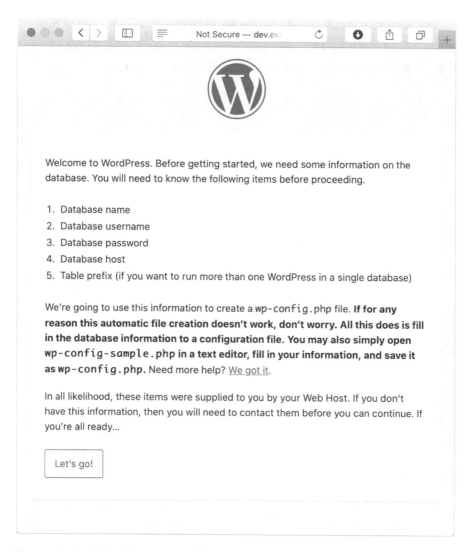

Figure 8-4. *WordPress installation*

We need the details we set earlier to fill in the form that is shown in Figure 8-5. Everything will be the same as here, except for the database name, if you changed it, and the password, if you set one.

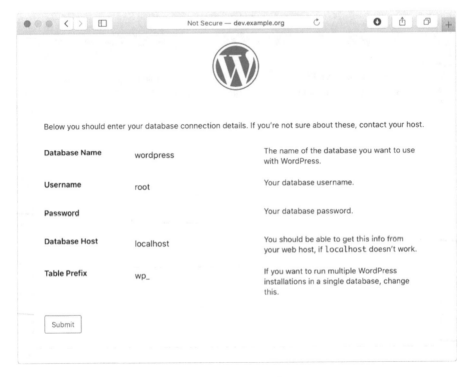

Figure 8-5. *WordPress installation details*

If everything checks out for installation, you should see the screen in Figure 8-6. If you get an error, you will need to address it before you finally see this screen. Common problems you might encounter are:

- MySQL is not running

- Wrong password

- Forgot to create the database

- Typo

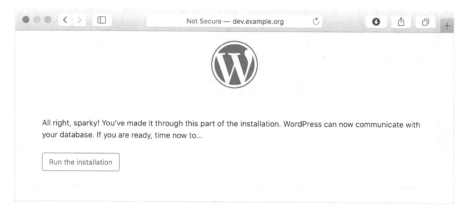

Figure 8-6. *WordPress installation final check*

Finally, we can install WordPress and get on with customizing it, as shown in Figure 8-7.

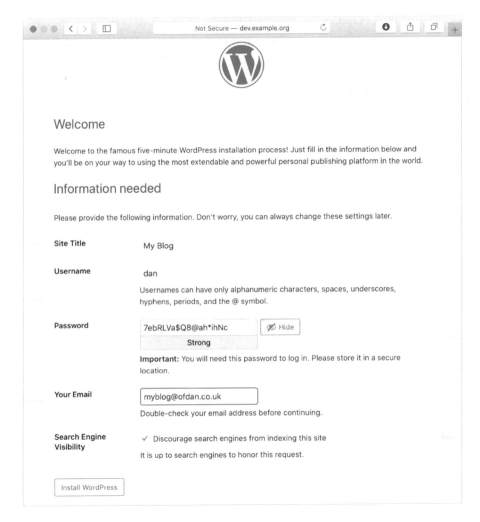

Figure 8-7. *WordPress blog setup*

Don't worry if you make a mistake at this stage; you can always change these details later from within WordPress. However, make a note of the username and password, as you need them to log in to WordPress and the password won't be shown again.

Finally, we can click the Install WordPress button.

When WordPress finishes installing and setting up the database, you will be shown your username, but not your password, as shown in Figure 8-8.

Figure 8-8. *WordPress installation is complete*

This tutorial covered the basics of installing WordPress. A more detailed installation guide is available from the makers of WordPress, at `https://wordpress.org/support/article/how-to-install-wordpress/`.

Using WordPress

Now everything is installed and you can log in, as shown in Figure 8-9. Logging in is easy the first time round, but keep a note of the URL so you don't forget. For future reference, the login URL to this blog is `http://dev.example.org/wp-admin/`.

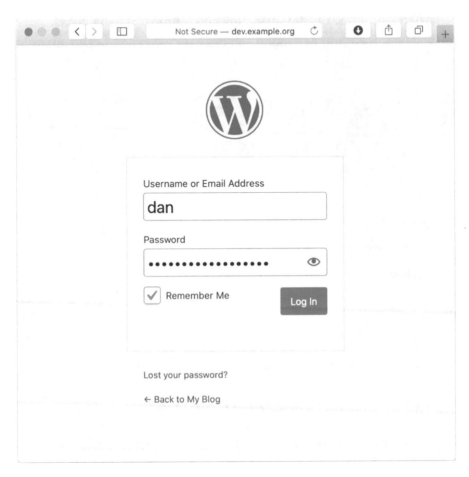

Figure 8-9. *WordPress login*

The Dashboard

Welcome to the admin of your new blog, as shown in Figure 8-10. You can see that I have one page, one post, and one one comment.

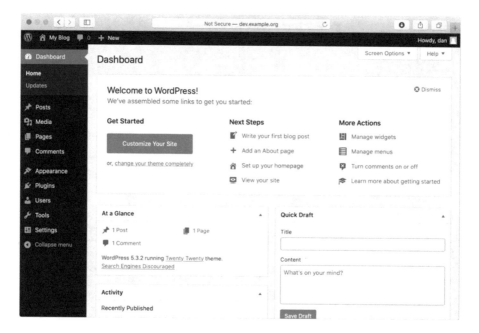

Figure 8-10. *WordPress admin Dashboard*

Settings

When I installed WordPress, I was asked some questions that I said could be changed later. These settings are in the General Settings tab, as shown in Figure 8-11.

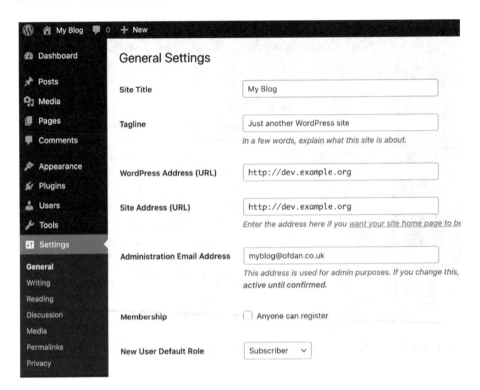

Figure 8-11. *WordPress General Settings tab*

Viewing the Blog

Now, when you go to `http://dev.example.org/`, you will see what your visitors see, as shown in Figure 8-12. This is also available by clicking My Blog, at the top right. If you are logged in, you will also see the WordPress toolbar at the top.

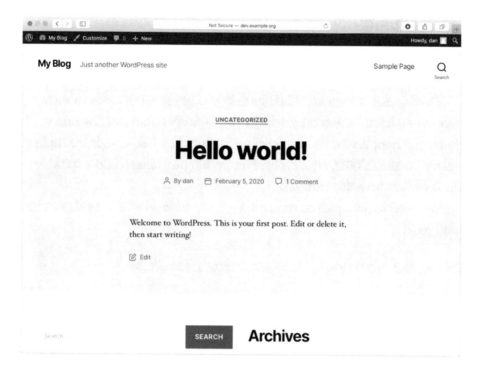

Figure 8-12.   *The default WordPress blog*

Permalinks

If you looked at any of the links in the previous example, you would have noticed that the links are based on the query string, rather than the name of the post or the category. For example:

```
http://dev.example.org/?p=1
```

These links work and are the easiest to get working, which is why they are the default. However, I prefer links that are much more readable, such as `http://dev.example.org/hello-world/`. To get this to work, we need to make two changes—one to the nginx configuration and the other to WordPress.

471

nginx Change

At the moment, when nginx gets a request, it checks to see if that file exists on the filesystem.

This is perfect for static files like CSS and images, but it doesn't work with dynamic URLs that only exist in WordPress's database. The other check that happens is, if you access a directory like / or `wp-admin/`, nginx will try the default file, `index.php`. Finally, if nginx fails to find a suitable file, it will return a 404 instead.

We need to tell nginx to return `index.php` instead of 404, as shown in Listing 8-3.

Listing 8-3. */usr/local/etc/nginx/servers/localhost*

```
server {
    listen 80;
    server_name dev.example.org;

    root /usr/local/var/www;

    location / {
        try_files $uri $uri/ /index.php$is_args$args;
    }

    location ~ .php$ {
        fastcgi_pass    127.0.0.1:9000;
        fastcgi_index   index.php;

        include fastcgi.conf;
    }
}
```

Don't forget to restart nginx.

```
% sudo brew services restart nginx
```

WordPress Changes

In the Permalink Settings tab in WordPress, there are many different ways to reference a post. My favorite is by the post name, as shown in Figure 8-13.

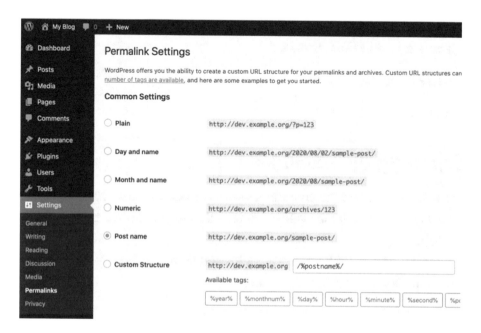

Figure 8-13. *WordPress permalink settings*

Now all your links on your blog look a lot better:

```
http://dev.example.org/hello-world/
```

Taking It Live

When you are ready, you can put this blog on the Internet. However, you will need to purchase some web hosting and a domain name. You will probably use scp to upload the web files.

```
% scp -r /usr/local/var/www/* user@webhost:~/public_html/
```

Sometimes you will have to upload files using a web interface, and then you will find it easier to zip up your web files for uploading.

```
% cd /usr/local/var/www
```

For GZip, use this:

```
% tar -czf webfiles.tar.gz *
```

As Zip, use this:

```
% zip -r webfiles.zip *
```

Exporting the Database

You now need to upload your database to the hosting site. This isn't as easy as just copying the database files. You need to extract the database from MySQL.

MySQL comes with a tool that helps you do this, called mysqldump, which saves your database a text file.

Note   wordpress is the name of your database.

```
% mysqldump -uroot wordpress
-- MySQL dump 10.13 Distrib 8.0.19, for osx10.15 (x86_64)
--
-- Host: localhost   Database: wordpress
-- ------------------------------------------------------
-- Server version 8.0.19
```

Note   If you set a password for MySQL, you will need the -p option for mysqldump.

Although outputting the database to your screen is interesting, saving it to a file is better.

```
% mysqldump -uroot wordpress > wordpress.sql
```

The hosting company will be able to help you upload your files and database.

WordPress Config

Your web host database login details for MySQL are different from your local database. If you try to see what your blog looks like before updating your database credentials, you will get an error message like Figure 8-14.

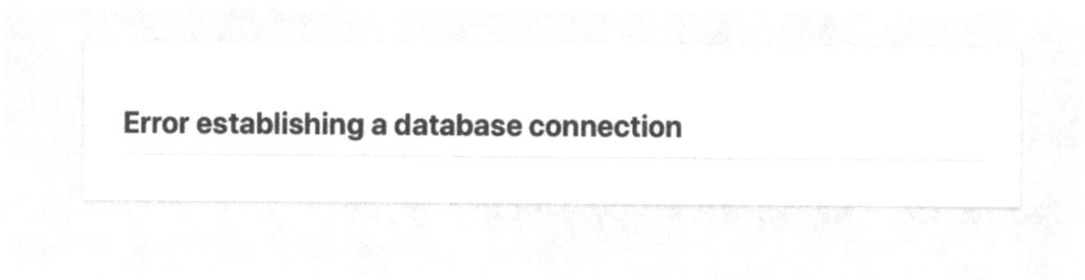

Error establishing a database connection

Figure 8-14. *WordPress with a database error*

WordPress database credentials are very easy to change. They live in a file called wp-config.php, as shown in Figure 8-15.

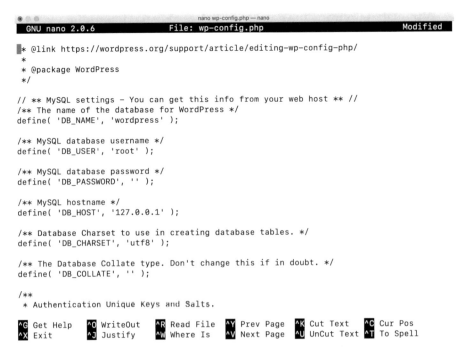

```
●  ●  ●                    nano wp-config.php — nano
  GNU nano 2.0.6            File: wp-config.php                     Modified
* @link https://wordpress.org/support/article/editing-wp-config-php/
 *
 * @package WordPress
 */

// ** MySQL settings - You can get this info from your web host ** //
/** The name of the database for WordPress */
define( 'DB_NAME', 'wordpress' );

/** MySQL database username */
define( 'DB_USER', 'root' );

/** MySQL database password */
define( 'DB_PASSWORD', '' );

/** MySQL hostname */
define( 'DB_HOST', '127.0.0.1' );

/** Database Charset to use in creating database tables. */
define( 'DB_CHARSET', 'utf8' );

/** The Database Collate type. Don't change this if in doubt. */
define( 'DB_COLLATE', '' );

/**
 * Authentication Unique Keys and Salts.

^G Get Help   ^O WriteOut   ^R Read File   ^Y Prev Page   ^K Cut Text    ^C Cur Pos
^X Exit       ^J Justify    ^W Where Is    ^V Next Page   ^U UnCut Text  ^T To Spell
```

Figure 8-15. *The WordPress wp-config.php file*

You need to update this file to match the details that your hosting company gives. When you originally installed WordPress, you gave it a domain name that it worked on. When you bring the site live, you will be using a different domain name.

The issue you will face is when you try to log in, WordPress will try to log you in using the old domain name. You need to tell WordPress about the new domain name so that you can log in.

Normally, I would tell you to edit either the wordpress.sql file or the database directly. The change you need to make is to a couple of records in the wp_options table. The records are siteurl and home. They contain the domain name that WordPress will redirect you to upon login, and when you click the Home button.

However, there is a much easier way to achieve the same effect, and that is by editing the wp-config.php file. We can override the values that WordPress gets from the database with whatever we specify in the wp-config.php file.

The lines that we need to add are these, and it doesn't matter where they go in the file:

```
define( 'WP_HOME', 'http://dev.example.org' );
define( 'WP_SITEURL', 'http://dev.example.org' );
```

Figure 8-16 shows an example where I've added these lines just after the database details.

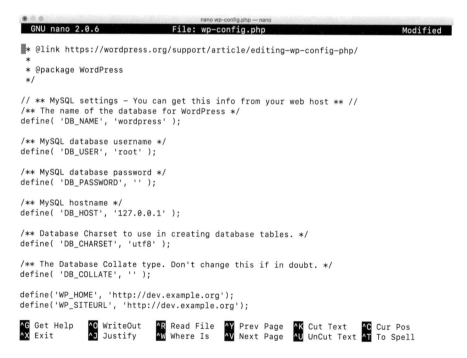

Figure 8-16. *Telling WordPress about the new domain name to log in*

Now, you either need to upload the new `wp-config.php` file or edit it directly on your server. Whichever way you do it, you will have your very own blog that you developed on your own computer!

Summary

In this chapter we installed everything needed to run WordPress—this included a web server, PHP, and a database. We covered how to install WordPress and log in. We also talked about how you can upload your WordPress installation to a public hosting site.

CHAPTER 9

Going Further

This final chapter covers what to do if you have problems with Brew. I will show you how to interact with a weather and stock service using only Terminal, as well as how to use Oh My Zsh to customize your Terminal. This chapter shows you how I use my Terminal.

Brew Clean Up

Now that you're able to search for commands, install them, and keep them up-to-date, what could go wrong?

Well, you could find yourself running out of space, depending on how large your computer drive is. Originally, when one upgraded a formula in Brew, Brew didn't remove the old version. I ended up with all the versions I had ever installed. At one point, I had 4GB of installed commands that were redundant.

In recent years, Brew started running maintenance commands automatically. When I upgrade a formula, Brew will now remove all previous versions that had been installed automatically. It will also attempt to clean up all formulas every 30 days.

However, it is helpful to know about these versions, as you might need them or want more control of when your cleanup runs. Occasionally, Brew's automatic cleanup doesn't run.

© Daniel Platt 2021
D. Platt, *Tweak Your Mac Terminal*, https://doi.org/10.1007/978-1-4842-6171-2_9

Opting Out

It is entirely possible that you'll want to keep your old versions of a command. If you do, you can opt out of the automatic cleanup by setting the `HOMEBREW_NO_INSTALL_CLEANUP` environment variable before running the `brew upgrade` command.

```
% HOMEBREW_NO_INSTALL_CLEANUP=1 brew upgrade
```

Or, you can add the variable to your `.zshrc` file.

```
export HOMEBREW_NO_INSTALL_CLEANUP=1
```

Manual Clean Up

You can manually run the `brew cleanup` command with the `-n` option, which means it's a dry run.

```
% brew cleanup -n
```

This will show you a list of everything that will be cleaned up and the space you'll save. I've just run the command and Brew tells me I will reclaim 4GB of disk space. If you are happy to proceed, you can run the same command, but without the `-n` argument.

```
% brew cleanup
```

You can also remove the applications one at a time with this command:

```
% brew cleanup <application/formula>
```

Either way, you won't have to worry about Brew storing all the versions of your installed commands.

When Things Go Wrong

If things start to go awry and things won't install or upgrades fail, or maybe you're just curious to know if everything is working correctly, you're in luck. There is a command called brew doctor that will run tests on your Brew installation to see if there is anything obviously wrong.

```
% brew doctor
Please note that these warnings are just used to help the
Homebrew maintainers
with debugging if you file an issue. If everything you use
Homebrew for is
working fine: please don't worry or file an issue; just ignore
this. Thanks!

Warning: A newer Command Line Tools release is available.
Update them from Software Update in System Preferences or run:
  softwareupdate --all --install --force

If that doesn't show you an update run:
  sudo rm -rf /Library/Developer/CommandLineTools
  sudo xcode-select --install

Alternatively, manually download them from:
  https://developer.apple.com/download/more/.

Warning: Homebrew's sbin was not found in your PATH but you
have installed
formulae that put executables in /usr/local/sbin.
Consider setting the PATH for example like so:
  echo 'export PATH="/usr/local/sbin:$PATH"' >> ~/.zshrc
```

The output is saying everything is okay, except that I need to update my command-line tools and there is a path missing from the PATH variable. Updating the command-line tools was straightforward by using the commands that were specified in the brew doctor message.

The PATH variable is special, as it contains all the locations where your computer will check for installed applications. By default, the shell will check /usr/local/bin, but not /usr/local/sbin. This isn't a problem at the moment, because the only items that I have in the /usr/local/sbin folder are unbound and php-fpm. However, if I were to install any commands that feature an sbin command, they won't be found by typing their name until this folder is searched.

Brew is telling us what is wrong and how it can be fixed. We can either do what it says to fix the whole thing, or you can copy and paste the extra bit and edit .zshrc manually.

It's up to you, both will work, but if you do it manually, you'll control the formatting and the order of preference and you will end up with fewer lines in your .zshrc file.

Let's assume you want to control what's in your .zshrc file, rather than just copying and pasting the echo command.

First, you need to edit your .zshrc file.

```
% nano .zshrc
```

If you don't have a line starting with export PATH, you will need to paste in this command.

```
export PATH="/usr/local/sbin:$PATH"
```

What if you already have a PATH defined? The PATH variable is simply a list of directories, separated by the : symbol. When you specify the $PATH variable within itself, you are saying, I want the system directories, plus these extra ones. For example, PATH="/dir/1:/dir/2:$PATH". Look in your .zshrc file and you see this line. What do you do?

```
PATH=/usr/local/bin:$PATH;
```

You should notice that the pattern is: directory, colon, directory. I recommend that you put the new directory in front of the existing one, because you are overriding the built-in macOS commands. Note that there might be a use case for the directory to go at the end of the variable.

Paste it in here (don't forget the semicolon). You will end up with a PATH that looks like this:

```
PATH="/usr/local/sbin:/usr/local/bin:$PATH";
```

Exit out of the .zshrc file, but don't forget to save. To save, you need to press Control+X to exit and then press the Y key to confirm saving.

You will need to rerun your .zshrc, and then run brew doctor (either open a new tab or type source .zshrc). Now, when you rerun brew doctor, that error should go away.

Sometimes you'll get warnings about files that are there but aren't hurting anything. They were put there by applications that Brew is not aware of. Those files won't do any harm.

Now that the error has gone away, we can move on.

Broken Applications

Occasionally, the applications you install will have an annoying bug in them. Let's take archey as an example.

```
% brew info archey
archey: stable 1.6.0, HEAD
Graphical system information display for macOS
https://obihann.github.io/archey-osx/
```

At the time of this writing, archey is at version 1.6.0. If you installed archey before November 30, 2018, then version 1.6.0 has a small bug in it. Let's look at the buggy output of archey, shown in Figure 9-1. This is from a couple of years ago, before the fix was applied.

```
        ###                       User: danielplatt
       ####                       Hostname: MacPro
        ###                       Distro: OS X 10.12.6
   #######    #######             Kernel: Darwin
 ####################             Uptime: 23:04
 ###################              Shell: /bin/bash
 ##################               Terminal: xterm-256color Apple Terminal
 #################                CPU: Intel Core i7-2760QM CPU @ 2.40GHz
 ###################              Memory: 16 GB
  ###################             Disk: 60%
   #################              Battery: 91.31%%
    ###############               IP Address: 80. .  .
     ####     #####
```

Figure 9-1. *Archey with typo output*

You can see that I use a laptop from this output, as it shows a battery status. The output for the battery percentage includes two percent signs. This is a small bug, but it illustrates my point of an application with a bug. The trouble is we were using the latest version.

However, there was another version that Brew didn't install by default, called HEAD. It's the bleeding edge of the project, and may not be 100% ready for use. That said, a lot of projects like to keep the *head* (referred to master branch) bug-free. Now, let's figure out if the HEAD version fixes our problem.

When we ran brew info archey another piece of information was the project URL, at https://obihann.github.io/archey-osx/. However, we are looking for the project repository, which is different. It is the project documentation, as shown in Figure 9-2.

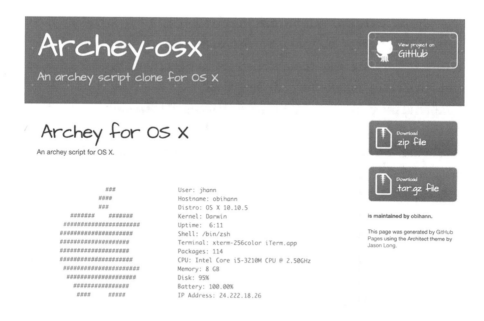

Figure 9-2. Archey project page

There is a link to the repository, which you can access using the View Project on GitHub button. The page you should end up on is https://github.com/obihann/archey-osx, as shown in Figure 9-3.

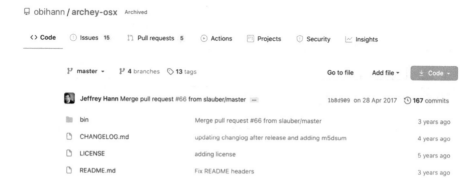

Figure 9-3. Archey GitHub page

In the Releases section, you can see that version 1.6.0 was released on April 4, 2016 and that is 22 commits behind the master branch. Now we know that there has been more work on this project since version 1.6.0, so there is a chance that our bug has been fixed.

Look at the project's commits to see if using the HEAD will benefit us. You can see the commits by clicking on Code and then choosing Commits. You should end up with the `https://github.com/obihann/archey-osx/commits/master` URL.

To find out where version 1.6.0 ends, you can either count down 22 commits or you can just look for all commits that have been committed after April 4, 2016. Looking at the commit message, I can see that the battery percent sign was fixed on the April 5, 2016 by ramlev, or on April 14, by meowgorithm. (It was a pull request, either #51 or #53, and they were merged on September 12.)

As our issue has been fixed in the master branch, let's rebuild `archey` using that.

```
% brew reinstall --HEAD archey
```

This will reinstall `archey`, using the master branch. Now when you run archey the double percent issue has gone. This won't work for every bug you experience, but it's worth a shot.

You might find that the version you install is not as stable as you'd like. How do you get back to the latest stable release?

```
% brew remove archey
% brew install archey
```

If the project doesn't have a fix, check the "Issues" to see if anyone has reported it. If you can't find an issue, consider opening your own issue.

Internet Services from Terminal

Not everything has to reside on your computer. There are services on the Internet that you can access from Terminal. In this section, we will explore how we can use them.

Weather

Knowing the weather should be as simple as looking outside, but maybe your computer isn't near a window. Being able to see the latest weather forecast could be useful. There is a website that provides a simple weather forecast, which also works well in Terminal, as shown in Figure 9-4.

```
% curl --max-time 1 http://wttr.in/andover,uk
```

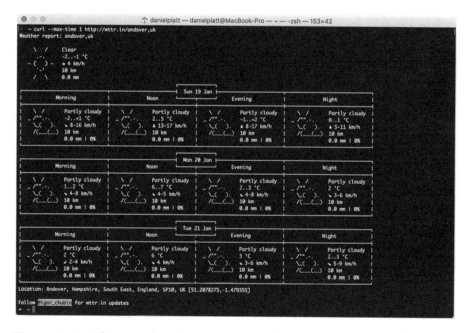

Figure 9-4. *The weather forecast for Andover, UK*

The location is specified as part of the URL. Each component is separated with a comma, such as andover,uk. The location can also be the three-letter airport codes. Landmarks are also supported if you prefix them with the tilde symbol (~), as follows:

http://wttr.in/~stonehenge

Note   If you need to use a space, replace it with the plus symbol (+).

You might not need the full weather forecast. Maybe you just need the current weather.

`% curl --max-time 1 http://wttr.in/andover,uk?days=0`

The output can be seen in Figure 9-5.

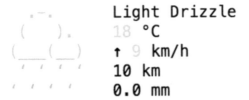

```
Weather report: Andover, United Kingdom

                      Light Drizzle
      ( ) .           18  °C
    (___(__)          ↑ 9  km/h
                      10 km
                      0.0 mm
```

Figure 9-5. *Current weather forecast*

--max-time is how long the curl command will wait before giving up. If you add this command to your .zshrc file, you could find out your local weather whenever you open your Terminal. Normally this service works really quickly, but if it's running slowly or you don't have an Internet connection, you wouldn't want this to hang your new Terminal window for the default timeout time.

Without `max-time`, `curl` could potentially cause you to wait up to five minutes before giving you a prompt. With a one second `max-time`, that's how long you'd have to wait in the worst case. There are more options available, and you can see them by invoking the help.

```
% curl wttr.in/:help
```

Stock Ticker

I like to keep my eye on the price of some of my shares, but I don't want to keep going to a website to see them. I use a ticker script that queries Yahoo Finance to return the latest stock and crypto prices directly to Terminal.

```
% curl -o ticker.sh https://raw.githubusercontent.com/pstadler/
ticker.sh/master/ticker.sh
% chmod +x ticker.sh
```

I like to move it into my local `bin` directory and drop the `.sh` file extension.

```
% mv ticker.sh /usr/local/bin/
```

Using the ticker is easy, but you do need to know the stock symbol in order to see anything. The usage information has a few suggestions.

```
% ticker
Usage: ./ticker.sh AAPL MSFT GOOG BTC-USD
```

When you run the ticker with the stock symbols, it will return the current price and how much the stock has changed that day, as an amount and as a percentage.

```
% ticker AAPL MSFT GOOG BTC-USD
AAPL       427.44       2.40      (0.56%)  *
MSFT       205.50       0.49      (0.24%)  *
GOOG      1482.01      -0.95      (-0.06%) *
BTC-USD  11316.80    -454.25      (-3.86%)
```

If you want to run this ticker command frequently, you can either add it to your `.zshrc` file or create an alias for it with the ticker symbols. For more information about this project, see its GitHub page at `https://github.com/pstadler/ticker.sh`.

Star Wars

This service is very different from the last one. With this, you can watch the first episode of *Star Wars* (retroactively called Episode IV) in Terminal, in ASCII. You will need to install a telnet client in order to be able to access it.

Telnet is how people used to connect to servers before SSH. However, the biggest problem with telnet was that everything that was sent across the Internet was in plain text. Therefore, anyone listening to your connection would have been able to see everything, including your password. It is safe to use telnet, but do not use it to send information that you wish to remain private.

```
% brew install telnet
```

All you need to do is telnet to `towel.blinkenlights.nl` and then you can sit back and watch Episode IV of *Star Wars,* as shown in Figure 9-6.

```
% telnet towel.blinkenlights.nl
```

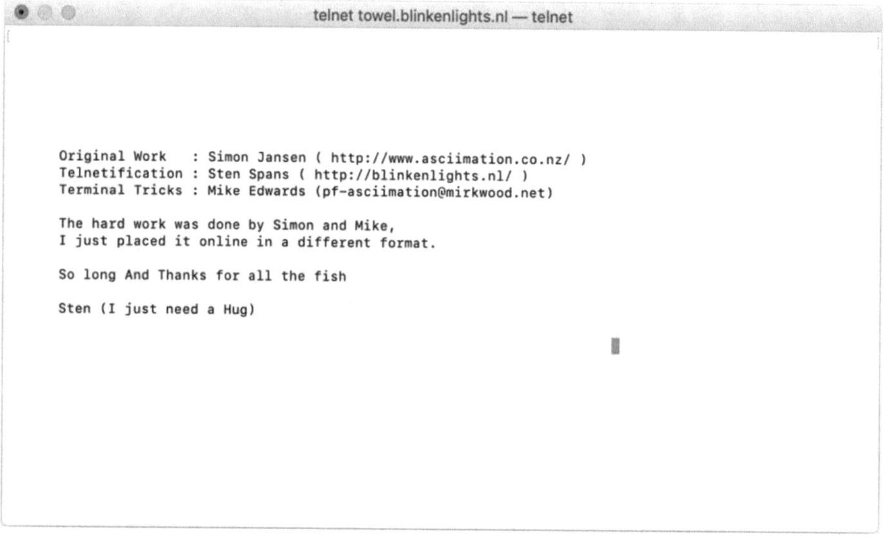

```
                      telnet towel.blinkenlights.nl — telnet



     Original Work    : Simon Jansen ( http://www.asciimation.co.nz/ )
     Telnetification : Sten Spans ( http://blinkenlights.nl/ )
     Terminal Tricks : Mike Edwards (pf-asciimation@mirkwood.net)

     The hard work was done by Simon and Mike,
     I just placed it online in a different format.

     So long And Thanks for all the fish

     Sten (I just need a Hug)
```

Figure 9-6. *Credit for ASCII Star Wars*

If you want to exit before the end, you can. However, you will find that Control+C will do nothing. You need to press Control+[to bring up the telnet prompt.

`telnet>`

At this telnet prompt, you can type `quit`, followed by the Return key, to drop back into Terminal.

Nyan Cat

This was going to be an online service that would display how long you've been watching Nyan Cat. If you are not in the know, Nyan Cat was a GIF created by `@prguitarman`; you can see it at `http://www.nyan.cat/`, as shown in Figure 9-7.

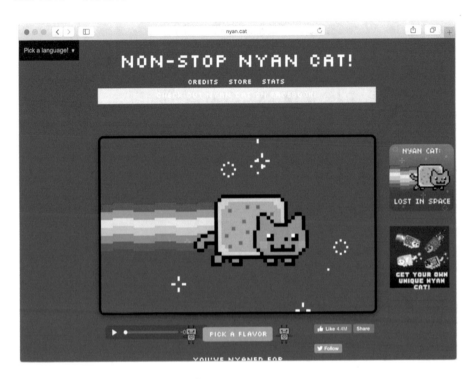

Figure 9-7. *Nonstop Nyan Cat*

Klange on GitHub created a Terminal version of the Nyan Cat GIF. Originally, I was going to show you that, but due to its popularity and huge bandwidth requirements, the server kept being taken down. If you want to visit Klange's nyancat repository, go to https://github.com/ klange/nyancat.

Instead, we will download the repo and build the application ourselves.

```
% git clone https://github.com/klange/nyancat.git
Cloning into 'nyancat'...
remote: Enumerating objects: 8, done.
remote: Counting objects: 100% (8/8), done.
remote: Compressing objects: 100% (5/5), done.
```

```
remote: Total 565 (delta 1), reused 1 (delta 1), pack-reused 557
Receiving objects: 100% (565/565), 139.10 KiB | 701.00 KiB/s, done.
Resolving deltas: 100% (327/327), done.
```

The repo has successfully been downloaded and placed into a folder called nyancat. Let's move into the nyancat directory.

% **cd nyancat**

This is a great project written in C. C is an early programming language that is powerful, but is beyond the scope of this book. However, there is a small example near the end of this chapter.

With Xcode installed, we can build this project without having to understand how it works. The hard work has been done with the inclusion of the makefile in the repo.

% **make**
```
cd src && /Library/Developer/CommandLineTools/usr/bin/make all
cc -g -Wall -Wextra -std=c99 -pedantic -Wwrite-strings    -c -o
nyancat.o nyancat.c
cc   -g -Wall -Wextra -std=c99 -pedantic -Wwrite-
strings   nyancat.o -o nyancat
```

That's all you need to do to build the command.

% **./src/nyancat**

The output is shown in Figure 9-8.

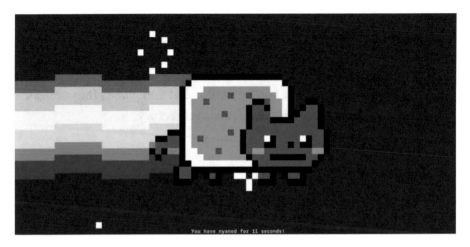

Figure 9-8. *Nyan Cat running in Terminal*

When you finish running this command, you have to use Control+C to end it. The repo even comes with a man page for nyancat. It's not built-in, though, so you need to refer to it by filename in order to load it.

```
% man ./nyancat.1
```

Oh My Zsh

"Oh My Zsh is a delightful, open source, community-driven framework for managing your Zsh configuration. It comes bundled with thousands of helpful functions, helpers, plugins, themes, and a few things that make you shout..."

Source: https://ohmyz.sh/

Installation

Just like with Brew, installing Oh My Zsh is achieved with a simple shell command.

```
% sh -c "$(curl -fsSL https://raw.githubusercontent.com/
ohmyzsh/ohmyzsh/master/tools/install.sh)"
Cloning Oh My Zsh...
Cloning into '/Users/danielplatt/.oh-my-zsh'...
remote: Enumerating objects: 1102, done.
remote: Counting objects: 100% (1102/1102), done.
remote: Compressing objects: 100% (1055/1055), done.
remote: Total 1102 (delta 23), reused 861 (delta 18), pack-reused 0
Receiving objects: 100% (1102/1102), 720.99 KiB | 351.00 KiB/s, done.
Resolving deltas: 100% (23/23), done.

Looking for an existing zsh config...
Using the Oh My Zsh template file and adding it to ~/.zshrc.
```

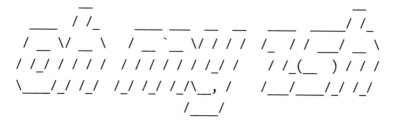

```
....is now installed!
```

Please look over the ~/.zshrc file to select plugins, themes, and options.

p.s. Follow us on https://twitter.com/ohmyzsh

p.p.s. Get stickers, shirts, and coffee mugs at https://shop.
planetargon.com/collections/oh-my-zsh

We are now running Oh My Zsh. Let's do what it suggests and look at
~/.zshrc. Let's look at ~/.zshrc in nano. The first item we see is about the
PATH.

```
# If you come from bash you might have to change your $PATH.
# export PATH=$HOME/bin:/usr/local/bin:$PATH
```

Next is the installation directory.

```
# Path to your oh-my-zsh installation.
export ZSH="/Users/danielplatt/.oh-my-zsh"
```

You shouldn't need to change this, unless you move the folder.

Customizing Oh My Zsh

There are many different ways to customize Oh My Zsh to make it your
own. The most dramatic way is by using themes to change how your
Terminal looks.

Themes

Oh My Zsh themes define the colors for Terminal. At the time of writing,
there are 140 themes and they all live in ~/.oh-my-zsh/themes. The next
part of the .zshrc file is the theme.

```
# See https://github.com/ohmyzsh/ohmyzsh/wiki/Themes
ZSH_THEME="robbyrussell"
```

It is easy to test new themes. You only need to put the theme name in,
and then save the file. Then you can open a new Terminal window or tab

and see what it looks like. If you are not happy with the theme, you can try the next one or enter the previous theme name.

Let's look at all the possible themes that Oh My Zsh comes with.

```
% ls ~/.oh-my-zsh/themes
3den.zsh-theme                  kafeitu.zsh-theme
Soliah.zsh-theme                kardan.zsh-theme
adben.zsh-theme                 kennethreitz.zsh-theme
af-magic.zsh-theme              kiwi.zsh-theme
```

Theme Previews

There are over 130 different themes, which can change the look and color of Terminal. This section discusses a selection of them. To see these previews, the git plugin has been enabled. When you are inside a git repository, it shows you which branch you are on.

Robbyrussell

I like this theme; it is simple but has a distinctive color scheme, as shown in Figure 9-9.

Figure 9-9. *The robbyrussell theme*

Clean

This theme is very similar to the robbyrussell theme. It displays the current user, the current directory, and the addition of the current time displayed to the right of the prompt, as shown in Figure 9-10.

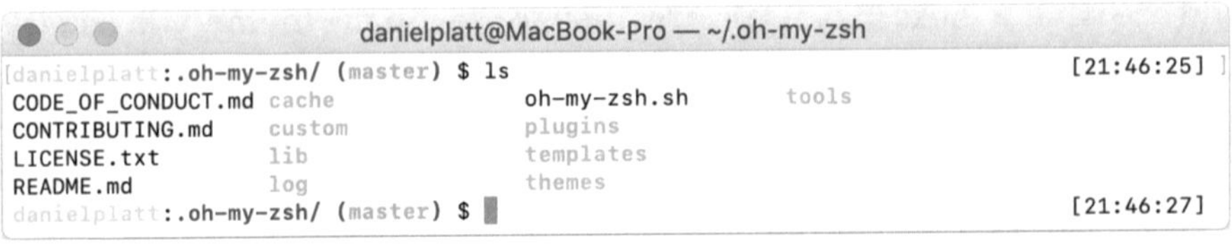

Figure 9-10. *The Clean theme*

Gallifrey

This is another good theme. It displays the hostname and current directory, as shown in Figure 9-11.

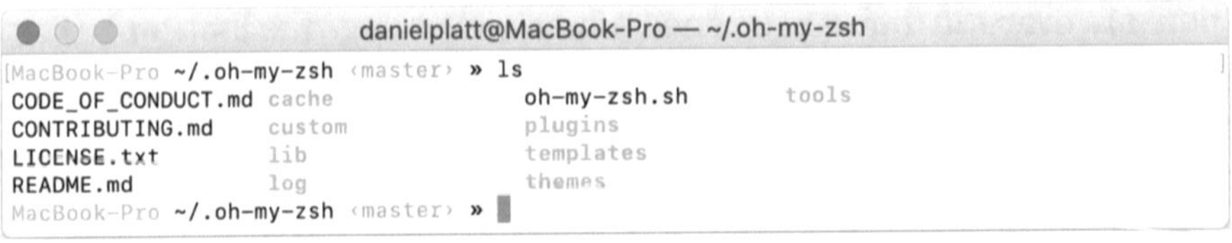

Figure 9-11. *The Gallifrey theme*

Nanotech

This theme is great at squeezing as much on your Terminal as possible. Compare this theme to the previous ones. Whereas the previous themes displayed the directory listing over four lines, this theme displays it using only two lines, as shown in Figure 9-12.

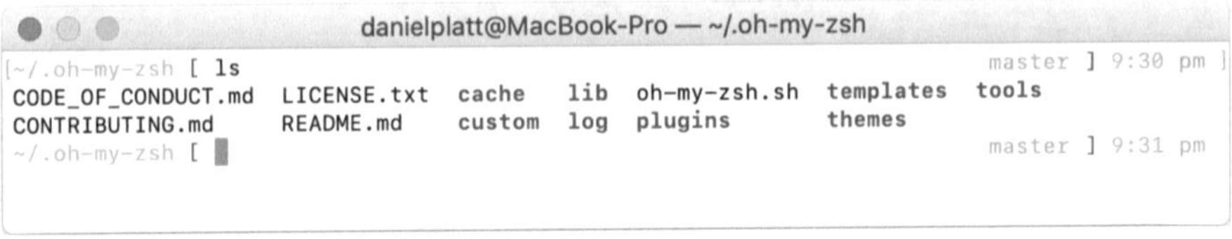

Figure 9-12. *The Nanotech theme*

Candy-Kingdom

I wanted to show you a theme that requires a plugin to be enabled before it works correctly. This theme takes advantage of the battery plugin. If it's not enabled, this theme won't work correctly, as shown in Figure 9-13.

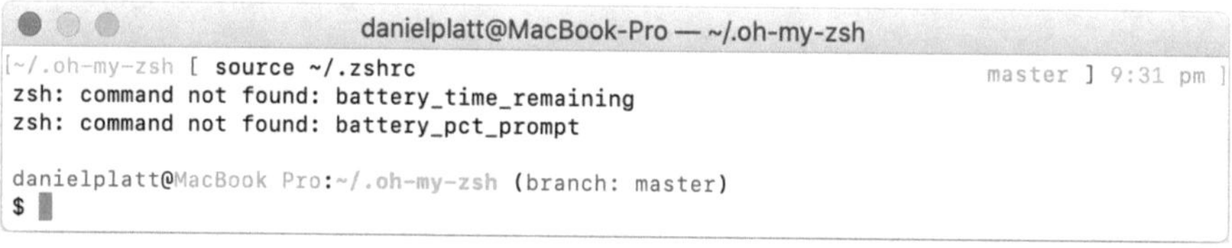

```
●  ●  ●                danielplatt@MacBook-Pro — ~/.oh-my-zsh
[~/.oh-my-zsh [ source ~/.zshrc                                  master ] 9:31 pm ]
zsh: command not found: battery_time_remaining
zsh: command not found: battery_pct_prompt

danielplatt@MacBook Pro:~/.oh-my-zsh (branch: master)
$ █
```

Figure 9-13. *The candy-kingdom Theme without the battery plugin enabled*

In the "Plugins" section, we cover the different plugins and discuss how to enable them, but when the battery plugin is enabled, it will look like Figure 9-14.

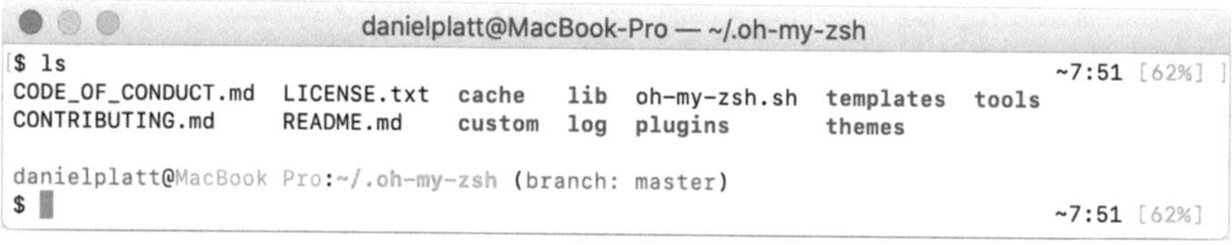

```
●  ●  ●                danielplatt@MacBook-Pro — ~/.oh-my-zsh
[$ ls                                                            ~7:51 [62%] ]
CODE_OF_CONDUCT.md  LICENSE.txt  cache   lib  oh-my-zsh.sh  templates  tools
CONTRIBUTING.md     README.md    custom  log  plugins       themes

danielplatt@MacBook Pro:~/.oh-my-zsh (branch: master)
$ █                                                             ~7:51 [62%]
```

Figure 9-14. *Theme candy-kingdom with the battery plugin enabled*

Agnoster

Another issue that you might encounter with themes is the colors not showing correctly, depending on your chosen Terminal profile, as shown in Figure 9-15.

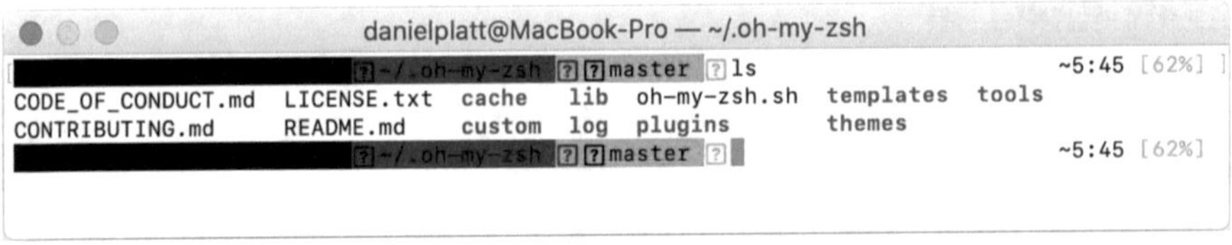

Figure 9-15. *The Agnoster theme*

Some themes work better with a different Terminal profile. This theme works better with the Silver Aerogel profile, as shown in Figure 9-16.

Figure 9-16. *The robbyrussell theme in silver*

Powerline Font

It's worth noting that some of these themes require Powerline fonts to work properly. You can tell by the question mark boxes that appear in Figure 9-16.

You can find out more about the Powerline font project at `https://github.com/Lokaltog/powerline-fonts` and you could follow the instructions there to install all the fonts. However, there is a good selection available within Brew, as shown in Figure 9-17. I prefer something to manage the items installed on my computer.

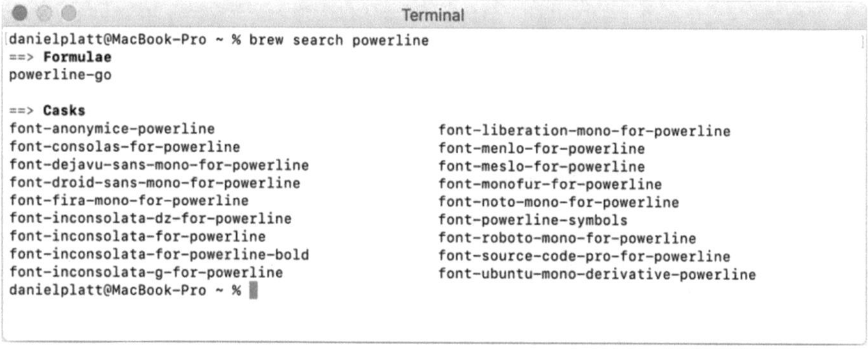

```
                                  Terminal
danielplatt@MacBook-Pro ~ % brew search powerline
==> Formulae
powerline-go

==> Casks
font-anonymice-powerline          font-liberation-mono-for-powerline
font-consolas-for-powerline       font-menlo-for-powerline
font-dejavu-sans-mono-for-powerline   font-meslo-for-powerline
font-droid-sans-mono-for-powerline    font-monofur-for-powerline
font-fira-mono-for-powerline      font-noto-mono-for-powerline
font-inconsolata-dz-for-powerline font-powerline-symbols
font-inconsolata-for-powerline    font-roboto-mono-for-powerline
font-inconsolata-for-powerline-bold   font-source-code-pro-for-powerline
font-inconsolata-g-for-powerline  font-ubuntu-mono-derivative-powerline
danielplatt@MacBook-Pro ~ %
```

Figure 9-17. *Powerline fonts available in Brew*

I picked the font called Meslo, as shown in Figure 9-18. You can install one or all of the fonts. If you do install more than one, it will be easier to decide which one you like in the next step.

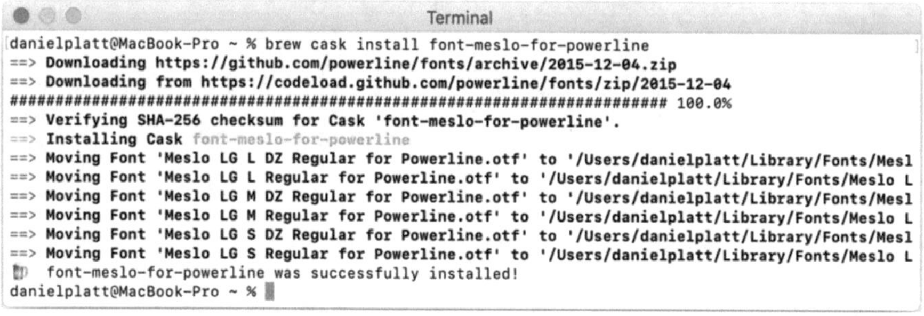

```
                                  Terminal
danielplatt@MacBook-Pro ~ % brew cask install font-meslo-for-powerline
==> Downloading https://github.com/powerline/fonts/archive/2015-12-04.zip
==> Downloading from https://codeload.github.com/powerline/fonts/zip/2015-12-04
######################################################### 100.0%
==> Verifying SHA-256 checksum for Cask 'font-meslo-for-powerline'.
==> Installing Cask font-meslo-for-powerline
==> Moving Font 'Meslo LG L DZ Regular for Powerline.otf' to '/Users/danielplatt/Library/Fonts/Mesl
==> Moving Font 'Meslo LG L Regular for Powerline.otf' to '/Users/danielplatt/Library/Fonts/Meslo L
==> Moving Font 'Meslo LG M DZ Regular for Powerline.otf' to '/Users/danielplatt/Library/Fonts/Mesl
==> Moving Font 'Meslo LG M Regular for Powerline.otf' to '/Users/danielplatt/Library/Fonts/Meslo L
==> Moving Font 'Meslo LG S DZ Regular for Powerline.otf' to '/Users/danielplatt/Library/Fonts/Mesl
==> Moving Font 'Meslo LG S Regular for Powerline.otf' to '/Users/danielplatt/Library/Fonts/Meslo L
    font-meslo-for-powerline was successfully installed!
danielplatt@MacBook-Pro ~ %
```

Figure 9-18. *Installing the Meslo font*

Changing to a Powerline Font

After Brew has installed the font, you can use it straight away. Go into Terminal preferences and select your new font, as shown in Figure 9-19.

Figure 9-19. *Selecting a new font for the profile*

When you go back to your Terminal window, the question marks are replaced with the symbols that theme developers intended, as shown in Figure 9-20.

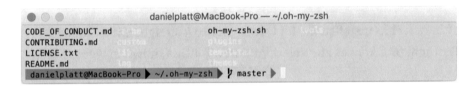

Figure 9-20. *Agnoster theme with the Powerline font enabled*

If for some reason you can't decide between two or more themes, you can set ZSH_THEME to random and put your favorite themes into ZSH_THEME_ RANDOM_CANDIDATES.

```
ZSH_THEME="random"
ZSH_THEME_RANDOM_CANDIDATES=( "robbyrussell" "agnoster" )
```

Note Remember to use double quotes around each theme name.

Plugins

The next section of the .zshrc file is about enabling plugins. The Oh My Zsh plugins provide extra terminal functionality. At the time of writing, there are 275 different plugins available.

```
# Which plugins would you like to load?
# Standard plugins can be found in ~/.oh-my-zsh/plugins/*
# Custom plugins may be added to ~/.oh-my-zsh/custom/plugins/
# Example format: plugins=(rails git textmate ruby lighthouse)
# Add wisely, as too many plugins slow down shell startup.
plugins=(git battery)
```

Here are a few plugins that I use. If you want more details, you can read the official wiki at https://github.com/ohmyzsh/ohmyzsh/wiki/Plugins. Inside each plugin is a README.md file, which explains more about how the plugin works. The following sections discuss a few plugins I recommend.

Alias-Finder

If you enable a lot of plugins, you will have a lot of aliases set up on your Terminal. Alias-finder helps you discover the best one.

```
% alias-finder "command"
```

Let's say you are looking for an alias that contains `git merge`.

```
% alias-finder "git merge"
gm='git merge'
g=git
```

There is also an option (`-e` or `--exact`) to limit results to exact matches.

```
% alias-finder -e "git merge"
gm='git merge'
```

There is also an option (`-l` or `--longer`) to include results that are longer than your search.

```
% alias-finder -l "git merge"
gm='git merge'
gma='git merge --abort'
gmom='git merge origin/master'
gmt='git mergetool --no-prompt'
gmtvim='git mergetool --no-prompt --tool=vimdiff'
gmum='git merge upstream/master'
```

BBEdit

I'm a great fan of BBEdit for editing text files. However, opening files in BBEdit can be tiresome, because you have to to type them out.

```
% open -a /Applications/BBEdit.app
```

BBEdit ships with Command Line Tools, but they are not available by default. You can install them from the BBEdit application menu (see Figure 9-21).

Figure 9-21. *Installing BBEdit's Command Line Tools*

This will install a command called bbedit. You can launch it.

% **bbedit --launch**

Or you can use it to open a file or a directory

% **bbedit <file|directory>**

If you use the BBEdit plugin for Oh My Zsh, you will get an alias called bb, which is a little quicker to type.

% **bb**

To open a file or directory:

% **bb <file|directory>**

Note   The BBEdit plugin requires the Command Line Tools to function.

OSX

This plugin is useful for simplifying some of the Terminal commands that interact with macOS, such as QuickLook .

Note   Some of these commands may cause security popups, as shown in Figure 9-22.

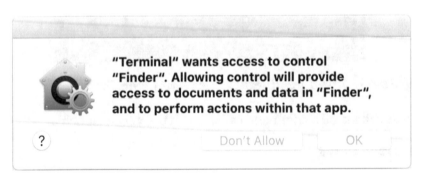

Figure 9-22. *Terminal requesting access to control Finder*

Print Finder Directory

The pfd command prints the directory of the last folder used in Finder, which is useful if you are in a directory many levels deep. I can never remember where my iCloud Drive is on the filesystem, so I can open the iCloud drive in Finder and then type pfd to see where it on the filesystem.

```
% pfd
/Users/danielplatt/Library/Mobile Documents/com~apple~CloudDocs/
```

To pass the output into another command, you must surround the command with *backticks*.

```
% cd `pfd`
```

Now my current directory is my iCloud Drive.

Print Finder Selection

With pfs, all you need to do is select a file in Finder. When you run pfs, the full path will be printed.

```
% pfs
/Users/danielplatt/Library/Mobile Documents/
com~apple~CloudDocs/
```

As with the pfd, if you want to do something with this, you can use the backtick symbol to insert the output into another command.

```
% ls -l "`pfs`"
-rw-r--r-- 1 danielplatt staff 64 23 Nov 20:31 /Users/
danielplatt/random-files-master/Readme.md
```

Note   It's best to also use quotes, because the path could have symbols that don't work well without being escaped. For example, the iCloud Drive path has a space in Mobile Documents.

Change Directory - Finder

The cdf command is pretty neat. You navigate to a directory in Finder, and you then run cdf in your Terminal, If by magic, you change the directory into the same directory you were in, in Finder.

QuickLook

We've seen how to use QuickLook before; however, it produced a lot of unnecessary debugging information. The `osx` plugin includes the command to perform a QuickLook as well. You access it with `quick-look`, followed by the file you want to quickly look at. This version of command will produce much less output.

```
% quick-look ~/.oh-my-zsh/plugins/osx/osx.plugin.zsh
[2] 98294
[2]  + 98294 done    qlmanage -p $* &> /dev/null
```

Manual Preview

Like the `quick-look` command, we've seen the manual in preview command before. This command (which is really an alias) is something you could set up yourself, but it is convenient to have a plugin do it for you.

```
% man-preview zsh
```

Hidden Files

If you've ever listed the contents of your home directory, you may have noticed that some of the files are not shown in the Finder. Earlier, we looked at files that are hidden, because they start with a dot. However, it is also possible to see all these files in the Finder.

```
% showfiles
```

This command changes a setting to show hidden files, and then relaunches the Finder. You might notice that all the icons disappear from the Desktop for a brief moment.

I find having the hidden files in the Finder visible all the time a bit too messy. To revert to them being hidden, you can use `hidefiles`.

```
% hidefiles
```

Remove .DS_Store Files

Have you ever transferred files to another type of computer (such as Windows), and noticed the hidden files being shown? The most common file like this is .DS_Store. If this bothers you, you can run rmdsstore on the directory or drive to have them stripped out.

```
% rmdsstore /Volumes/USBDrive
```

Warning   Using rmdsstore will remove all customization on the folder layout, so it's not recommended you run it on your user folder.

Preferences

The next section of the .zshrc file is all about tweaking how Oh My Zsh works. These comments are copied into the .zshrc file once you install Oh My Zsh.

Case-Sensitive Completion

```
# Uncomment the following line to use case-sensitive
completion.
# CASE_SENSITIVE="true"
```

By default, using Tab to complete commands is case insensitive. This means if you type NAN and then press Tab, you get nano. If CASE_SENSITIVE is enabled and true, then there would be no matches.

Hyphen Sensitivity

```
# Uncomment the following line to use hyphen-insensitive
  completion.
# Case-sensitive completion must be off. _ and - will be
  interchangeable.
# HYPHEN_INSENSITIVE="true"
```

By default, autocomplete will treat dashes and the underscore symbols differently. If you want them to be interchangeable, you should enable HYPHEN_INSENSITIVE.

Auto Update

```
# Uncomment the following line to disable bi-weekly auto-update
  checks.
# DISABLE_AUTO_UPDATE="true"

# Uncomment the following line to automatically update without
  prompting.
# DISABLE_UPDATE_PROMPT="true"

# Uncomment the following line to change how often to auto-
  update (in days).
# export UPDATE_ZSH_DAYS=13
```

Manual Update

With these options, you can decide to stop the automatic update of Oh My Zsh, or apply the updates without question. To manually upgrade Oh My Zsh, use the upgrade_oh_my_zsh command.

```
% upgrade_oh_my_zsh
Updating Oh My Zsh
remote: Enumerating objects: 39, done.
```

```
remote: Counting objects: 100% (39/39), done.
remote: Compressing objects: 100% (17/17), done.
remote: Total 27 (delta 18), reused 18 (delta 10), pack-reused 0
Unpacking objects: 100% (27/27), done.
From https://github.com/ohmyzsh/ohmyzsh
 * branch              master          -> FETCH_HEAD
   78b07e92..4e45e12d  master          -> origin/master
Updating 78b07e92..4e45e12d
Fast-forward
 lib/clipboard.zsh                                         | 4 ++--
 oh-my-zsh.sh                                              | 4 ++--
 plugins/colored-man-pages/colored-man-pages.plugin.zsh | 2 +-
 plugins/pyenv/pyenv.plugin.zsh                           | 3 ++-
 plugins/virtualenvwrapper/virtualenvwrapper.plugin.zsh |
7 +++++++
 plugins/yarn/_yarn                                       |
8 +++++---
 6 files changed, 19 insertions(+), 9 deletions(-)
Current branch master is up to date.

      __                                         __
 ___  / /_        ___ ___  _  _     ___  ____/ /_
/ _ \/ _ \     / _ `_ \/ / / /    / _  / / __/ _ \
/ /_/ / / /    / / / / / /_/ /    / /_(__  ) / / /
\___/_/ /_/    /_/ /_/ /_/\__, /    /___/____/_/ /_/
                         /___/

Hooray! Oh My Zsh has been updated and/or is at the current
version.
```

Magic Function

```
# Uncomment the following line if pasting URLs and other text
  is messed up.
# DISABLE_MAGIC_FUNCTIONS=true
```

This feature is useful for escaping text as you paste it into Terminal. If you paste `https://www.google.com/search?q=zsh` into your Terminal, it will be escaped as `https://www.google.com/search\?q\=zsh`. The downside of leaving this option enabled is that pasted text will be processed slower than when it is disabled.

Colors

```
# Uncomment the following line to disable colors in ls.
# DISABLE_LS_COLORS="true"
```

This controls whether to use color in the directory listings with `ls`. Folders, aliases, and executables by default will have color. If this is disabled, then they will revert to the same color as the standard files.

Terminal Window Title

```
# Uncomment the following line to disable auto-setting terminal
  title.
# DISABLE_AUTO_TITLE="true"
```

In Terminal preferences, I normally turn off all the options for the title. I like my title bar to be very simple, as shown in Figure 9-23.

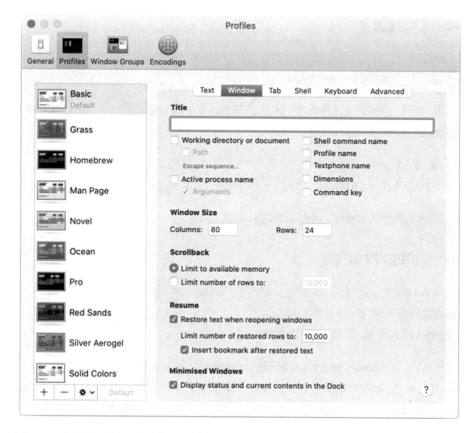

Figure 9-23. *Terminal profile with an empty title bar*

However, without `DISABLE_AUTO_TITLE`, the title bar will be updated with the current command, as shown in Figure 9-24.

Figure 9-24. *Oh My Zsh changing the title to the running command*

Auto-Correct

```
# Uncomment the following line to enable command auto-correction.
# ENABLE_CORRECTION="true"
```

If this is enabled, Oh My Zsh will look for a close match before issuing a command not found error.

% **tai high.sh**
```
zsh: correct 'tai' to 'tail' [nyae]?
```

The options are no, yes, always, and edit.

Completion Pending

```
# Uncomment the following line to display red dots while
  waiting for completion.
# COMPLETION_WAITING_DOTS="true"
```

This will display red dots while the system is waiting for information about how to complete a command. They will show up briefly when using Tab to complete paths.

Command History

```
# Uncomment the following line if you want to change the
  command execution time
# stamp shown in the history command output.
# You can set one of the optional three formats:
# "mm/dd/yyyy"|"dd.mm.yyyy"|"yyyy-mm-dd"
# or set a custom format using the strftime function format
  specifications,
# see 'man strftime' for details.
# HIST_STAMPS="mm/dd/yyyy"
```

By default, when you use the `history` command, you will see a list of the commands you have typed and an incrementing number.

```
1   ls
2   cd
3   sudo whoami
```

If you enable the format shown here, you will see the date and time as well.

```
1   12/21/2019 12:16   ls
2   12/21/2019 12:16   cd
3   12/21/2019 12:16   sudo whoami
```

Custom Directory

With the whole `~/.oh-my-zsh` directory managed by git, it is unwise to edit any files stored within. That includes the themes. What happens if there is a theme that you like, but you want to change it? This is where the custom directory comes in. Anything in this directory is ignored by git. If you wanted to tweak a theme, you can copy it to `~/.oh-my-zsh/custom/themes/`.

If for some reason you wanted to move your custom directory to outside of `~/.oh-my-zsh`, you can use `ZSH_CUSTOM` to specify where that is.

```
# Would you like to use another custom folder than $ZSH/custom?
# ZSH_CUSTOM=/path/to/new-custom-folder
```

The default location is `~/.oh-my-zsh/custom/`.

Ideas for Terminal

This section covers various Terminal tweaks that can make parts of your job easier.

Mistyping

Do you find that you mistype the same commands again and again? Maybe you could do with a tip to help you recognize when you do so. You could also adapt this tip to prank other people. Not that I condone that sort of thing.

Recall that we installed the `sl` command for the steam locomotive, and the point of this command is to display an animated steam locomotive that travels across your Terminal. We found out that this command is run by typing `sl`, which is a common mistyping of the `ls` command. The command cannot be cancelled and the wider your screen, the longer it takes.

So, how can this help with other mistyped commands? You can use aliases to run the locomotive command. Let's see an example. When I type commands, I sometimes type them too quickly, missing a space. This becomes problematic when I'm changing directories. I should type `cd ..` (cd *space*) to go up a directory.

However, I often end up with `cd..` without the trailing space, which will return the dreaded message, "`command not found`". So let's alias that. Type this command into your Terminal or add it to your `.zshrc` file.

```
% alias 'cd..'='sl'
```

Now when you type `cd..`, the locomotive will help remind you to type the correct command.

Identify Other Computers

As a systems administrator, I spend a lot of time logging into different computers using my Terminal.

```
% ssh user@example.org
```

Some of them are production systems and others are staging environments. If I'm quickly switching tabs, it can be easy to lose track of which environment I'm in. So, how can we make it easier to know which environment we're in? We can use figlet to tell us.

```
% figlet "Staging"
```

After a while, that would get lost in the scroll back. Now, because most remote systems are using Bash, we can also change the color, and that will persist, no matter how much we type. The production colors are shown in Listing 9-1 and the staging colors are shown in Listing 9-2.

Note   Instead of looking in .zshrc, Bash will look in a file called .bash_profile.

Listing 9-1. The .bash_profile Production

```
printf '\e[38;5;215m\n' # Foreground color
printf '\e[48;5;88m\n' # Background color
```

Listing 9-2. The .bash_profile Staging

```
printf '\e[38;5;237m\n' # Foreground color
printf '\e[48;5;208m\n' # Background color
```

However, this only works for the current line and any subsequent lines. We can use the clear command to force the whole screen to empty. This has the effect of applying the colors to the whole window. With a staging server, you would end up with something like Listing 9-3 in your users .bash_profile.

Listing 9-3. The .bash_profile

```
printf '\e[38;5;237m\n' # Foreground color
printf '\e[48;5;208m\n' # Background color
clear

figlet "Staging"
```

This would be displayed like Figure 9-25.

Figure 9-25. *An example of connecting the staging configuration to a server*

If I then connect to the production account, I would see a different screen, as shown in Figure 9-26.

Figure 9-26. *An example of connecting the production configuration to a server*

If you close the window when you are finished connecting to the remote server, it works really well. However, when you log out from the remote server, the colors aren't reset. It leaves you with the same color scheme from the remote server, on your local Terminal. This is far from ideal.

When you log out, the .bash_logout file is executed by Bash. If we put the tput init command into .bash_logout, that will cause the colors to reset to the defaults. Now when disconnect, your colors will be as they were before you connected.

Filtering Log Files

Recently, one of our websites was being flooded by bot traffic, which I could see in the nginx access logs. Some automated programs cause unnecessary load on the websites. Here's an example of a line in the access log:

```
127.0.0.1 - - [14/Feb/2020:07:55:23 +0000] "GET /info.
php HTTP/1.1" 200 90885 "-" "Mozilla/5.0 (Macintosh; Intel
Mac OS X 10_15_3) AppleWebKit/605.1.15 (KHTML, like Gecko)
Version/13.0.5 Safari/605.1.15"
```

Note   The log line shows the remote IP address, the HTTP user, the date and time of the event, the request, the HTTP status code, the total bytes sent, and the user agent.

I needed to filter the web servers access log for something, but the traffic was coming from lots of different sources. However, there was one commonality—they all had HeadlessChrome in the user agent string in the nginx access log. The user agent string is a piece of text that tells you about the browser that is connecting to your server. This is what my user agent for Safari looks like.

```
"Mozilla/5.0 (Macintosh; Intel Mac OS X 10_15_3)
AppleWebKit/605.1.15 (KHTML, like Gecko) Version/13.0.5
Safari/605.1.15"
```

The first thing I did was confirm what was returned when I filtered for HeadlessChrome.

```
% grep HeadlessChrome /usr/local/var/log/nginx/access.log
```

The list had everything on it that I wanted. If I could turn that list into just the IP addresses, I could block it from accessing my servers.

```
% grep HeadlessChrome /usr/local/var/log/nginx/access.log | awk
'{print $1}'
10.2.2.2
10.1.1.1
10.3.3.3
10.2.2.2
10.3.3.3
```

Note   These IP addresses are made up to illustrate the point.

The problem now was that I had a list of IP addresses, but they needed to be deduped. Thankfully, we've already seen some commands that do this by using sort and uniq.

```
% grep HeadlessChrome /usr/local/var/log/nginx/access.log | awk
'{print $1}' | sort | uniq
10.1.1.1
10.2.2.2
10.3.3.3
```

Great, I sorted list that I can block. However, I wanted to make it a little more difficult for the attacker and remove potential false positives. I thought it would be good to only include IP addresses that have accessed the server more than 100 times. By using uniq to produce a count, I could then use awk to filter on that count.

```
% grep HeadlessChrome /usr/local/var/log/nginx/access.log | awk
'{print $1}' | sort | uniq -c | awk '$1 >= 100 '
120 10.1.1.1
131 10.2.2.2
110 10.3.3.3
90 10.4.4.4
```

Finally, all I needed to do was return the IP address and sort the list again.

```
% grep HeadlessChrome /usr/local/var/log/nginx/access.log | awk
'{print $1}' | sort | uniq -c | awk '$1 >= 100 {print $2}' |
sort -rh
10.1.1.1
10.2.2.2
10.3.3.3
```

Now, with this list of IP addresses that I was confident were not our customers, I could block them. I managed to block 1,157 IP addresses using this method.

Programming Languages

There are more programming languages available to you than the ones I have shown. These can be used without having to install anything extra on your computer.

Python

There are many uses for Python. It can be used to make websites, build system commands, and research artificial intelligence.

```
% python3 -V
Python 3.7.6
```

macOS also ships with version 2, but this version has been deprecated and will eventually be removed. The simplest Python script is a hello world, as shown in Listing 9-4.

Listing 9-4. hello.py

```
print("Hello World")
```

```
% python3 hello.py
Hello World
```

C and C++

C and C++ are typically used to create very efficient applications and games. I don't recommend them for beginner users. I suggest that a beginner try Python instead. A very simple example of a C program is the hello world, shown in Listing 9-5.

Listing 9-5. hello.c

```
#include <stdio.h>

int main()
{
    printf("Hello World\n");
    return 0;
}
```

You then can use gcc to compile the program into a command and save it to the hello command.

```
% gcc hello.c -o hello
```

```
% ./hello
Hello World
```

Swift

Swift is used to create applications for the Apple ecosystem. Recently it has also been ported to Linux, to allow for some cross-platform apps. Listing 9-6 provides a simple hello world example of Swift.

Listing 9-6. hello.swift

```
print("Hello World")
```

Running a Swift program is simple.

```
% swift hello.swift
Hello World
```

Or you can compile the program, just as we did with C, into a command called `hello`.

```
% swiftc hello.swift -o hello
```

Summary

With this book, I have tried to give you a nice overview of lots of different Terminal options. There are lots of different applications you can install and services you can call to customize your Terminal. If you get into programming, there is a whole new world of customization you will be able to perform with your computer as well.

Index

A

B

C

Printed in the United States
By Bookmasters